A First Course in Information Technology

Leslie Cowan Jane Higgins

Oxford University Press 1988

Contents

8 Applications software

Oxford University Press, Walton Street, Oxford OX2 6DP

Oxford New York Toronto
Delhi Bombay Calcutta Madras Karachi
Petaling Jaya Singapore Hong Kong Tokyo
Nairobi Dar es Salaam Cape Town
Melbourne Auckland

and associated companies in
Berlin Ibadan

Oxford is a trade mark of Oxford University Press

ISBN 0 19 832736 6

Acknowledgements

We never planned to write this book. We never would have done so but for the encouragement of Rob Scriven in the early stages. The meticulous work of Lucy Hooper i transforming the text into a form which we hope you will find easily readable is warmly acknowledged; perhaps above all, we appreciate the tolerance of Doreen, Margaret and Donald, who have been so patient with our preoccupation with this text over a long perio

Our overall experience and teaching ideas are a reflection of all that we have gained from working with others and reading others' contributions to a particular field of activity, as well as from personal experience. We would be less than fair if we did not acknowledge th unconscious contribution of all these people to the substance of this book and the accompanying Tutor's Manual.

The publishers would like to thank the following for supplying photographs or illustratio

ASEA Limited: p.46;
AST Europe Ltd: p.143 (bottom right);
INMAC (UK) Ltd: p.123, p.143 (top left);
J Sainsbury PLC: p.123 (top right);
Epson UK Ltd: p.41, p.43;
Borland UK: p.137;
The British Standards Institute: p.173–174;
The Controller of Her Majesty's Stationery Office: p.148.

Additional photography by Chris Honeywell.

Illustrations by David Birdsall, Marie-Hélène Jeeves and Oxford Illustrators.

Typeset by Pentacor Limited, High Wycombe Bucks

Printed in Great Britain by Cambridge University Press, Cambridge

CHAPTER 1 About this book

Practical computing

This is a book for people who need to (or want to) use computers. It is not for computer whiz-kids or theoreticians, but for the vast majority of people who just need to be able to use computers with sufficient understanding to make the most of them in their employment.

We have never yet met anyone who gained much knowledge about computing and computer applications just by reading books. So we haven't even tried to write a book which attempts to stand alone as an information source. This book needs to be studied, so far as possible, with a computer system of some kind immediately to hand. What kind? We deal with this in Chapter 2, but we have been as undemanding as possible.

We have also tried to make our approach as practical as possible, so that by the time you have finished you have actually experienced word processing, used (and indeed constructed) simple spreadsheets and a database; handled some applications software, and perhaps found out a little about the construction of programs which make such applications possible.

No programming emphasis

But the book makes no attempt to teach programming as such. The emphasis which has in past years been given to programming has stopped many people using computers. Programming is a skill which provides a great deal of pleasure and satisfaction for some. But it is not essential for those who want just to use computers for a range of information processing tasks.

However, we have not turned our back on programming completely for we feel that an understanding of what is involved is useful, and you will find the second half of Chapter 8 deals with programming. To the extent that coding aspects are touched on, the language used is BASIC, but our purpose is to illustrate some programming principles, not teach coding. It is expected that readers who tackle the exercises in this part of the text will already have undertaken some simple coding practice. What we try to do is to help you, at an introductory level, to understand the need for a systematic approach to program design and to see what is involved in such an approach, rather than just to sit down at a computer and bash in code, trusting that the logic will work out!

The basics

But whether you use a programming language interpreter or compiler, applications software or more general purpose software for spreadsheets, database or word processing, there are some quite basic things you need to know about the computer system which enables these complex pieces of software to be effective.

A computer is no more than a very well organized collection of inter-connected electronic switches, and as such it can only do what it has been programmed to do. The fundamental programs which enable the computer to undertake input and output operations for us, to organize its memory and store so that it knows where it has put data which we have asked it to keep, together make up the Operating System.

Chapters 2 and 3 are largely about data representation, input, output, processing and storage and the things the user needs to know about an operating system and its utilities. Don't believe that by the time you get to the end of it you will know all about these topics! The book is an *introductory* text, designed to get you off the ground. There is much more to be said about operating systems (and especially about the use of some of the associated utilities), but you do not need it at this stage.

How to use the book

We strongly recommend that you should work through Chapters 2 and 3 before you explore the rest of the book. Do not rely on doing just once or twice the various copying, deleting, formatting and other techniques which are described in the chapters. You should practice using these facilities until they become second nature to you.

Once you have worked through Chapters 2 and 3, dodge around as you please, because Chapters 4–8 are free standing with little or no cross-reference. But the work in each of these chapters will make some assumptions about the basics covered in Chapters 2 and 3. This is why we would like you to work through these chapters first.

Use of shoulder headings

In presenting the text, we have endeavoured to use shoulder headings fairly liberally, so that if you are coming to the book for re-inforcement of a topic on which you have some knowledge, you should be able to locate the relevant section of text fairly readily.

Definition of terms

There are very many terms associated with computers and computing. Where key words or phrases have been used for the first time, they have been printed in ***bold italics*** and their meaning explained, if not immediately clear from the context. If you come across a term which we have not explained and about which you are uncertain, try *A Glossary of Computing Terms* published by Cambridge University Press on behalf of the British Computer Society. It is concise and regularly updated.

Use of summaries

Another feature of the presentation is the end-of-chapter summary: a learning checklist. There are summaries in the middle of long chapters as well. In these summaries we try to express things in terms of what you should then be able to do – again, putting the emphasis on *doing* rather than *knowing about*.

Proprietary software

Books which try to be practical quickly run into difficulty, because of wanting to make specific reference to particular software packages and particular operating systems. There are many books on the market which do just this, specializing in dBase or Lotus 1–2–3, WordStar or any of a dozen other popular packages. Amongst them, there are some excellent books, which if followed through will give a very detailed knowledge of the workings of a particular package.

Our book does not do this. We have found it necessary (or thought it helpful) to make some reference to specific packages or operating systems, but so far as possible have laid emphasis on the principles involved, making specific references only to illustrate a principle. To the extent that we have done this, we have referred mainly to MSDOS/PCDOS and CP/M operating systems, WordStar and Wordcraft word processing, Multiplan spreadsheet software and Delta database software.

There were several reasons for selecting these particular applications packages, but there were two very important ones. Firstly, we expect that this book will meet a need in many educational establishments offering vocational courses, and we needed to choose packages which are both actually used in real business, and most likely to be found in schools and colleges.

Secondly, we were influenced by the way the chosen packages operate, because they allow many principles to be illustrated. Some recent and more sophisticated software (particularly in the database field) may combine several operations in one blanket instruction, thus concealing some of the steps which form part of a particular process. While such software is a joy to use, it does not help to develop an understanding of what is actually going on so readily as a package where the user has to undertake each step of the operation.

Principles emphasized

But readers of this book may be working through it with any of twenty or more spreadsheets, word processing or database packages which never get a mention in these pages. How will they cope?

The straight answer is that if they are looking for a 'cookbook' approach – first press this key, then press that – a procedure to follow blindly rather than an understanding of what is to be achieved and why, then this book will not provide what they are seeking. Such an approach does nothing to encourage the learner to recognize the transferability of skills which is possible when the concepts are understood and the approach is not merely mechanistic. And skill transferability is vital in the business world. Not only will a change of job probably involve dealing with different software and hardware, but even if one stays in the same post, technological advances will lead to changes over a period of time.

So we would encourage readers to look up software handbooks to check commands which will produce the desired effects, or if this approach fails, to approach a tutor who is familiar with the software to which the learner has access. Above all, it will be essential to read screen prompts carefully and use on-screen help.

Tutorial support and support for tutors

Because we believe that there is no substitute for good tutorial support, we have written a companion volume for tutors. To help with the problem of handling specific software packages, this companion volume contains, amongst other things, partly completed photocopyable charts listing the functions you will need to use, and with a blank space opposite each for the tutor to enter the way in which it is achieved with the system you are using. It also contains much other material to support the tutor in providing a well-rounded course centred on this book.

There is still further support for the book in the form of software available on 5¼ inch and 3½ inch floppy disks for use with any IBM PC compatible machine and on 5¼ inch disk for RML 380/480Z computers. These disks include the accounts system referred to in Chapter 8, several programs in BASIC, and software to be used in association with WordStar, Multiplan and Lotus 1–2–3. These proprietary packages are not, of course, included on our disks. A 5¼ inch disk for BBC systems is also available, but does not carry the accounts software or the spreadsheet exercises, due to the limited capacity of BBC systems. With the exception of the accounts software and the program BIRTHDAY. BAS, the material on disk could be replaced by tutor-devised software, but we hope that in making software available, we are providing a useful support for tutors so that they in turn can support their students.

Learning outcomes

Some users of this book will be happy if, by the end of it, they have gained a sufficient grounding to develop greater expertise in one or more of the areas to which we have provided an introduction. They will have used the book for purely practical purposes.

Coverage of published syllabuses

Others may wish also to use it as a means of working towards a paper qualification of some kind. We have not moulded the content of the book around any particular set of syllabuses; our main consideration has been to produce something of practical value to those working (or hoping to work) in a clerical/secretarial/administrative environment.

Examination courses

That said, there are some examination syllabuses which have the same broad aim. We have in mind especially introductory level modules in the excellent Information Technology series (CGLI 726) produced by the City & Guilds of London Institute, and the RSA Computer Literacy and Information Technology Scheme. There is also substantial coverage of some CPVE modules – for example, the preparatory module on Word Processing. More generally, many of the aims under the broad heading of Information Technology within CPVE are covered.

The practical skills acquired in working through the book in the manner suggested will more than meet the practical requirements associated with the AEB Basic Test in Computer Awareness. The book will also be of value in relation to studies leading to GCSE qualifications in computer studies, but it does not aim to cover fully the syllabuses published by the several examining boards. As we said at the outset, we are primarily concerned with people who wish to acquire practical skills.

YTS core skills

The book is an ideal basis for tuition designed to cover core skills in Computer and Information Technology as defined by the Training Commission for the Youth Training Scheme. If the minimum time of 30 hours of off-the-job training for this area of study is applied one would have to be quite selective about the depth of study, and the flexible structure of the book allows this.

New Syllabuses

New syllabuses are continually being developed – for example, the joint initiative by the CBI and CGLI launched in Industry Year, leading to a certificate of Basic Competence in Information Technology. This is intended for use by sixth-form students following courses which lead to higher education or direct entry into industry or commerce, who would not have much access to computers in the course of their main studies. The book covers substantial areas of this syllabus too, and it seems almost inevitable that all syllabuses at this level should have a substantial amount of common ground. Our belief is that the way in which we have presented ideas in the following chapters allows sufficient flexibility for a wide range of needs to be met. But now is your chance to find out. Remember . . . Chapters 2 and 3 first and then take the others in an order which suits your purposes.

CHAPTER 2 Introduction to computer systems

Basic hardware for practical work

Have you got a computer handy? You are going to need it. This book is essentially practical and when working through it you will never want to be far away from a micro of some kind.

But what kind? Our aim has been to produce a text which is helpful regardless of the computer system to which you have access, but there is a minimum specification if you are to be able to undertake all the practical work we suggest.

The essential components of any computer system are shown here:

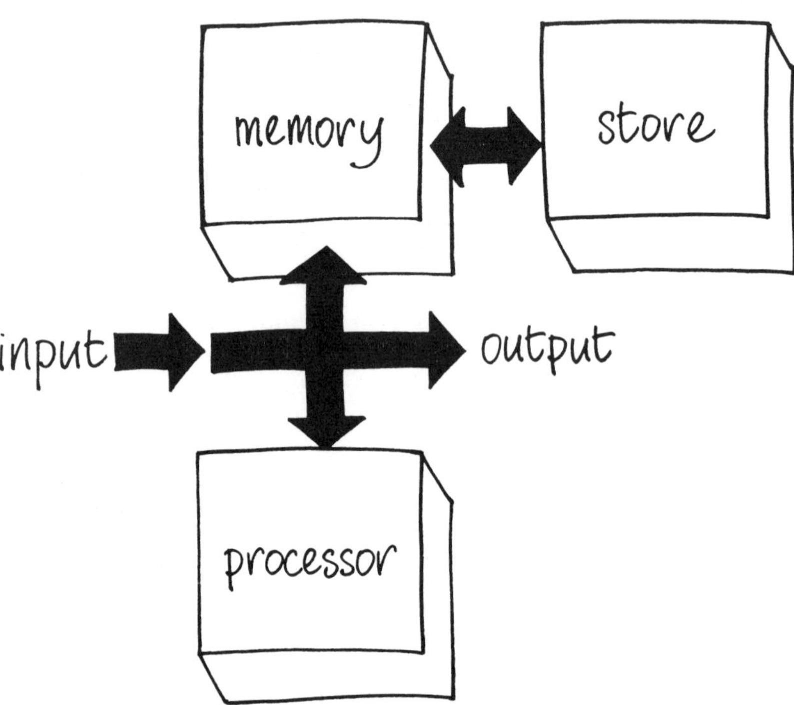

The basic components of a computer system

As we shall see, there are a number of ways of inputting either data or instructions to a computer system; the essential ***input device*** which all computers have is a ***keyboard***, for typing in both data and instructions, thereby telling the computer what to do with the data. So your computer system has the first essential component – a keyboard for input.

It also has the second component – a ***processor*** with temporary memory associated with it. The amount of memory doesn't matter too much, but if you have access to commercial software such as WordStar or Multiplan (which are ideally suited for some of the practical work), you will need at least 64 Kbytes of memory. Later versions of Multiplan require more.

Byte is a term that will be discussed again later; for now, remember that byte is used as a measure of memory or storage capacity; the K in front stands for *kilo*. You are probably used to using a lower case k prefix to mean a thousand, as in km (1000 metres) or kg (1000 grammes). In the computer world we deal in multiples of 2, and if you develop the series 1, 2, 4, 8, 16 . . . you soon come to 1024. Being roughly a thousand, we use the term *kilo* when speaking about it, but to distinguish between it and the exact kilo, we indicate it with a capital K in print. So, when we talk of a 64 Kbyte memory we mean it has the capacity to hold as much data or instructions as can be contained in 64 × 1024 (i.e. 65536 bytes). The handbook for your computer will undoubtedly tell you how much memory is available, or if you are using this text in the context of an organized course of study, your tutor will ensure that you are using an appropriate combination of hardware and software. Word processing, spreadsheet and simple data management software exists for machines with memories of smaller capacity than 64 Kbytes, but it is necessarily very limited in its scope. The tendency is for the most recent versions of commercially used software packages to become ever more demanding on memory, and memories of 512 Kbytes or more are common in business micros today.

Next, your system must have an ***output device***, and preferably more than one. The essential one is a screen or monitor, because this does two jobs for you. It *echoes* what you input through the keyboard so that you can check that you have in fact input what you intended, and it provides output for you to read when you are running a program. (Notice the American spelling of *program*, by the way. This is the accepted convention when referring to computer programs.)

You may have access to a printer as another output device and this would be useful so that you could have a permanent record of your work. If you are working towards an examination at this introductory level, you will probably find that you need to produce printed output and to be able to handle the loading of printer stationery, so try to include a printer of some kind in your computer system if you possibly can.

The final component of your system must be some kind of ***store*** for your data and programs, so that they can be kept from day to day or week to week in a form which can be accessed and understood by your computer. This might be ***magnetic tape*** or ***disk***. Tape is cheaper but has a severe disadvantage in that programs and data can only be accessed ***serially***, so that every time you want to get a program or data which is stored at the far end of the tape, you have to work right through the tape to get at it.

With storage on a disk, however, the computer can locate and read data from any point on the disk within a few milliseconds. Also, with a disk, the computer controls the entire search operation. With a tape, if you wish to access a file which is located on a part of the tape which is already on the take-up spool, you have to rewind. Having rewound to a point just before the start of the required file (you use the counter on the tape player to keep a record of each file's starting point), then set the tape recorder to *play* before the computer reads into its memory the file you have specified. File access using tape is not automatic – it requires your intervention.

For this reason, tape is not an appropriate storage medium for serious work (other than for ***back up*** or archival purposes) and we shall assume that you have access to a disk drive. Ideally, your system would have twin disk drives, but this is not essential.

You will notice that in describing the kind of computer system you need in order to make best use of the material in this book we have referred to ***memory*** and to ***storage***. You may well be saying to yourself, 'Presumably a memory remembers, so why do we need a store as well?' There are two points to make in answer to that question. The first is that memory that is available to you, ***Random Access Memory (RAM)***, is ***volatile*** – that is, the computer stops remembering what you have told it as soon as it is switched off. Storage is ***permanent***: once a file has been written to disk it is there for as long as you care to keep it.

The second point is that memory is limited in size. Even if it didn't 'forget' when we turned the machine off, it could not possibly contain all the programs and data we wish to use over a period of time. But we can have as many disks as we like, each containing *some* of our programs and associated data. The computer can then call into memory just those programs and data files it needs.

Review

So, we have now established the minimum computer system you should be working with. It consists of a processor with a reasonable amount of local memory, a keyboard to act as an input device, a monitor or screen (sometimes called a VDU – Visual Display Unit) to act as an output device, and a disk drive to make storage easier. The disk drive is both an input and an output device, because the computer may read in programs or data from the disk into memory, and may save programs or data in memory by outputting them to disk. To this bare minimum computer system, we add a printer as an additional output device if at all possible.

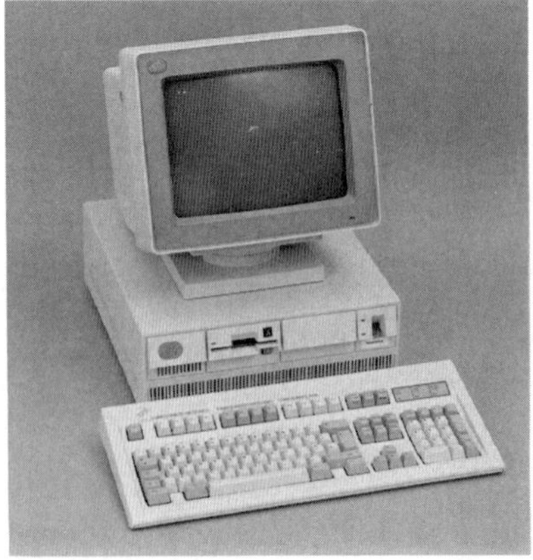

A linked unit computer system (left)

Computer system units as a single unit (right)

Sometimes the various parts of the system are all in separate units linked together by cables; often the keyboard and VDU are separate, but normally the disk drives are fitted into the same box as the processor boards. In some cases – particularly with portable computers – all the various parts are built into the same box.

Before we go any further, take a look at your computer system. Make sure you can identify each of the parts we have mentioned and that you know how they all plug together and get their power.

Computers and information processing

The structure of any processing activity

We haven't quite got to the stage of switching on yet, but we shall soon. Just before we do, it may be worth considering the question 'Why does a computer system have the basic form of ***input – processing*** (with local memory) – ***output***?' The simple answer is that all our systems of human activity work in this way and the computer system is designed to copy our way of working. For example, think about a typical office worker sitting at his/her desk.

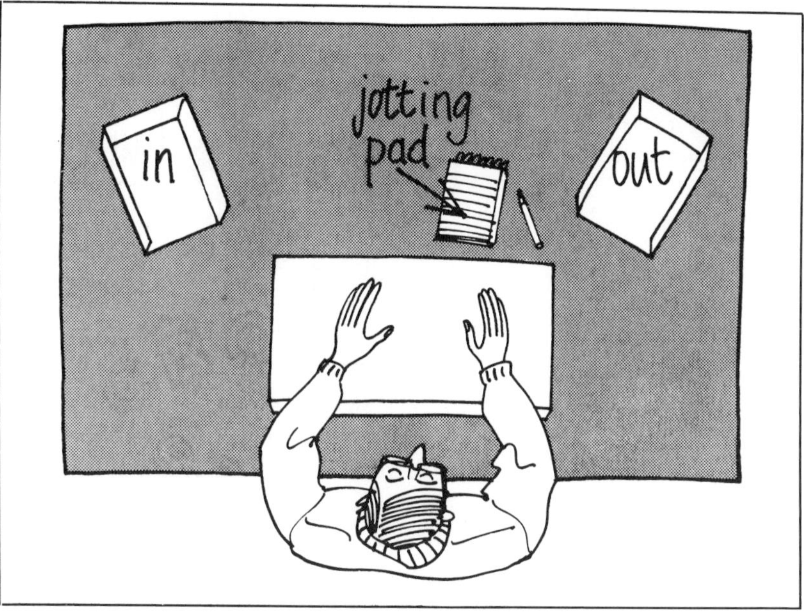

Input-processing-output in a manual system

Work comes in the form of pieces of paper which someone keeps putting in the In-tray. S/he has some process to carry out on this input. S/he might, for example, be the accountant who writes the cheques to settle the company's bills, and the input would be the invoices which have been received and are due to be paid.

The process might have several parts to it. For example:

1 Checking that the goods/services have actually been received and are satisfactory.
2 When payment is to be made, entering details in the purchase ledger.
3 Writing the cheque.
4 Marking up the invoice in some way to identify the payment date and cheque number.
5 Producing a remittance advice so that the person receiving the payment knows what it is for and who has sent it.

There are two outputs:

1 The cheques with their remittance advice slips. These will form the input for another process – that of addressing, stuffing, sealing and franking the envelopes; and that process will output to the outgoing mail service.
2 The paid invoices. These will be output to appropriate files and be kept available for any queries arising, or for audit purposes.

Try a similar analysis for yourself. Think about a check-out point in a supermarket and see if you can identify all the inputs, the processing and use of temporary memory, and the outputs arising from this activity.

The components of an information system

In these and many other examples, the activity we are describing is broadly covered by the term ***information processing*** and the system which allows this activity to take place (perhaps as part of a larger overall activity) is called an ***information system***. In basic terms, an information system will have these features:

- □ *data capture* from a live situation
- □ *storage* of the data
- □ later *retrieval* of the data
- □ *processing* of the data
- □ producing *output* of information in the required form

Let's see how these features apply in the case of the invoice payment routine described above.

The main stages in information processing

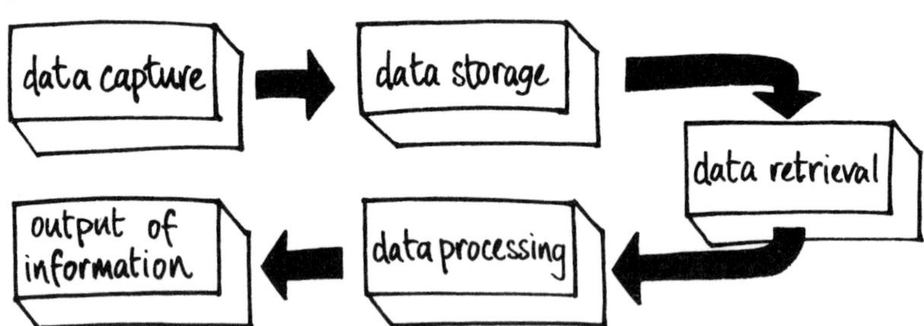

Data capture

This is fairly easy in this case. The invoice arrives through the post; the mailroom clerk knows that all incoming invoices should be directed to the Finance Section. The Finance Section logs it in, checks it against the original order, attaches a payment authorization slip to it and sends it to the department which should have received the goods or services to verify that they have in fact been satisfactorily received. The documents are returned to the Finance Section, and now all the data required by our accountant is to hand.

Storage of data

The accountant doesn't spend all day every day paying bills; s/he has other jobs to do as well. So s/he reserves a period, say once a fortnight, for settling accounts. In this way, s/he can deal with a whole batch at a time. But until that time comes round, the checked and verified invoices have to be stored (in this case in a file in a drawer of a filing cabinet). The ability to store data is an essential feature of the system.

Retrieval of data

Obviously, there would be no point in storing data if we never wanted to get it back. In our example, we want to open the file containing invoices passed for payment once a fortnight to extract and process all the invoices it contains. Data retrieval is another essential feature of an information system.

Processing of data

We have already looked at many of the processing activities associated with this particular example, but if we had chosen a different example, the processing activities would have been quite different. Suppose we had been looking at an activity in the personnel department of our organization: then the process might have been one of selecting the records of employees who met certain criteria – for example, those under the age of 45 with sales experience who could speak German. It may have been a counting process, e.g. finding out the number of people in each of five salary brackets. It may have been no more than an alphabetic sort on surnames. But processing is always an essential component of an information system.

Output of information

In our example, the output included cheques accompanied by information saying what the payment was for. In other cases, the outputs might be a list of names and addresses, or tables of statistics. Or it might be more appropriate to have an output in a graphical form of some kind, because quite often information can be given more effectively by graphs, bar charts or pie charts, rather than by tables of figures. But note that information is quite different from data: *information is derived from data, through the analysis, selection or reorganization of data.*

Typical graphical outputs

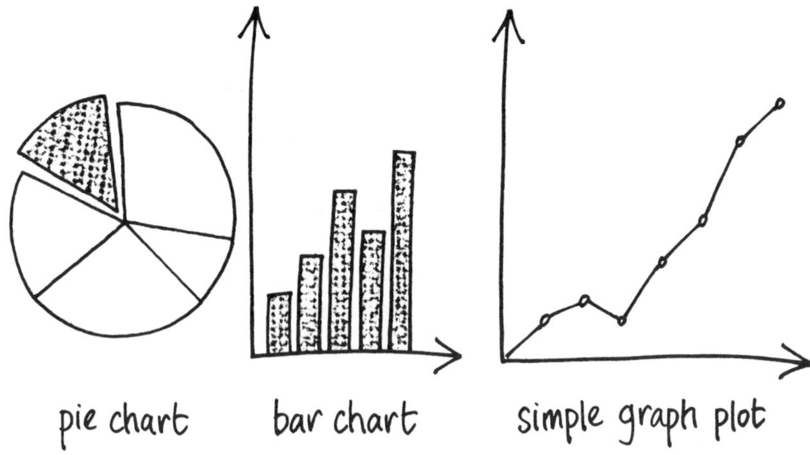

Standard facilities allow alphanumeric information and graph scales to be added to these.

So, an information system is made up of

- ☐ data capture
- ☐ data storage
- ☐ data retrieval
- ☐ data processing
- ☐ information output

Information processing activity handled by computer

As we have seen, all the parts of a computer system are present in any manual (i.e. non-computer) system, so why not ask: 'If information processing can be achieved without using a computer, why buy this expensive and complicated equipment to achieve the same results?'

The answer is simply that a computer is much better than any manual system in the way it can

> *store data* efficiently and compactly, *retrieve data* selectively and quickly, *process data* by sorting, selecting, counting and calculating at high speed, *output information* in any desired format and in any required location.

Data capture is something which must take place before the computer system can start its job, and there are some very efficient ways of capturing data for computer systems. But for the moment, we shall look at those aspects of information processing which follow on from data capture.

Let's look at these features one by one.

The storage and retrieval of data

Data storage is achieved using disks or tapes coated with a material which can be easily magnetized, and once magnetized, will hold the magnetic pattern imprinted in it for an indefinite period, unless you choose deliberately to erase it or overwrite it with something else. Disks and tapes are described as ***magnetic media.***

Magnets are an example of what are known as 2-state, or ***binary***, devices. If you use the magnetic field which is set up when an electric current flows in a circuit to magnetise something, the resulting magnet is polarized either N-S (North-South) or S-N (South-North), depending on the direction of the current. So the magnet may be considered to have two possible states: N-S or S-N. It is a 2-state or binary element.

Now, a binary element can only represent two things because it has only two states. But suppose we had two such elements in combination. How many things can be represented then? If we take the symbol '0' as one binary state and '1' as the other, then the possible combinations are:

```
00
01
10
11
```

As we see, four different things can be represented. If we take three binary elements in combination we can represent eight different things:

```
000
001
010
011
100
101
110
111
```

Representation of characters by binary digits

Each time we add another element, we double the number of things we can represent, and by the time we have reached seven elements we can represent 128 different things. This is more than the number of characters available to us on a computer keyboard, for we need to represent only the letters A-Z and a-z, the figures 0-9, punctuation and mathematical characters like + and =, and some control functions like line feed (LF) and carriage return (CR). In all, there could be about 110, so the 128 different combinations available from a group of seven binary digits (known as ***bits***, for short) adequately cover all the keyboard characters and control symbols we need.

In fact, a computer system uses groups of eight bits rather than seven to represent each character, and these groups of eight bits are called ***bytes***. The eighth bit is used for error checking purposes.

There has been international agreement on which binary patterns shall represent which characters; the coding system which has been adopted is the American Standard Code for Information Interchange, known as the ***ASCII code***.

We shall look rather more closely at ASCII code later on, but for the moment we want to concentrate on the way characters coded in a binary pattern are stored on a disk.

Disk handling

Have you got a floppy disk you can look at? *Take care how you handle it!* Always hold the disk by the labelled end. Keep your fingers (and anything else) well clear of the window. Don't lay the disk down anywhere until you have put it back in its envelope. The coating of the magnetic material is so thin that it could be very easily damaged.

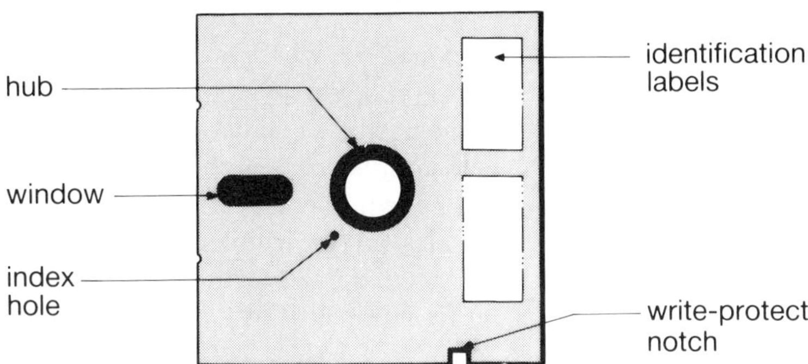

A standard 5¼ inch disk

If you happen to be looking at a 3½ inch disk, you won't see the window because it is covered by a spring-loaded metal shutter which stays in place until the disk is placed in the disk drive, at which point the shield is pushed to one side.

Handling the disk carefully
a do not use magnetized objects near the disk
b do not place heavy objects on the disk
c do not make erasures near the disk
d do not expose the disk to excessive heat or sunlight
e do not fold or bend the disk or use paper clips on it
f do not touch or clean the exposed disk surface
g do not eat, drink or smoke while handling the disk

Representation of data by magnetic patterns on disk

When you switch your computer on and place your disk in the disk drive and close the latch (if there is one), the disk drive grips the disk by its central hub. The jacket stays still, but the disk is free to move within it and the drive will rotate the disk at a rate of several hundred revolutions a minute when storage or retrieval is taking place.

The part of the disk drive unit that creates the magnetic fields which form the patterns representing characters on the disk is called the ***read/write head***. When the head is writing, what is actually happening is that a series of small electrical pulses, each representing one bit of a byte, are sent to the read/write head by the ***Central Processing Unit (CPU)***.

On receiving a pulse, the read/write head creates a very localized magnetic field which lasts only as long as the pulse which creates it. The direction of the magnetic field depends on the sense of the pulse (positive going or negative going) sent to the read/write head.

Any material which is easily magnetized (like the surface coating of a disk) and which happens to be under the read/write head at the moment that a magnetic field exists, will be magnetized by that field and, because of the nature of the material, it will retain its magnetism. Depending on the field direction, the very small part of the disk surface influenced by a particular magnetic pulse, may be magnetized in a North-South sense or a South-North sense (one representing a '1' bit, the other a '0' bit).

The same head which writes this magnetic pattern to the disk can also be used to read it back at some later stage because the process we have described for converting a pattern of electrical pulses into a corresponding pattern of magnetic pulses is reversible. When operating in ***read mode***, the changes in magnetic field strength under the read/write head as the disk rotates cause electrical voltages to be generated in the head and these voltage pulses will be positive or negative going depending on the polarities of the magnetic pattern (i.e. North-South or South-North). The read/write head when reading, sends back to the computer electrical signals which exactly reproduce the magnetic pattern recorded on the surface of the disk.

This diagram shows the way in which a read/write head can move to cover any part of the active surface of the disk in the line of the window. And in the lower part of the diagram, you see how the head in ***write mode*** leaves a pattern of very small magnets representing each character stored on the disk.

Writing to disk

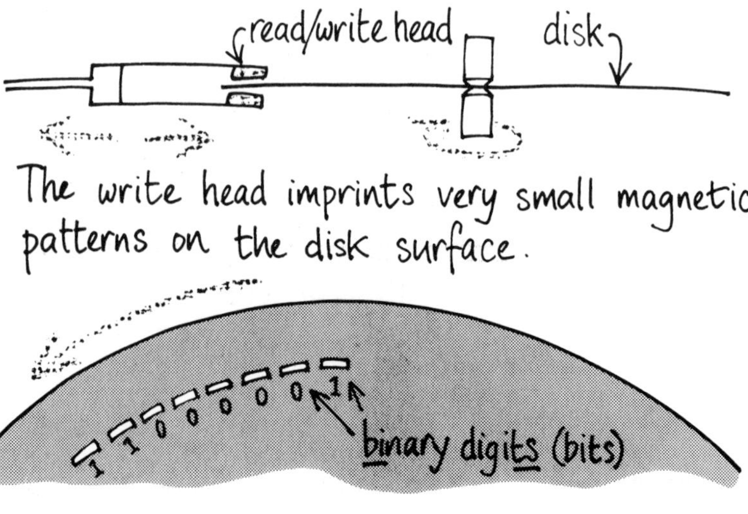

The manufacturers of disks and disk drives are always striving to compress the room taken by the very small magnets representing bits, and to pack them closer together. Thus a disk may be described as ***double sided, double density*** (often abbreviated to ***DSDD***), meaning that both sides of the disk can be used to store data and that the packing of the very small magnetized areas representing bits is twice as dense as the original standard.

At the time of writing this book, DSDD disks are still widely used, but there are already quadruple density disks in use, and leading companies are now producing 5¼ inch floppy disks and drives to handle the storage of more than 6 million bytes (6 Mbytes) on one disk.

A full page of A4 paper, closely typed, may contain about 3000 characters, and since a byte contains the code for one character it follows that a 6 Mbyte disk holds the equivalent of at least 2000 A4 pages. That's a lot of filing cabinet space! One way which manufacturers have found of increasing the packing density is to form the magnets vertically in the magnetic coating of the disk instead of horizontally on the surface.

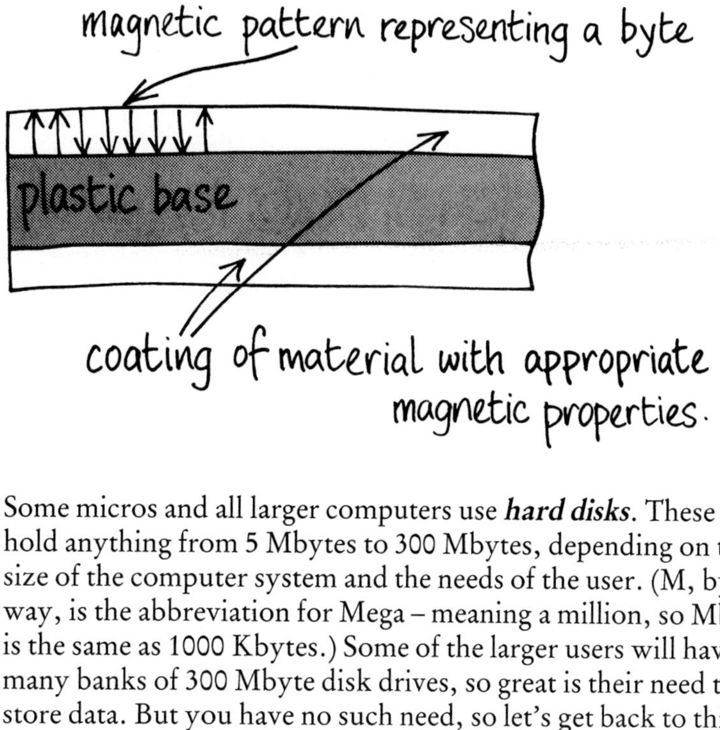

Section view through a disk (greatly enlarged)

Some micros and all larger computers use ***hard disks***. These may hold anything from 5 Mbytes to 300 Mbytes, depending on the size of the computer system and the needs of the user. (M, by the way, is the abbreviation for Mega – meaning a million, so Mbyte is the same as 1000 Kbytes.) Some of the larger users will have many banks of 300 Mbyte disk drives, so great is their need to store data. But you have no such need, so let's get back to thinking about floppy disks. The principles involved are just the same whether we consider hard disks or floppies. The two differences from the user's viewpoint are:

1 The volume of data which can be stored.
2 The speed at which it can be accessed (a hard disk is several times faster than a floppy, mainly due to the fact that it can be rotated much faster than a floppy).

We have seen, in outline at least, how the small electrical pulses representing bits can create a corresponding pattern in the magnetizable coating on a floppy disk. We have also seen how the process can be reversed so that the magnetic pattern can generate small electrical voltages in the read/write head operating in read mode and thereby transmit stored data patterns back into the computer.

The need for formatting

But in order to read back the data that you want, and not any old piece of data, two things have got to happen:

1 The surface of the disk must be mapped in some way by the computer so that a location may be defined. This is rather like the use of grid references on maps, where a point may be referenced by the intersection of two grid lines, one running E-W, the other running N-S. In the case of a disk, we use ***tracks*** and ***sectors***.

2 The computer operating system must ensure that a record is kept of the reference where your data file starts and of the sector it uses. (The functions of an operating system are described more fully a little later in this chapter. For now, just think of it as something which stands between a user's software and the computer hardware; its job is to control input to and output from the system and from the disks.)

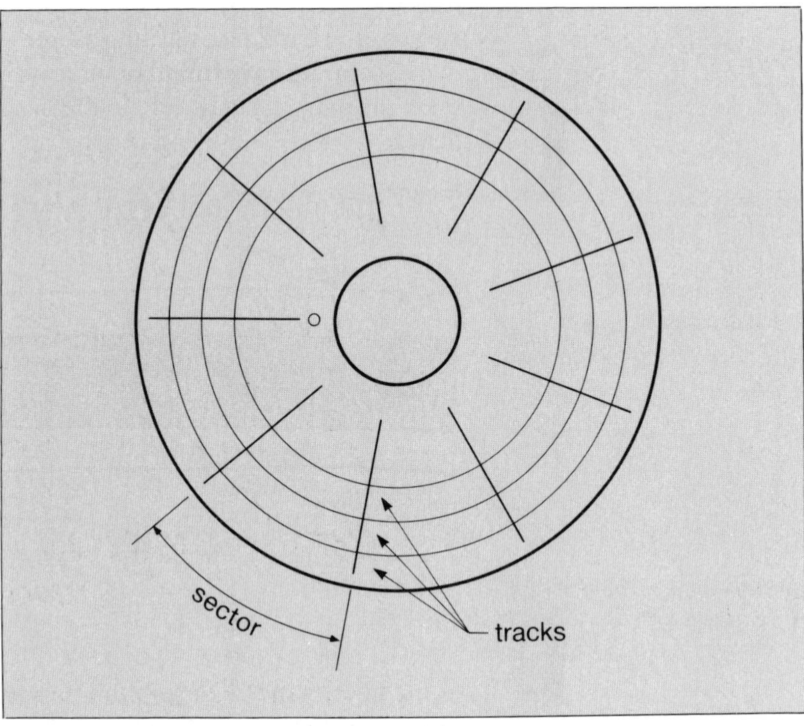

A disk format

You cannot see the tracks and sectors; there is nothing to see because they are simply a magnetic pattern imprinted on to the disk during a process called ***formatting***. Each track is identified by a number, as is each sector. Sector numbering starts from the point where the index hole in the disk allows light to pass from a source on one side of the disk to a light receptor on the other side. This brief pulse of light, converted into an electrical pulse, tells the computer that the first sector is just coming under the read/write head and, from that point on, it can count the magnetic sector markers as they pass the head.

There is no single standard relating to the numbers of tracks and sectors to be used in a disk format. Different computer manufacturers may use different formats (although a good many have in recent years fixed on the standards adopted by IBM, whose products have greatly influenced the business microcomputer market). So that disk manufacturers may sell identical disks to be used on many different makes and models of computers, the disks are normally sold unformatted. The formatting process is left to the user, who is provided with appropriate software to do the job.

Starting up a computer having disk drive(s)

If you can lay hands on a blank disk (i.e. one that has never been used before), try this little experiment. Switch on your computer, insert the ***system disk*** in the disk drive (if you are using a *twin floppy-disk machine* then put it in drive A) and close the latch. A system disk is one which carries files containing the operating system programs. Incidentally, if you don't know where to switch your computer on, the best thing to do is to trace the lead from the power plug to the computer. The on/off switch is usually close to where the power supply lead plugs into the computer (and it is almost always in some awkward place at the back of the machine!).

If you put in the right disk, the computer will, after a few seconds in which it is testing its more important circuits, start to read in the operating system. Some systems require the user to type B (for Boot) before the reading of the system into memory can start. The expression 'booting the system' which is sometimes used to describe the start-up process needs a little explanation. It comes from a rather old-fashioned expression for someone who has made progress in life by his own effort; the person is said to have 'pulled himself up by his own bootstraps'. The idea is a good one in terms of computer start-up. In the case of typical business micros with built-in disk-drives, the machine has a very few built-in instructions which it holds permanently: it keeps those instructions in a fixed memory called ***Read Only Memory (ROM)***. When the machine is switched on, these stored instructions tell the computer to read in the main part of the operating system from disk. As these further instructions are read in, so the computer gains in power, until the full operating system is loaded into memory.

As we have indicated, the operating system is a group of programs that enable the computer to control a large number of essential functions which we would otherwise have to look after ourselves. To take just one example: we do not want to have to specify all the tracks and sectors to be used in storing one of our data files; we leave it to the computer to file it in a sensible unoccupied place on the disk, and to retrieve it for us when we want it. This is only one of very many jobs the operating system does for us; indeed, the computer cannot read in and execute any other program until the operating system is installed in memory. With small, very basic computers which do not have to worry about controlling disk drives, the operating systems have many fewer instructions and are totally contained in ROM. Many home computers are of this kind.

Date and time

During the loading of the operating system, the computer may well pause, displaying a date and inviting you either to accept the date (by pressing the ENTER key) or correct it. Some computers have batteries which keep the clock going even when the computer is switched off, and these machines will normally display the correct date.

It is not essential to give the computer the correct date, but it is good practice, so do it. You will see later on why it is useful. Note the example display on the screen, and enter the correct date in the same way. A good many systems use the American format, putting the month before the day.

After the date, the machine will display the current time and invite you to accept it or correct it. Correct it if necessary and press the ENTER key.

Changing the logged drive

With these preliminaries completed, your operating system is now ready for use, and a ***system prompt***, for example, A> will appear on the screen. What this is saying to us is that the operating system is now fully loaded into the computer memory and the computer is ready for us to load a program file from a disk in drive A.

We refer to A as the ***logged drive***. The computer logs on to whichever drive it was that held the system files read into memory. It may be your only disk drive anyway, but if you have a twin disk machine, change the logged drive to B by typing B: and pressing the ENTER key; then insert the blank disk in drive B. You will notice that having changed the *logged drive* to B, the system prompt has changed to B>. This is telling the user that unless specifically instructed otherwise, the computer will write to the disk in drive B any files that need to be saved and if asked to read a file from disk into memory, it will look for that file on drive B. If you only have a single disk drive, remove the system disk and replace it with the blank one.

Dealing with new disks

Now type DIR, which is a widely accepted abbreviation for DIRECTORY. (DIR may be entered in either upper or lower case.) The computer will search the disk – you will notice that a red light associated with the disk comes on during this time. But search as it may, not only will it *not* find any files, because there aren't any on the disk yet, but it cannot read the disk at all because the format pattern has not yet been imprinted on it. An ***error message*** will be displayed on the screen. Note it down so that if you get it again you know the likely cause. If you have access to a system handbook for your computer, you will find error messages and their likely causes listed in it. A similar message would have been displayed if you had used a disk formatted for a non-compatible machine (i.e. one using different numbers of tracks and/or sectors).

The next part of the experiment is to format the blank disk. For this you will need to load a ***system utility program*** usually called FORMAT: if you are working in a tutored group, your tutor will ensure that you have the right disk and the correct program name.

System utility programs are all part of the software supplied with the operating system. But unlike the operating system, which must be present in the computer memory before any other program can be run, utilities are not needed all the time and are just loaded when required.

Place the utility disk in drive A. If you wish to format a new disk in drive A, you would simply enter the command FORMAT (assuming this is the program name used for the formatting operation on your system) next to the A> system prompt. If the new disk to be formatted is in drive B, the command would be modified to FORMAT B:

In either case, pressing the ENTER key will cause the formatting program to be read from disk into memory and you will be prompted by a message on the screen to place the blank disk in the appropriate drive. When you are ready, follow the screen prompt – usually 'Press any key to continue' – and format your disk.

When formatting is complete, you return to the operating system by telling the machine, in response to on-screen questions, that you have finished with formatting and do not wish to format any more disks.

You can now *call the directory* of your newly formatted disk. (Remember how? You do this by typing DIR and pressing the ENTER key.)

If, on a twin-disk machine, you are logged on to drive A and you want to see the directory of the disk in drive B, then type DIR B: Of course, there still aren't any files on the disk, so the directory will still be empty; but this time you will not get an error message, whereas with the unformatted disk you did.

Sometimes we reformat old disks containing data or program files we no longer want. If ever you do this, check the directory first to make quite sure there is nothing on the disk that you want because formatting erases any existing files! Nothing remains on it after formatting except the pattern of tracks and sectors.

So now you know not only how data is represented and stored on disk, but you know how the computer can reference the point at which it started to store it. This brings us on to a more detailed look at ***retrieval***.

File names

Simply, retrieval is reading the contents of a file stored on disk back into the computer memory so they are ready for use. If the file contains a program (i.e. a list of instructions which the computer is to obey), it must be read into memory before it can be ***run*** (i.e. used). If it contains data, it must be read into memory before the data can be processed or output. Either way, what we are doing is the computer equivalent of going to a filing cabinet, opening a drawer and pulling out the wanted file.

A disk may carry many files, and each is identified by a name which we give it.

File names may be made up of either alphabetic or numeric characters or a mixture of the two; the usual way to express this fact is to say that ***alphanumeric*** characters may be used for file names.

Most operating systems will only allow file names to be up to eight characters long. A few non-alphanumeric characters are also allowable in file names, but some are not, so it is best to avoid them unless you can refer to your operating system handbook to determine which are safe to use. In particular, note that spaces are not allowed. So a file named MYFILE would not be permissible, but MYFILE would be. Not that it would not be a very useful file name, because it gives no clue as to whether it is a program file or a data file, and no idea as to the contents.

File names may have ***extensions*** of up to three characters and these extensions can be very useful in telling us more about a file. For example, you could give the extension .DTA to MYFILE, so that it would be known as MYFILE.DTA (notice that the full stop tells the system where the file name ends and the extension begins). If we listed the directory of a disk containing this file, it would be listed with both the file name and the extension (although the full stop would be omitted by most systems and a number of spaces inserted instead so that the extensions of all files on the disk appeared one under the other in a column). The .DTA extension tells anyone coming to use the disk that MYFILE is a data file. You will find some people use the extension .DAT to mean the same thing.

'WHAT SHALL WE CALL
OUR FIRST FILE NAME
DARLING ?'
A–Z
Computer
File
Names

Having identified it as a data file, it remains to choose a more helpful name for it. For example, if it contained records of all your income during the year 1988 you might call it INCOME88.DTA; it is immediately identifiable as a data file containing records relating to income in 1988.

You should be aware that some file names are given extensions automatically by the software with which they are created. You will find reference to these in your operating system handbook, and you should avoid using them for any purpose other than that for which they are intended. To give you one or two examples: if you were to write a program in BASIC (one of several programming languages which you are likely to come across) and then save your program to disk, you would find that the extension .BAS had been automatically added to whatever file name you chose for your program.

Similarly, if you wrote your program in a language called PASCAL, the Pascal software would add the file name extension .PAS when you saved it to disk.

Saving to disk simply means copying a record of your program from memory which is volatile (i.e. not permanent) on to a disk where it can be stored permanently. This is something which we do frequently when inputting programs, so as to minimize the risk of loosing valuable work in the event of a power failure, or something unexpected happening when we try out part of our program with test data.

There are a number of other file name extensions which you will come across, but not all of them are common to the several operating systems which are likely to be used by readers of this book. There is just one more file extension you should become familiar with at this time: it is the extension used by your system to identify a command file. With many operating systems, the file name extension is .COM; with others it is .CMD. Most systems use one or other of these conventions for command files.

Command files

What is a command file anyway? What characteristics does it have? And why do we need to know?

The first point about a command file is that it contains program information rather than data.

Secondly, it contains this information in machine-readable (i.e. binary) code. So there is no need for any other software to stand between a command file and the computer system itself.

If you wish to load and run a .COM or .CMD file, all you have to do is to type in the file name against the operating system prompt, for example, A>, and press the ENTER key. The computer immediately searches the directory of the disk in drive A until it finds the ***address*** of the file you have requested. Once found, the command file is loaded into the computer memory and automatically executed (i.e. run).

Only command files and batch files (which we will discuss more fully in a later chapter) can be run in this way – and that is at least one very good reason for knowing a command file when you meet one!

Directory tracks and file allocation tables

On each disk, the operating system uses special tracks to house directory information, so the read/write head does not have to scan the whole disk to see if the requested file is present and, if so, where it starts.

When a file is first created, the system automatically adds the file name (with any extension used) to the directory, together with the address (track and sector) where the operating system has started to store the file. It also records the total length of the file in bytes and the date/time when the file was created – assuming that you set the date and time correctly when you loaded the operating system.

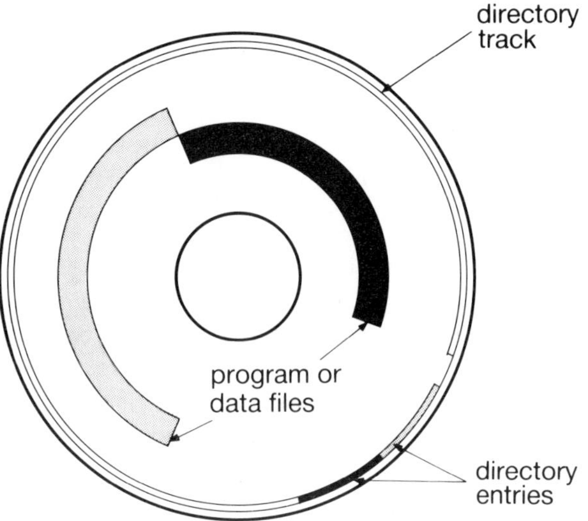

Disk use by computer

The diagram above illustrates the way the directory works. The system area on each disk also contains a ***file allocation table***. The system uses this to allocate free sectors to new files as they are created and it keeps track of the locations which belong to each file. Both the file allocation table and an empty directory are created on disk during the formatting process.

From what has been said, it begins to appear that retrieval of information from a computer system is quite like the manual process we would go to get back information stored on paper in a filing cabinet, except that the computer system is much faster. Putting the correct disk into the disk drive is like selecting the right drawer of the filing cabinet. Within that drawer there many files, just as on a disk there may be many files. But there are differences.

Differences between:	**Manual System**	**Computer system**
1	Files arranged alphabetically and numerically.	Files stored wherever there happens to be space on disk.
2	A clerk searching for one file would start looking in the filing cabinet around the letter or number area of the file.	The computer moves straight to the point on disk where the disk file allocation table tells it the file is stored and reads the file into the computer memory.
3	The file, when found, is taken to the clerk's desk where s/he works on it. It is removed from the system and another clerk may not use it at the same time.	The computer copies the file or part of the file into the computer memory. The original file remains in the system on disk for others to use and the operator has an exact copy to work with.

We have now covered as much ground as we need to for the time being with regard to storage and retrieval; we shall next look at processing and output, the two other key areas of any information system. But we want to do this through the medium of practical work, and for you to be able to do this with confidence and understanding, you first need to know more about system commands and utilities.

Some useful operating system commands

Internal and external system commands

You have already used one utility – a program file usually called FORMAT. All you did was to type in the file name against the system prompt and enter the drive where you were placing the disk to be formatted. The computer immediately loaded the program into memory and ran it because it was a command file, written in machine code.

Why not have a look at the directory of your utilities disk to see if you can identify some other command files? Remember how? Make sure the computer is logged on to the disk drive in which you have placed the disk (if you want to change the logged drive, just type in the drive letter of the required drive followed by a colon and then press ENTER); then type the command DIR and press the ENTER key.

The name, extension and, with many systems, the size (in bytes), date and time of creation or last amendment, will be displayed for each file. If there are more than a couple of dozen files on the disk, you will not be able to see them all listed at once. Some systems will pause at the end of a screen-full (sometimes referred to as a 'page') and not move to the next screen-full until prompted to do so by the user; others will scroll straight through to the end of the list unless the DIR command is qualified by some further instruction. For example, when using the MSDOS operating system, DIR/P will list the directory a screen-full at a time. (MSDOS: Microsoft Disk Operating System – a very widely used operating system with business microcomputers.) If you cannot make the listing do what you want it to do, check in your system handbook.

Bearing in mind that you used exactly the same approach with the command DIR as you did with FORMAT, you might expect to find DIR in your listing as a command file. But you know from what you have done already that you can use the DIR command without there being a DIR.COM file on the disk because it is an ***internal*** or ***resident command***, meaning that it is built into the operating system itself. You will quickly discover why software engineers have designed it this way. It would be annoying if we had to insert a utilities disk every time we wanted to check the directory of a disk. In the same way, we would not wish to copy a utility called DIR.COM on to every disk we used. So the obvious thing to do is to make it part of the operating system which is read into memory when the machine is powered up. It is then available for use at any time.

DIR is not the only internal command; commands for copying files (e.g. COPY in MSDOS, PIP in CP/M*), deleting files (DEL in MSDOS, ERA in CP/M), setting date and time (DATE, TIME in MSDOS, TOD in

* Another microcomputer operating system, produced by Microsoft's main rival, Digital Research. CP/M stands for Control Program for Micros, and it was the first operating system to receive general acceptance as an unofficial standard in the microcomputer field.

CP/M) and displaying on screen the contents of an ASCII file (the command is usually TYPE) – all these are internal commands, built into the operating system. There are others, but these are the ones you are most likely to use at present.

Copying files

You can use some internal commands right away. If you are working in a tutored group, ask your tutor for a disk containing the files TELEDIR.DTA and BIRTHDAY.BAS and copy these onto the disk you formatted earlier. If you are not working under tutorial guidance and do not have access to the disk which is a part of the total package associated with this book, you will not have files TELEDIR.DTA and BIRTHDAY.BAS to copy. But that will not prevent you from practising. Try copying one or two of the files from your utilities disk onto the disk you formatted. With a twin floppy disk system, you could put your ***source disk*** (the one containing the file you want to copy) in drive A, the ***destination disk*** (the one you are copying to) in drive B, and use a command of the form

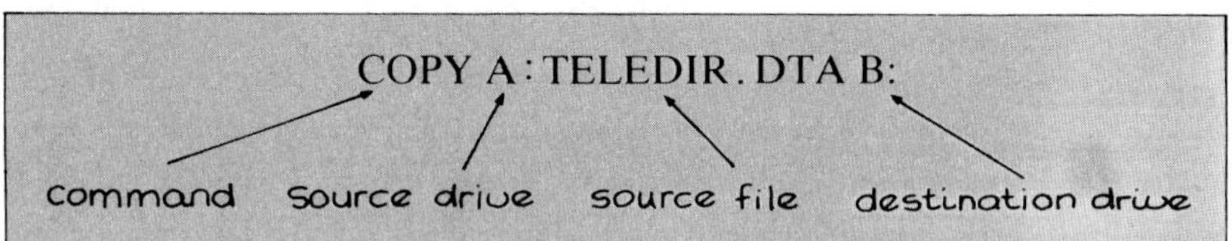

if the operating system is MSDOS, or in the case of CP/M, a command of the form

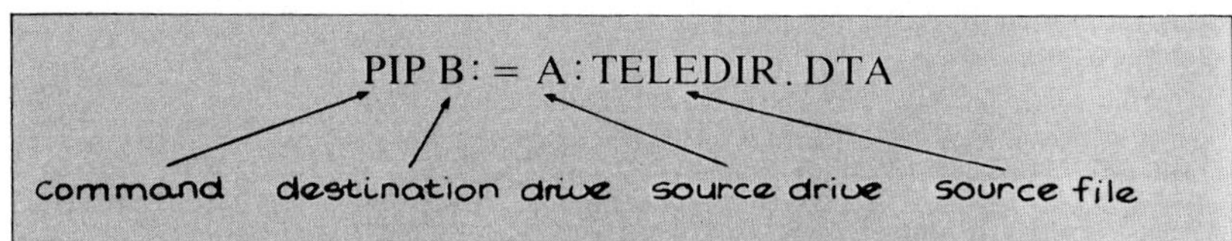

The command PIP, by the way, is derived from the expression Peripheral Interchange Program.

In both the examples given above we are using a short form of command, because we have not specified the file name to be used for the new copy on drive B. In these circumstances, the computer assumes that we wish to use the same file name. Had we wished to call the copy by a different name – e.g. FONELIST.DTA – then the commands would have been

```
COPY A:TELEDIR.DTA B:FONELIST.DTA
PIP B:FONELIST.DTA=A:TELEDIR.DTA
```

Sometimes – especially during program development and testing – it is useful to have the same file twice on the same disk under different names so that you can always get back to the original data or program if you need to. To duplicate a file under another name on the same disk, make sure that the logged drive is the same one that holds your disk and then use the shortened command

```
   COPY TELEDIR.DTA FONELIST.DTA
or PIP FONELIST.DTA =TELEDIR.DTA
```

If you have a system with only one disk drive, use commands just like those we have illustrated above; you will find that the system views the two disks (rather than the disk drives) as A and B, and prompts you when you need to change from one disk to the other. It will want the source disk first, and will copy the required file (or as much of it as it can) into memory; then it will ask for the destination disk and write to it the file contents which it is holding in memory. With a large file and a small memory, this process may have to be repeated many times to copy the complete file.

The use of wild cards

If you needed to copy or delete a whole batch of files, it would take a long time to have to input individual commands for each file, and operating system designers have recognized this by providing a ***wild card*** facility. There are two wild card characters: the question mark (?) and the asterisk (*). A ? in a file name or extension indicates that any single valid character may occupy that position.

For example, if you had on drive A a group of files

```
DEPT1DIR.DTA
DEPT2DIR.DTA
DEPT3DIR.DTA
```

then we could copy them all on to a disk in drive B by one command in which the file name would be written DEPT?DIR.

Thus the command using an MSDOS operating system would be

```
COPY A:DEPT?DIR.DTA B:
```

or with a CP/M operating system:

```
PIP B:=A:DEPT?DIR.DTA
```

In both cases, all three files would be copied, one after the other.

The * is used in just the same way except that it represents not just a single character, but a group of characters. By way of illustration, consider a disk containing a group of files associated with a database. They might all have a common file name, e.g. MEMLIST, but with different extensions, depending on the nature of the file contents in each case. Some typical file specifications might be:

```
MEMLIST.DEF
MEMLIST.INX
MEMLIST.DAO
MEMLIST.MSK
MEMLIST.PRC
MEMLIST.CEL
etc.
```

and if one wanted to copy or delete these with just one command, it would simply be a matter of using the asterisk wild card to represent *any* extension.

Deleting files

The MSDOS command DEL A:MEMLIST.* (or the CP/M command ERA A:MEMLIST.*) would delete every file on the disk in drive A having the file name MEMLIST, regardless of the extension. If you wanted to delete every file on the disk you could use two wild cards:

```
DEL A:*.*
```

– But take great care that you mean it! Once your files are gone, you can't get them back. This is one reason why you should keep back-up copies of all important work.

Of course, the idea of using two wild cards, one to represent any file name and the other to represent any extension, is not restricted to deletion. We often use this method to copy the entire contents of one disk on to another. But more of that in a moment. First, let us consider a little more closely a term we introduced in the previous paragraph: ***file specification***.

Up to this point we have talked about file names and extensions; file specification is a term meaning the file name with its extension. Remember that the extension incorporates a leading dot or full stop. Thus in the list of database files which we gave above, we would refer to MEMLIST as a file name (which happens in this case to be common to a number of files); whilst MEMLIST.DEF would be referred to as the file specification (often abbreviated to 'filespec') of the first file in the list.

The three internal commands which we have now considered in some detail – DIR, COPY (or PIP) and DEL (or ERA) are so useful that it is important that you are able to use them (or their equivalents) fluently.

So break off for a while and practise:

1 Copy files to another disk keeping the same filespecs.
2 Copy files to another disk using a different (but appropriate) filespec for the files on the destination disk.
3 Copy files to the same disk, using different filespecs.
4 Use both forms of wild card to copy or delete groups of files.

Call for the DIRectory from time to time to check that the copying or deletion commands have been carried out as intended. (Some files suitable for this practise are included on the disk associated with this book.)

Other forms of disk copying

Some operating systems include an external command DISKCOPY or FASTCOPY in their utilities. These work quite differently from COPY or PIP and need to be used with care. We would suggest that you avoid using them at this stage: they do nothing which cannot be achieved by the FORMAT and COPY commands (or their equivalents) and we shall not consider them further in this book. The important point is, if you should come across them, don't think they are just other names for the COPY or PIP commands. They are not.

Legal and illegal copying

Let us look at one or two applications of the COPY command. Whenever you buy a new piece of software – for example, a word processing package – it is supplied to you on a disk, or sometimes with a large package, on several disks. Before you attempt to use the software, the first thing to do is to make a copy of the disk(s). Then put the original disk(s) away in a safe place and work with the copies. Thus, if anything unfortunate happens and the working copy of your software is ***corrupted*** (i.e. something either you or the computer system has done has introduced errors into the programs), you can go back to the original source which you know to be error free, and recopy it.

Making single copies of software for the purpose we have described is legitimate, but be warned! Copying of software for any other purpose (like giving it to your friends) is illegal. It is an infringement of copyright commonly called *software piracy*. Don't do it.

Software producers have found a number of ways of combatting illegal copying; for example, some encode into the original disk something which is essential to the running of the program, but which cannot be copied. In such cases, still take a copy of the purchased disk, but keep the *copy* safe and work with the original. If the original becomes corrupted, copy the copy back over it and, short of physical damage to the original disk, you will be able to continue working satisfactorily. Software companies which take this approach will supply a new disk in exchange for a damaged one, but all this takes time, during which you are without your software. Software protection is a subject in its own right, and outside the scope of this book; we have mentioned it only in the context of applications of disk copying.

The need for back-up copies of data

Maintaining regular back-up copies of your data disks is also vitally important. At this stage, whilst you are still at an introductory level, you will not generate much data and it will not have so much significance as would, say, financial data in a business system.

But in a real system, totally dependent on computer-based records, it is essential that proper precautions are taken to ensure that a failure of any kind does not have catastrophic effects.

Get used to backing up your work frequently. Back-up systems which will enable you to reconstruct data in the event of file corruption will vary according to the particular applications you are dealing with, and we shall touch on this subject again in later chapters.

Now that you have mastered the commands necessary to format disks, call for directory listings, copy or delete individual files or blocks of files, we are all but ready to go back and take a closer look at processing and output. There is just one thing we need to do first: the formatted disk you prepared, and on to which you copied (and probably deleted!) TELEDIR.DTA, BIRTHDAY.BAS and perhaps other files, is probably getting in a bit of a mess by now. In any case, it has not had the operating system transferred to it, and it would be useful to have it there so that you can boot the system from your own disk.

Transferring systems files on to a newly formatted disk

Depending on the operating system you have, we may be able to kill two birds with one stone. The simplest way of cleaning down a disk and starting again, is to use the FORMAT utility (or its equivalent). This leaves nothing but the magnetic pattern of tracks and sectors on the disk. With some operating systems, e.g. MSDOS or PCDOS (virtually the same as MSDOS, but supplied by IBM, the biggest computer company in the world, for its own micros), the FORMAT command can be modified by adding /S to the end of it, and if this is done, the operating system is automatically transferred to the newly formatted disk.

Other systems require a separate command to transfer the system; for example, with a RML480Z running CP/M you would first use FORMAT and then SYSGEN. Check with your tutor the correct procedure for your system and make a note of it for future use.

When you have reformatted your disk and transferred the operating system to it, close down the computer. To do this, first ensure that the screen is displaying the system prompt, then carefully take out the disk(s) and place them immediately in their sleeves to ensure that the active surface does not get damaged. Then switch the computer off and the printer too if you have one.

You may wish to switch the computer on again in a minute, but it is bad practice to switch it back on immediately after switching off, so we will take the opportunity to say a little more about disk care whilst you give the machine a break.

Care of disks

Great care must be taken of the active surface of your floppy disks. But as well as avoiding physical damage, you must also beware of invisible dangers in the form of stray magnetic fields. Remember that data is stored in the form of a magnetic pattern in the disk coating; any strong magnetic field could destroy this. Such fields may be produced by television receivers, electric fan motors, electric typewriter motors or any unshielded mains transformers; so keep your disks away from these potential sources of trouble.

Give a thought too to the temperature of the environment in which you keep your disks. You will weaken the magnetic strength of the data pattern if you subject the disks to extremes of temperature, either too hot or too cold. In general, if the temperature is comfortable enough for you, it is all right for your disks too. So your working disks may be in no danger so far as temperature is concerned; but remember your master disks, which you have stored in a 'safe place', may become damaged if the environment is not suitable.

A learning checklist

Here is an opportunity for you to check just what you have learned so far. What the checklist does is to suggest what you should be able to *do*. Measure yourself against it and go back for further revision and practice if necessary. By now you should be able to:

1 Identify four units of hardware which together could form a microcomputer system.
2 Power up and power down a complete microcomputer system in an appropriate sequence.
3 Classify different units of a microcomputer system into categories of input devices, output devices, input/output devices and processing units.
4 State environments likely to damage microcomputer equipment, storage media, or data.
5 Explain how characters are coded and stored on magnetic disks.
6 Explain the need for formatting and use the terms track and sector correctly.
7 Use the system utility FORMAT or its equivalent to format a disk and, if required, transfer the operating system to the newly formatted disk.
8 Explain how the Disk Operating System uses directory tracks and a file allocation table to facilitate efficient storage and retrieval of files.
9 Create file specifications which indicate whether the files are program files or data files, and which provide an unambiguous description of the file content.
10 State the difference between a program file and a data file.

11 Recognize the significance of some commonly used file name extensions.
12 Recognize simple error messages or interpret them using an appropriate manual.
13 Use the operating system internal commands to produce, one page at a time, a catalogue containing extended definitions and detail about the files on a disk.
14 Use the operating system internal commands to copy a single file and a group of related files from one disk to another.
15 Use the operating system internal commands to duplicate a file under another name on the same disk or a different disk.
16 State reasons for producing regular back-up copies of important work.
17 Produce back-up copies of disks.
18 Delete files held on magnetic media.

CHAPTER 3 Processing and output

The function of a programming language interpreter

There is more practical work ahead of you, so switch on your computer and load the operating system, but this time use your own disk – the one you formatted and copied the system files on to when working through the last pages of the previous chapter. If you have done the job correctly, the computer will load the operating system from your disk.

Once the system prompt A> appears, you will do some more file copying – but this is not just practice, it's for real. What you are going to do is copy from the utilities disk on to your disk the command file (and any associated files) containing the BASIC interpreter. An ***interpreter*** is a program or group of programs which translate into machine code instructions which we write in a language not far removed from a limited form of English.

For example, if we wanted the computer to work out the VAT and total price we would have to pay for an article costing £p plus VAT, we could write a small program of instructions to the computer which would include:

```
VAT = PRICE * 0.15 : TOTAL = PRICE + VAT
```

(Notice that the asterisk (*) is used for a multiplication sign rather than x so that there is no risk of confusion between the letter x and the mathematical function of multiplication.)

Now the computer only understands machine code (binary) instructions, and the purpose of the interpreter is to translate our statements about the relationships of PRICE, VAT and TOTAL into machine code.

Different systems provide BASIC interpreters under a variety of names, and again you must refer to your tutor or the documentation supplied with your computer to find the name which is appropriate in your own case. If you cannot get help in this way, place the utilities disk in disk drive A, call the directory and look for such file names as BASIC, MSBASIC, BASICA, GWBASIC. You can be sure that the acronym BASIC (which stands for Beginners' All-purpose Symbolic Instruction Code) will appear somewhere in the file name. And, of course, the file(s) you are looking for will include at least one with a .COM (or equivalent) extension.

You cannot interpret a high-level language to the machine if the interpreter is not itself in machine language, and you will remember that one of the features of command files is that their contents are written in machine code.

Whatever means you use, when you have found the appropriate command file, copy it and any others obviously associated with it on to your own system disk. Finally, copy BIRTHDAY.BAS back on to your disk. After this copying, make sure that your working disk is in drive A and that the system is logged to drive A. You should know by now how to change the logged drive if you need to, but see page 22 if you are unsure.

Now BIRTHDAY.BAS is written in the high-level language BASIC, as the file name extension tells us. It has therefore to be interpreted to enable the computer system to understand it and act on its instructions. So, with the system prompt showing on the screen, type in the file name of your BASIC interpreter and press the ENTER key. You will see the machine activate the disk drive (usually a red light on the drive comes on whilst the drive is active); what is happening is that the interpreter file is being read into the computer memory.

As soon as this operation is complete, control passes to the interpreter; if you look at the screen, you will see displayed some brief information about the interpreter, and the cursor is ready on the left-hand side of the screen, waiting for your command. The system prompt is no longer displayed because control has passed to the interpreter.

The BASIC interpreter recognizes certain ***keywords*** which include the commands LOAD (which is used to read into memory a BASIC program stored on disk) and RUN (which starts the operation of the program once it has been loaded into memory). We shall now use these to load and run the program BIRTHDAY.BAS (see Chapter 2 page 27). In BASIC, all strings of characters are enclosed within inverted commas (double quotes – some people call them 'speech marks') so that the interpreter can recognize that it is dealing with a group of characters as such and not the name of a variable, such as VAT or TOTAL in the very small example we gave above. Since the file name BIRTHDAY is to be treated as a group of characters, we must enclose it in inverted commas when using it in the LOAD command. So type in the command

LOAD "BIRTHDAY"

and press the ENTER key.

From now on, when we want you to type something in at the keyboard and then press the ENTER key, we shall simply ask you to *enter* whatever it is. For example

Enter LOAD "BIRTHDAY"

meaning: type LOAD "BIRTHDAY" in at the keyboard and, when you are satisfied that you have typed it correctly, tell the machine to accept it by pressing the ENTER key.

Just as when you were entering command file names at system level, you did not have to enter the .COM or similar extension, so with the control passed to the BASIC interpreter, you do not have to enter the .BAS extension to BASIC program file names.

Now enter the command RUN.

We do not have to specify what is to be run, because there is only one BASIC program file loaded into memory. Whereas, with the LOAD command the file had to be distinguished from many.

The processing of data in a computer system

You should now have before you a screen displaying an opening menu. The software you are using is an example of what is called ***menu-driven*** software. By this we mean that the user guides the program through his choice of a number of pre-determined processes for which the program has been designed.

In the present case the menu gives you a choice of five options:

```
1 Enter new names and birthdays
2 Delete entries
3 Interrogate the data file
4 List all records on file
5 Exit from the program
```

The menu options screen

There is no data held in the computer yet, because this is the first time you have used this software. Therefore you must enter some names and birth dates; to do this choose option 1.

On entering 1 you will be presented with a new screen which will enable you to make data enteries. Type in data – surname, first name and birthday – as indicated by the screen prompts, pressing the ENTER key after entry; you will then see a question appear on the screen which requires a yes/no answer.

With virtually all professionally written software, it is sufficient to enter either Y or N in either upper or lower case. Depending on the facilities available to the software writer and his program writing style, you may find that the computer reacts immediately to the typing of a single appropriate character without waiting for you to press the ENTER key as you would normally do when confirming that what you have keyed in is correct and ready for entry. So be prepared for this to happen, but equally, be prepared to press the ENTER key if the machine does not respond when you think it should. This illustration shows a completed screen.

```
BIRTHDAY LIST - NEW ENTRIES

SURNAME? Robinson

FIRST NAME? Leslie

BIRTH DATE? (dd/mm/yy) 08/02/72
(It is important to use this format)

CHECK! Are these entries correct? (Y/N)

More entries to make (Y/N)
```

The BIRTHDAY.BAS program new entries screen

The point of the question "Are these entries correct?" – is to allow users to discard an incorrect entry screen before the data ever gets as far as being filed. It is a feature which is always to be found in one form or another in all professional software, because there must be the opportunity for users to check their entries and revise them if they are wrong before the data is filed or processed.

Fields and records

Continue using this screen until you have created a dozen or so records; they needn't of course relate to real people if you don't know enough actual birthdays. In fact it would be a good idea to have some made-up entries, because you cannot explore the software to the full without having several (say three or four) birthdays in the same month and two or more individuals with the same surname. The software is designed to accept the entry of up to 30 records in one batch.

We have started to use the term ***record***, and it needs to be defined. It is more fully defined in Chapter 4, but for now, think of it as a row in a table which contains related data about people, places or things. Everything in the row refers to one person, place or thing. In another row the data refers to a different person, place or thing, and this is another record. Each data item is held in a ***field*** and all data items of the same kind are in the same field.

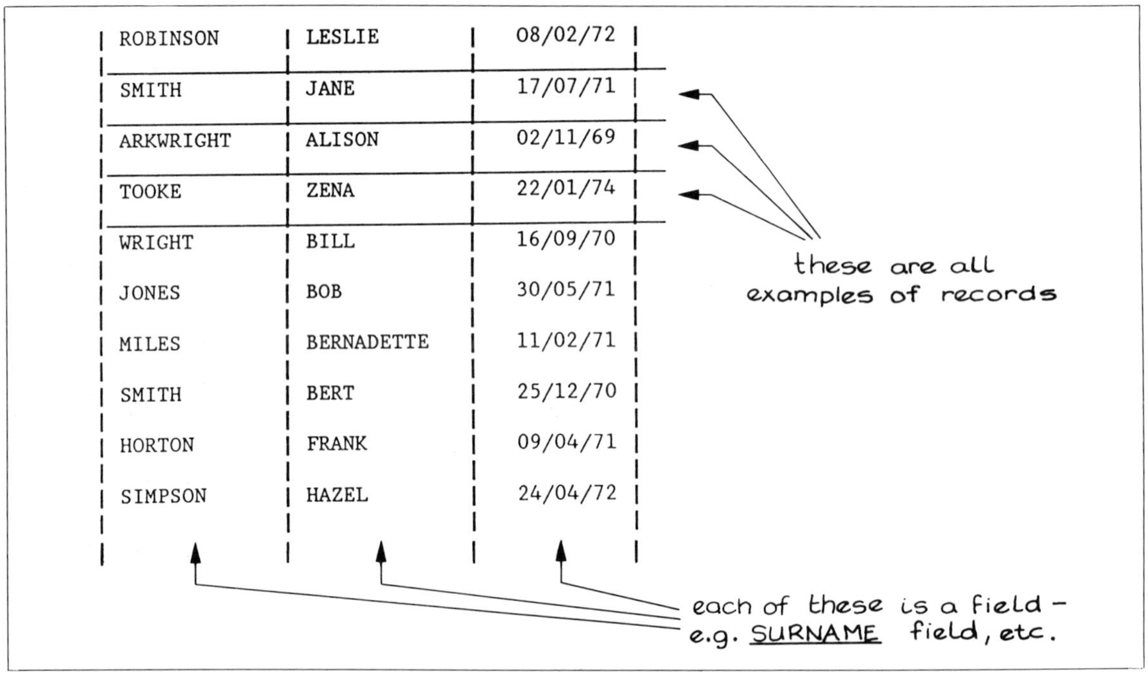

ROBINSON	LESLIE	08/02/72
SMITH	JANE	17/07/71
ARKWRIGHT	ALISON	02/11/69
TOOKE	ZENA	22/01/74
WRIGHT	BILL	16/09/70
JONES	BOB	30/05/71
MILES	BERNADETTE	11/02/71
SMITH	BERT	25/12/70
HORTON	FRANK	09/04/71
SIMPSON	HAZEL	24/04/72

these are all examples of records

each of these is a field – e.g. SURNAME field, etc.

A records listing for *BIRTHDAY.DTA file*

When you have completed your batch of entries and finally respond to the question "More entries?" with N, then all the entries which you have made, and which have been kept temporarily in memory, are appended to a file called BIRTHDAY.DTA. This means that they are added on to the end of whatever data is already in that file. When you started, there wasn't even a file of that name on the disk because this was the first time you had run the program. So when the program reached an instruction to append your entries to the file BIRTHDAY.DTA, the first thing it did was to create the file; then it appended your records to the end of an empty file.

Records processing

The sort of filing just done for you by the BIRTHDAY.BAS program is one kind of processing undertaken by computers. It is part of a group of activities known collectively as ***records processing***. Within records processing, you can: write records to file which amend or replace existing records; add new records to the end of a file or insert them at any point in the file you choose; delete records; read all or selected records from the disk back into computer memory.

Let's do some more processing. You will notice that since we told the computer we had no more entries to make at this time, it automatically returned us to the main menu. Choose option 3 this time. You are presented with a different screen, carrying an explanatory note and inviting you to choose from what is, in essence, a second-level menu.

In this case there are only two options: you can seek information regarding a named individual or regarding all individuals whose birthdays fall in a named month. You will enter either I or M.

Try entering a different character and see what happens. You will find that the system refuses to accept it, because the program has been designed to reject all ***illegal*** entries (this is the term used in computing to describe unacceptable responses to questions). What you have just demonstrated to yourself is an example of ***input validation***; only four possible responses – I, i, M, m – are acceptable, and the program is designed to ensure that only valid inputs are accepted.

Now use both the I and M options to provide outputs to screen of the desired birthday information. In both cases you are using the *processing* power of the computer to select all records in the file which have a specified characteristic, and to read these selected records back into memory prior to outputting them to screen.

We shall say more about outputting a little later on; first, let's look at another aspect of file processing – deleting a specified record. There are many occasions in practice when we want to do this. For example, if we kept stock records in a computer file and in the course of time we decided not to stock a particular item in future, the record for that item would need to be deleted from the stock file. Or, if we are running an accounts system on a computer, we need to be able to delete a record from the debtors' file when the debt has been paid. So let's try this aspect of processing.

Return to the main menu (look at the message at the foot of the screen, which tells you what to enter to do this) and then select option 4. This will enable you to see all the records you have on your file at present, and it gives you the option of outputting the list of records to your printer (if you have one connected) or to screen.

Since we haven't used the printer yet, it might be worth doing so. Make sure that the ***multicore cable*** which carries the data output from the printer port to the printer is properly plugged in at both ends; that the printer is connected to a power supply and switched on; and that paper has been loaded. (A ***port*** is the name we give to the multi-pin socket which is often, but not always, at the back of the computer and which has fed to it from the computer electrical signals representing the ASCII codes of characters to be output from the computer. In this case, the electrical signals will be used to control the operation of the printer.)

Following the screen prompts, print your list of records. It doesn't matter whether you have listed on paper (***hard copy***) or to screen (***soft copy***); the purpose of listing is so that you can pick a record – any one you like – to try out record deletion. Having chosen the record you want to delete, note the records either side of it because, when you have used the software to delete the selected record, you will want to check back on the file listing to satisfy yourself that it really has been deleted.

So from the main menu choose option 2, and by following the prompts on the subsequent screen, delete your chosen record. By responding N to the question "Any more deletions?" you will return to the opening menu.

Now take option 3 and specify the name you have deleted; the system sends you a message to say that it has no data relating to the named individual.

Just to be quite sure that the record has been deleted, go back to option 4 and list the file contents again. You will find that it really has gone, and that the records which were either side of it are now next to each other. So you have achieved successfully another aspect of records processing.

File and records processing are the most important kinds of processing from the point of view of business applications, although some straight-forward arithmetic processing is also required. With engineering and scientific applications, the emphasis is often different. Here the processing frequently involves doing difficult and repetitive calculations very quickly and very accurately; it is sometimes referred to as 'number crunching'.

The work on processing leads naturally into a consideration of output. There would be no point in processing if the result were not to be output somewhere.

The output of information using a computer system

So far, you have seen output to screen, and you may also have output to printer. For example, when you asked for the birth date of a named individual, the information was presented to you on the

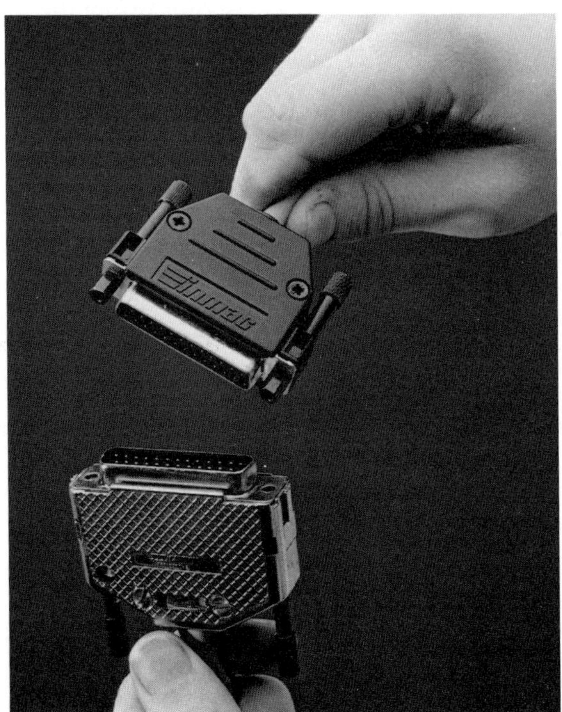

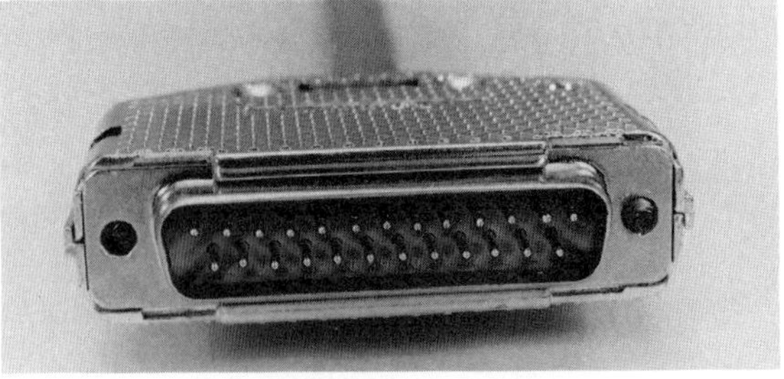

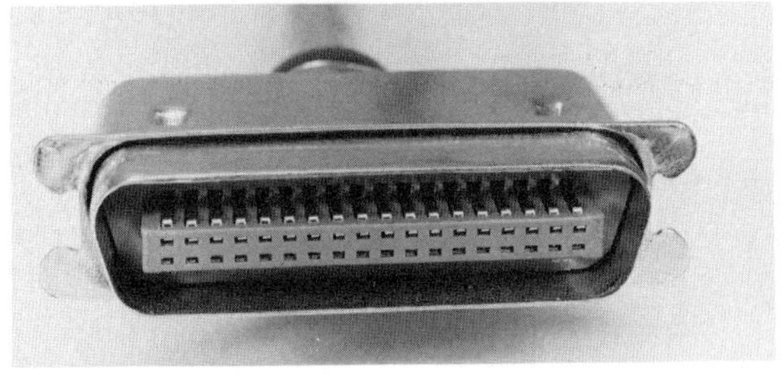

Two male connectors, the RS232 (V24) (top right) and the Centronics type (bottom right)

A male and female RS232 (V24) connector (left)

screen. When you listed the contents of your data file, you had the choice of outputting to screen or to printer.

You have also used the disk as an ***input/output*** (***I/O***) device; when you input data about your friends and their birth dates, this was held temporarily in the computer memory until you indicated that there was no more data to enter. Then the data was *output* to a disk file. (Later when you interrogated that file, data was *input* from it into the computer.)

A form of output which you have not yet had the opportunity to try is to another computer. This might perhaps be close by, or thousands of miles away, with connection effected over telephone lines and other communications circuits. It may be that your computer and the one to which you are outputting are both connected to a common Local Area Network (LAN) which is the kind of linking one would use in a large building or within a single site containing several buildings.

In all these cases, as in the case of connection to a printer, the data output signals leave the computer through multi-pin sockets (usually situated at the rear of micro-computers) and are normally one of the two shapes shown in the photographs opposite. Look around your computer and see if you can locate one or more output ports looking like them.

Serial and Parallel transmission of data

Remember that a byte, which represents a character, comprises eight bits. Within the computer, each bit is represented by an electrical voltage level – for example, it might be a + 5 Volts for a '1' and 0 Volts for a '0'. If we wished to transmit this electrical information to control a printer, and we wanted to transmit every bit of the byte at the same time, then we would have to use separate wires for each bit of the byte. This is called ***parallel transmission*** and the multi-pin plugs and sockets usually (but not always) used for parallel transmission are of the Centronics design.

The other way of delivering the electrical signals to a device at the other end of a transmission line is to queue the bits up and send them one after the other down the same pair of wires. The receiving device – it may be a printer or another computer – collects the bits and then reforms the byte. This is called ***serial transmission*** and for this the serial port uses RS232 plugs and sockets. ***RS232*** is the American code for this kind of connector; the European standard is called ***V24***. Physically, it is the same thing.

Printers may, and connection to non-local (remote) computers will, require serial transmission. In such cases, attention has to be given to a number of technical matters, such as the rate at which the bits are to be sent down the line – but these matters are outside the scope of this book. Fortunately, nearly all printers accept parallel transmission of the electrical signals representing bytes and these are generally easier to handle.

Using a screen dump facility

In the case of the program BIRTHDAY.BAS which you ran, there was an opportunity built into menu option 4 for you to produce a printed output. This facility was not available to you when using option 3, and it may be that you wanted a printed record of the information you obtained through this screen. With most business micros the keyboard includes a dedicated PRINT SCREEN key, by means of which it is possible to produce in hard copy an exact echo of the text displayed on the screen. If you have this facility on your computer, try it out.

This is called taking a ***screen dump***; everything displayed on the screen is printed, whether or not you want it. But at least the print-out includes the information you want. By the way, do make sure if you call for something to be printed that your printer is connected to the computer, loaded with paper and switched on. If it is not 'ready' the computer will wait and it will not accept any other instruction until is has received the 'ready' signal from the printer and has sent the data which you asked to be printed.

Printers

There are a number of quite different printer types which you may come across, and some others which you will only see if you have the opportunity to visit a large computer installation. We shall only look at those which you are most likely to come across.

Daisywheel printers

The ***daisywheel*** printer takes its name from the shape of its printwheel.

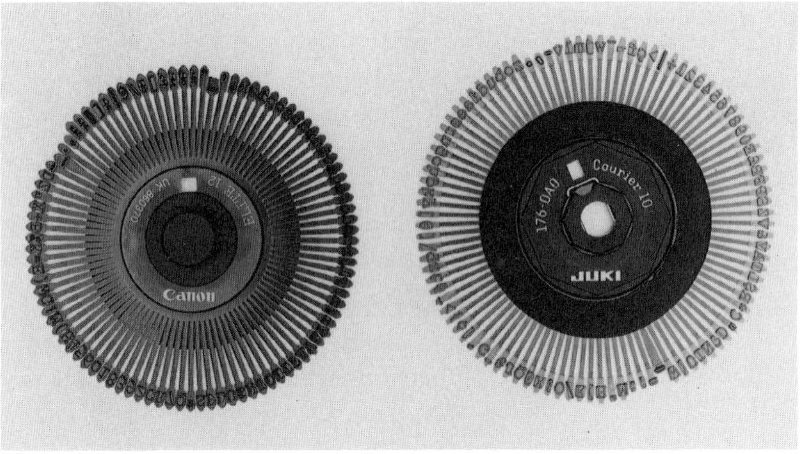

Print wheels from a daisy wheel printer

At the end of each 'petal' of the daisywheel a character is moulded in just the same way that is would be at the end of a type-bar in a conventional typewriter. The daisywheel will only fit in one position on the print head, because there is a spigot on the head which engages in the square cut-out which you can see in the printwheel in the illustration.

When the printer is in use, the print head rotates the daisywheel at several hundred revolutions per minute, and as the required character comes round to the print position it is struck sharply by a small solenoid with a hammer-like action. The moulded character at the end of the petal in turn strikes the ribbon and an image of the character is left impressed on the paper.

Print speeds with this type of machine vary from about 17 characters per second for a relatively cheap, light-duty machine, through to about 90 characters per second for a top-quality office machine costing about six times as much.

The great merit of daisywheel printers is the excellent quality of the output. Daisywheels may be moulded in plastic or they may be made of metal. The metal ones are much more durable and give an even sharper print than the plastic ones – but then, they should be better because they cost five or six times as much.

A very wide range of typefaces is available and there are also daisywheels for scientific and mathematical symbols, foreign language characters, italics, etc. But if you wish to change typeface in the middle of a document, you must arrange for printing to be halted at that point in order to change daisywheels. Typically, you will want to change back again a few characters later! This is quite inconvenient, and the lack of flexibility is probably the largest disadvantage of daisywheel machines in relation to the most commonly found alternative – the matrix printer.

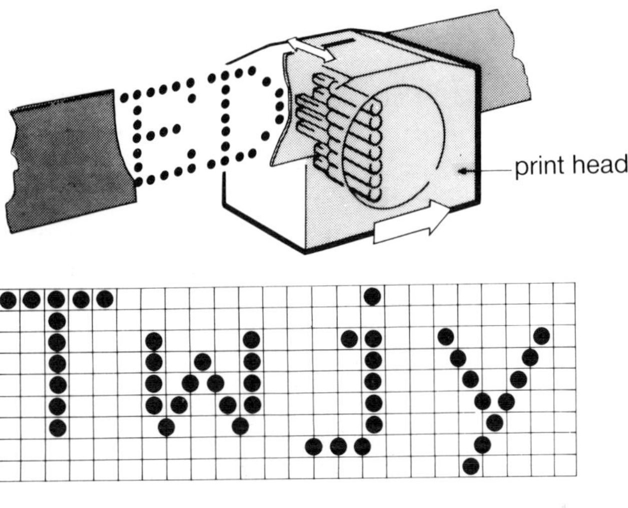

Matrix printer principles

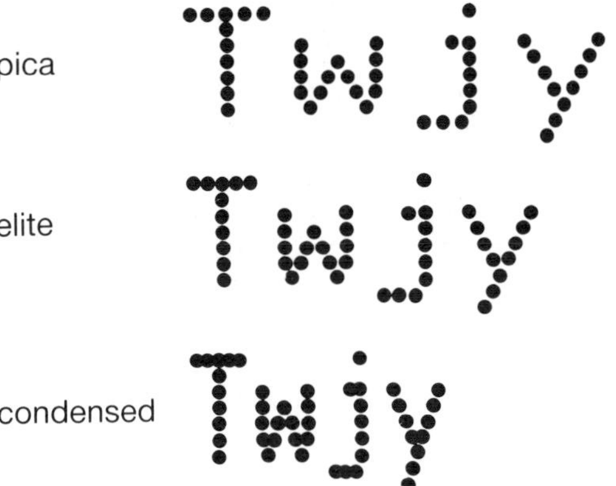

Dot matrix characters

pica
elite
condensed

How dot density changes print style

Matrix printers

In a ***matrix printer*** the print head carries a column of needles, each of which can be projected forward independently of the others. The effect of a needle being fired is that it pushes the ribbon against the paper at that point and leaves a small dot printed on the paper. So, by firing the pins in appropriate combinations and making the print head progress across the paper in very small steps, characters can be formed from the dot pattern. In many current printers, a character is contained with a 9 × 6 dot matrix – a standard which results from having 9 needles in the print head and making the head take six small steps during the formation of each character.

Because of the way characters are made up from dots, it is simple to change the type style – to go from standard characters to italics, for example, or to change the number of characters per inch, going into a condensed mode or into an enlarged mode. This flexibility is where the matrix printer scores over the daisywheel. But it does so at the expense of print quality, because the characters do not have the solid, sharp-edged appearance which is attainable with daisywheel elements.

In recent years a great deal of work has been done to improve the quality of the output from matrix printers and nearly every manufacturer now claims that his machines are able to produce text in ***near letter quality*** (***NLQ***). There are vast differences between what different manufactures call NLQ, but the best are very good indeed, being indistinguishable from daisywheel printing at a casual glance.

Several different techniques are employed to bring about the desired effect.

Some are hardware techniques; for example, a print head may contain a second column of needles slightly displaced vertically with respect to the first column so that they fill in some of the gaps between the dots of the first printing. Many manufacturers now use 24 needles of very small diameter so that a much denser image with less 'ripple' on the edge is obtained. All use smaller horizontal steps to increase the dot density in that direction. This horizontal motion is usually under software control, so that the user may select either ***draft*** quality, where the gaps between the dots are more obvious, but the print speed is substantially greater (typically 160 – 200 characters/second) or NLQ where the print speed will be reduced to perhaps 80 characters/second because of the smaller horizontal increases. Examples of these are shown below.

This shows the letter quality print of one of the better 24-pin matrix printers. It is very close to the quality obtainable from daisywheel printers.

This is the same printer operating in draft mode. The dot composition of the letters is apparent but less so than in the 9-pin printer example below.

This shows print quality of a cheaper 9-pin printer when operating in NLQ mode. It makes two passes to print each line.

This is the 9-pin printer operating in draft mode. Both the cheap and expensive printers offer more than one typeface for NLQ output.

Draft quality output and NLQ output

Cheap software is available which will control both horizontal and vertical movements and allow a good NLQ print to be obtained from a low-cost standard matrix printer; but the resulting output is produced very slowly – too slowly for serious use in an office environment, but acceptable for home use.

We will make brief reference to one or two other kinds of printers which you may come across, but since you are most likely to be using either a daisywheel or a matrix printer, let us first deal with one or two practical matters associated with these machines.

Paper-feed mechanisms

Some printers are supplied without any paper-feed arrangements at all. They rely solely on ***friction feed***, with the platen pulling the paper through as it turns. You feed in each page separately by hand, pulling the paper bail back out of the way until the top of the paper is high enough to pass behind the bail when it is put back in position. If you are dealing with a multi-page document, you must ensure that the software causes the printing to pause at each page end whilst you feed in the next sheet.

Although this can be an adequate arrangement for low-volume output, it is totally unsatisfactory in a busy office environment. Here a ***cut-sheet paper-feed attachment*** would be well worth its cost, simply on the grounds of increased productivity because the printing can proceed unattended.

There are many designs of cut sheet feeders, but there is one general principle which applies to them all: when in use, the roller pressure must be on, because the paper is drawn through into the printing position by the rotation of the platen.

The opposite rule applies if you are using continuous stationary with a sprocket or tractor feed (a sprocket feed is also sometimes called a pin feed). Here the paper must *not* be gripped tightly between the platen and the pressure roller, because it is being pulled through the printer at the correct rate by the sprockets engaging in the holes at the edge of the paper.

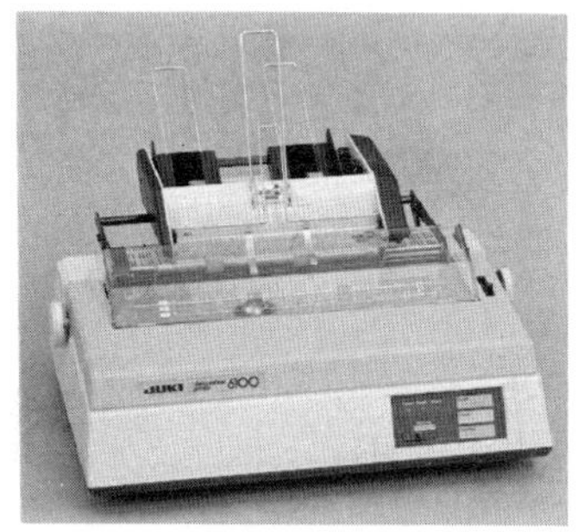

A cut-sheet paper-feed attachment

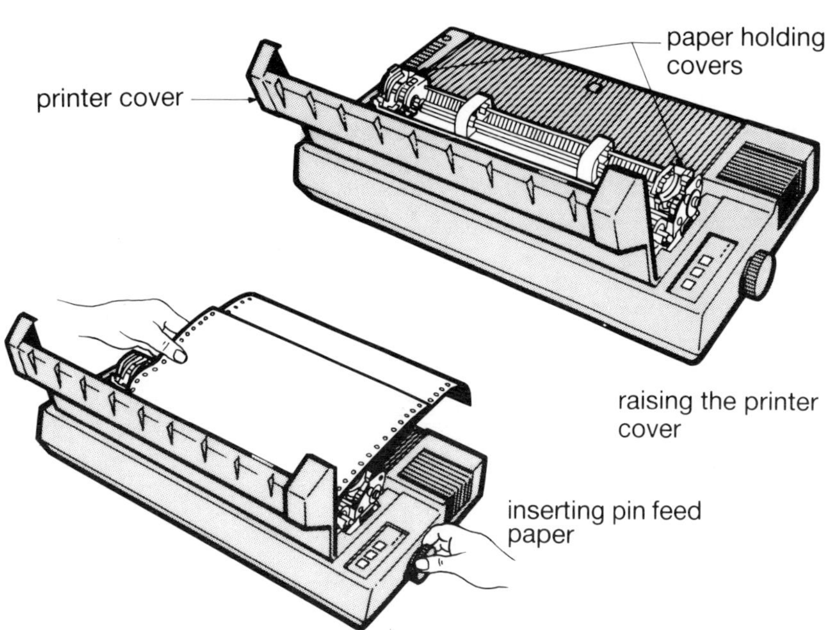

Tractor feed for continuous stationery (right)

It is possible to undertake very short print runs with continuous stationery using friction only and not using a sprocket feed, but this may cause misalignment or slippage and is not recommended.

With address labels there is a very little room for misalignment and these are invariably supplied mounted on a backing webb with sprocket holes for a tractor feed. When loading stationery with sprocket holes, always make sure that the paper is square in the machine before closing the gates which prevent the paper from riding off the sprockets. Also ensure that the distance between the sprocket wheels (which is adjustable) is just enough to prevent the paper falling slack in the centre, but not pulling tightly on the sprocket holes, since this is likely to tear the paper and cause a jam.

One last practical point about daisywheel and matrix printers: you may well be asked to change a ribbon at some time, and this is a fairly straight-forward thing to do because the ribbons are contained in cartridges which just snap into place. The only part of the job which is not always clearly explained in the handbooks is the actual path of the ribbon from the time it leaves the cartridge to the time it returns there. Two rules of thumb may help here. The first is to check carefully the ribbon path before you take the old cartridge out (and hope that the person who put the last cartridge in did it correctly!). The second is that you won't go far wrong if you make the ribbon pass immediately in front of the daisywheel, or in the case of matrix printers, next to the print head nose – *not* between the ribbon mask and the paper.

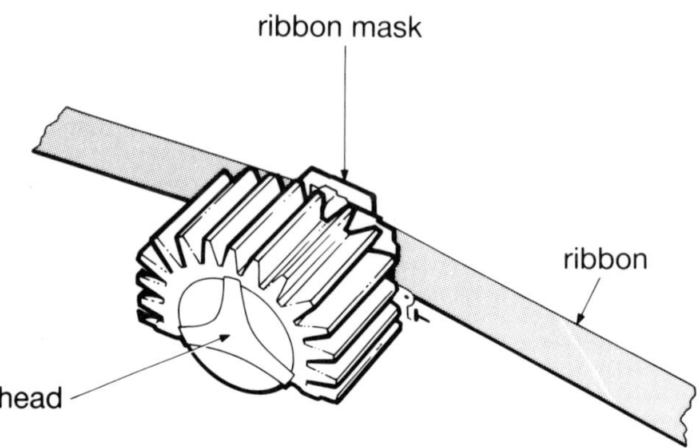

Examples of correct and incorrect ribbon setting

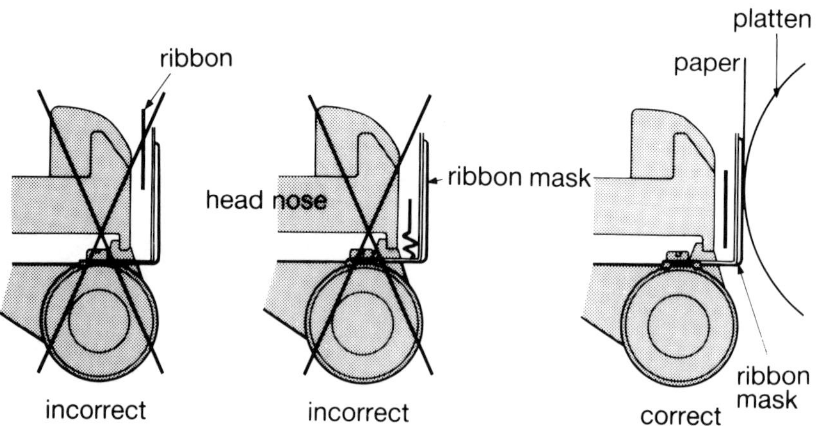

Thermal printers

Of other kinds of printers, the one you are perhaps most likely to come across is a ***thermal printer***. It forms characters from a series of dots like the matrix printer, but in this case, transfer from the ribbon to the paper is by a heat process rather than impact. In fact, you buy special heat-sensitive paper, there is no need for a ribbon at all. Thermal printers are slow and expensive in terms of running costs (although the initial cost can be quite low). Their great merit is that they are lightweight and compact, and for this reason they are often used with, and sometimes built into, small portable computers.

Laser printers

A printer which will be seen increasingly in the next few years is the ***laser printer***. When first developed, it was designed only for large-scale users with a massive throughput and a large budget. However, subsequent development and pricing structures have already brought the laser printer into serious competition with the high quality end of the daisywheel and matrix printer market.

Like matrix printers, laser printers form characters from groupings of dots, but in the case of laser printers, 300 dots to the inch is a common standard. The result is a character of such density and sharpness of definition that it is as good as the output from any daisywheel printer; and because of the way it is formed, there is all the flexibility of a matrix printer. Changing from one print style to another, or from one size of print to another, is no trouble at all. Add to that a throughput of 8 pages per minute or better, totally silent operation and rapidly falling prices, and you begin to see why you will be likely to come across them in many offices before too long.

So much for printed output. It is by no means the whole story, but it should provide enough information to satisfy your present needs.

Computer output to control physical systems

Another form of output which is of great importance in the broad context of information processing is one which produces physical movement of the output device, usually in two or three dimensions. When the output is in this form, the technology involved is usually referred to as ***robotics***.

You may well have come across some simple robotics examples; the 'turtle' graphic robot which is quite often controlled by the output from a BBC Model B computer is typical. The principle is simple. The robot has two drive wheels which are totally independent; if both are rotated at the same speed, the motion of the turtle is in a straight line, whereas if one drive wheel is not driven at all, the robot goes in an arc.

There is an infinite range of possibilities in between these two extremes, which enable the robot to follow any desired course, simple by varying the distance covered by the periphery of one drive wheel relative to the other in the same period of time. Each wheel is driven by a stepping motor – that is, a motor which turns its rotor though a small precisely defined angle each time it receives an electrical pulse. So the output from the computer to the robot must contain information which says which motor (i.e. *address information*) is to move how many (i.e. *data value information*) steps.

Other information must also be transmitted, because the robot must be told whether the pen is to be 'down' so that a line is drawn as the robot moves, or whether it is to be 'up' avoiding contact with the paper whilst the robot is repositioned.

Simple systems like this are not particularly accurate because they gradually build up errors due to slippage of the drive wheels, and in more complicated robotic systems the position of the robot relative to fixed points in the environment in which the robot is operating is constantly measured. Data derived from these measurements is fed back to the computer (this is another form of *input*) and as a result of this input the computer modifies its output to the robot in accordance with the instructions which have been built into the program it is running. In this way, the robot can be positioned very accurately. There are many industrial examples which you may have the opportunity to see; perhaps one of the most impressive is in the manufacture of motor vehicles.

A car assembly robot

A learning checklist

In our discussion of computer output, we have only just touched on output to non-local equipment; we will say more on this subject in a later chapter. What we have aimed to do in this chapter is to give you enough background to be able to:

1 Use prewritten software to create file records, delete file records, print file contents and extract data selectively to output requested information.
2 Recognize that these operations constitute file processing, which is part of the overall processing capability of the computer.
3 Identify the two principal types of output ports used on computers.
4 Distinguish between serial and parallel transmission of data from a computer to a printer or another computer.
5 Identify daisywheel and matrix printers by physical inspection, and explain the principle of operation of each.
6 Discuss the relative merits of at least three different kinds of printer appropriate for producing hard copy from microcomputer output.
7 Load, use and undertake simple maintenance operations (e.g. change ribbons) on at least one type of printer.
8 Use equipment handbooks to ascertain detailed information relevant to specific equipment or associated software.

CHAPTER 4

First steps in database design and use

What is a database?

At its simplest a database is a collection of related facts (*data*) held in files on magnetic disk. This is a very broad description of a database and we shall be more precise later in the chapter. But it is good enough for a starting point.

Database vs. simple data file

If you have been using the program BIRTHDAY.BAS in Chapters 2 and 3, it may have seemed to you that you were developing something like a database and then making enquiries of it. But in fact, this was not a real database. BIRTHDAY.BAS was a straightforward ***applications program***, not a ***Database Management System (DBMS)***. So, what's the difference?

Perhaps the most important difference is that software associated with a DBMS is reusable in many unrelated activities, whereas the program BIRTHDAY.BAS can only be used for the specific purposes for which it was designed. So with database software you could have a database covering all members of a large club, with all kinds of details about class of membership, the subscription level associated with it, the date by which it needs to be renewed, and many other details. Then using exactly the same software, you could have a database covering, say, stock records in a manufacturing company.

There is another major difference between a database management system and a system in which the software element is an applications program which enables the user to collect data and subsequently make enquiries of files containing that data.

With the applications program you are limited to the specific enquiries allowed by the program. For example, with BIRTHDAY.BAS you could make the program look at the data file contents to find the birthdate of a named person, or you could ask to see details of all those on file whose birthdays fell in a specified month. You could list the entire contents of the file. But that was all. You could not, for example, ask for a listing of all those whose eighteenth birthday was coming up in the next three months. To enable such an enquiry to be made, there would need to be substantial modifications to the program – not the sort of thing most users would either wish to perform or perhaps even be able to perform.

Database software, on the other hand, allows the user to set up simply and quickly any ***selection criteria*** and apply them to the database. It should allow the user to view his data in a number of different ways.

There are other differences too, but the main differences should now be clear: DBMS software stands between the user and the data s/he is working on and can be used easily to produce output to screen, to disk or to an output port (remember RS232 and Centronics? see page 39) which may be connected to a printer, or to other computers. This output can be in any specified format and selected on single or compound (i.e. multiple) criteria.

The enquiries one makes of the database may be routine ones which have been set up at the outset and are simply rerun from time to time when updated information is required from the latest values of data in the database. Or they may be specific enquiries to obtain information for a specific purpose on a single occasion.

The way in which an enquiry is made will depend on the database software. With the most expensive and complex software running on large computers, you can type in from the keyboard an information request in plain English – e.g. 'list all clients in Birmingham' – so that the user with little or no understanding of computer systems can nevertheless use it effectively to obtain the information s/he needs. But with simpler software and smaller systems, enquiries of the database must be made in a very structured and precise way which can be recognized and understood by the software. Such enquiries use a form of language which is very far removed from the 'natural language' which may be used with the big sophisticated systems.

The nature of data

We mentioned in the previous paragraph that data in the database will always be changing. Suppose it were a database about stock in a store. Items are being issued and new items are being added to stock every day. When data changes, it means either that new data has been *added* to the database, existing data has been *deleted* or existing data has been *amended*, and we shall practise all three in due course.

The fact that data may need to be amended from time to time, points to ***time*** as being an essential component in the make-up of any straightforward piece of data. In fact, four things are necessary to define a piece of data:

1 Object name.
2 A property of the named object.
3 The value of the property.
4 The time at which value is true.

Try writing down some elementary pieces of data for one or two objects; there are hundreds to choose from as these show:

Object name	Property	Value	Time at which value is true
Petrol tanker reg. C 123 VDU	Petrol on board	2000 galls	Prior to first delivery (an example of relative timing)
Jones & Co. Ltd retail store	Daily takings	£1234.56	01 December 1987
Your favourite football team	League table position	-	-

HAVE YOU BEEN
UPDATING ADMISSIONS
AGAIN?

Having established the idea that time is an essential component in describing an element of data, let's qualify that slightly by pointing out that ***relative time*** may sometimes be more important in practice than ***absolute time***.

Consider, for example, a database concerned with hospital patients; let's suppose that one day, two patients are due to leave a particular ward and so there is room for two new patients to be admitted to that ward. If the person responsible for updating the part of the database which deals with patient movements enters admissions before updating the records of those who are going home, there is a period when any manager making an enquiry of the database about the number of patients in wards would find that the number of patients in the ward exceeded the number of beds!

So even from the standpoint of someone who is just using a database system and is not concerned with its design, we need to have this appreciation of the part time plays in the definition of data.

But we can't perform operations on a database before we have set one up, and we cannot set one up until we have decided what ***fields*** we want and which of those fields is the most important or ***key field*** to which all the others relate. Decisions regarding the fields we want depend on decisions about the nature of the information which we wish to derive from the database and the ways in which we wish to use it.

Information, by the way, is not the same thing as data, as the following example will show.

Suppose you were a telephone manager with a database on all your exchange lines and the customers connected to them, together with details of the equipment rented out to the customer. From your point of view, the *key* data item is the exchange line number. All other data items ***relate uniquely*** to it. By that we mean that a particular user, his address, etc., relate to a particular number and no other user has that number. It is unique to that customer. So if we were to express the data in a table form, it might look something like this:

Field 1	Field 2	Field 3	Field 4	Field 5	Field 6	Field 7	Field 8
Exchange code	Number	User name	User ini-tials	User add1	User add2	User add3	User postcode
0865	245700	Smith	J	2 High Street	-	Oxford	OX1 100
0865	245701						
0865	245702	Jones	W R	10 Park Cres	-	Oxford	OX2 2AB
0865	245703	Robinson	A	21 The Larches	Kennington	Oxford	OX1 8PQ
..							
..							
..							
0993	323400	Adams	S F	32 Gypsy Road	-	Witney	OX8 7PZ
0993	323401	Brown	J	140 Witney Road	Ducklington	Witney	OX8 7TA

From such a tabulation you can see immediately that on exchange 0865, line 245701 is currently unallocated. In all other cases you have instantly available the name and address of the person to whom each line is currently allocated. Very useful information ... for the telephone manager.

But what about me? I want to find out the telephone number of a friend.

Distinction between data and information

Now all the *data* necessary is present in a tabulation of the kind shown above. But it doesn't give me useful *information* – information and data are not the same thing. We need to *process* the data to obtain the required information and, in this case, the essential process is to sort on fields 3 and 4, Surname and Initials. Then, if we wanted to make a listing looking just like a telephone directory, we would have to do some further processing. For example, a directory uses exchange names rather than codes, so we would have to undertake some processing based on conditional statements of the kind

IF Exchange code = "0865" THEN Exchange = "Oxford"
IF Exchange code = "0993" THEN Exchange = "Witney" etc

Also, if you examine a telephone directory, you will find that i) postcodes are omitted, and ii) where the town in the address has the same name as the exchange, it is omitted.

i) is easily achieved because with database software we simply print out those fields in which we are interested. ii) involves more conditional processing:

IF User Add3 = Exchange THEN User Add3 = " "
(This means that in any record where the field User Add3 initially contained a string of characters identical to the exchange name, – e.g. "Oxford" – there will now be an empty string, i.e. one with no characters in it)

Having obtained something looking much more like a telephone directory, it remains only to place Exchange and Number columns after the name and address; this again is simple, because database software allows us to print out reports in any format we choose, so we can have the fields in any order we please.

Setting up a database

Let's start to construct a very simple database because, as we do so, many of the points which you need to know about will be brought out. To do this, you are going to need commercial database software which will run on your micro; packages like Delta from Compsoft, dBase from Ashton Tate, Paradox from Ansa Software or Borland's Reflex would be admirable, even though they have the power to do much more than we shall attempt in this introductory text. You may have Cardbox or the database module from the Psion Exchange integrated software package, or any of some 20 or 30 packages currently on the market.

Because of the range of available software, we shall keep to principle. The exact way in which these principles are applied will depend on the software you are using. If it is a good quality product, the combination of documentation and helpful on-screen prompts

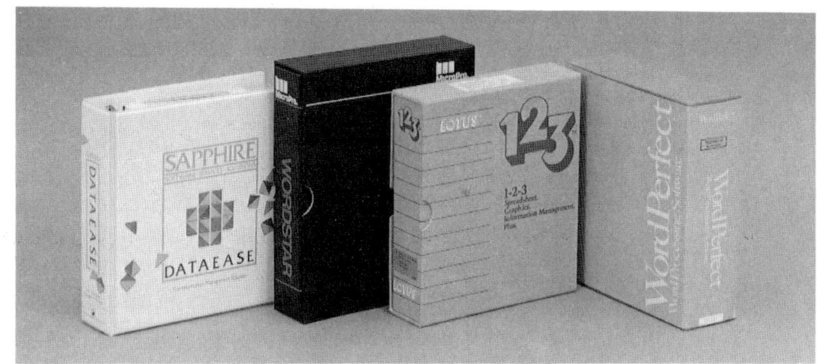

Popular software packages on the market

should give you all you need to convert the principles into successful practice. But if you find that your software isn't up to all the processing we suggest as we develop the example, don't despair. It will still be worth reading through the text to see what can be achieved with more powerful software, and you will find there are quite substantial and useful pieces of the project which you can tackle practically with more limited software.

Suppose you are a secretary to an organization which has a general area of activity – say, the arts – and specific interest groups within that general area. For this project we shall assume four interest groups: Music, Drama, Painting & drawing, and Films. There are a number of membership categories, each with its own annual membership fee; the fees may need to be changed from time to time, so the facility for doing this must be available.

Let's suppose that at the moment the membership categories and current annual fees are:

Individual	£10.00
Family	£18.00
Student	£5.00
Pensioners	£4.00

Consider what outputs are required

The jobs for which we wish to use the data are:

1 To produce from time to time a print-out of all current members' names, addresses and membership categories, listed in name alphabetic order.
2 To produce address labels (in name alphabetic order) for all current members.
3 To produce address labels (in name alphabetic order) for all members in a specified interest group.
4 To generate a standard letter to all members one month in advance of the date on which their subscription falls due.
5 To accumulate for accounting purposes the total fees received in each membership category and the overall total for the financial year.

Of these several tasks, even the simplest of data management software should be able to cope with jobs 1–3; a good many packages will allow you to generate personalized standard letters, and those which do not will probably allow you to ***export*** your data to a word processing package which will handle the situation. So one way or another, you should be able to tackle task 4. Whether or not you can do anything with the fifth task depends on the ability of your software to do numerical processing. If it is little more than an electronic replacement for a card index, you will have to leave that task out; but if you have software such as dBase, Delta, Reflex, or one of the many other comparable packages available, you will have all you need to do the fifth job.

You may well think of other uses which could be made of the data available – the above list is only indicative of the kind of uses which can be made.

There are things which you may *not* do with data, and the purpose of the Data Protection Act in this country (with its equivalent elsewhere) is to discourage abuse of data by imposing heavy penalties on individuals and organizations that do so. It is outside the scope of this book to cover the legalities involved in the keeping of live data which affects individuals; it is enough to say that it is an aspect which must be thoroughly investigated by anyone setting up a database in which records are kept about people.

Deduce what data input is required

We have now completed the first step – looking at what we want to achieve so that we can work out what data we need to hold. This process is also helping us to clarify our thoughts about what the *key field* should be. The key field is the one holding the data on which all other data in a given record depends. By dependency, we mean that each value of the key determines only one value of each attribute.

We are introducing one or two new terms here which need to be defined more closely.

A data file contains items of data concerning a particular object of interest – for example, the telephone directory of all people/organizations with telephones in a given exchange area – and such an object is referred to as an ***entity***.

Items of data which tell us different facts associated with an entity are called ***attributes***.

Within a data file, these items of data are contained in ***fields*** which are identified by ***field names***.

Records are groups of relevent attributes for specific occurrences of the entity. For example, in the telephone directory, pick any name at random – you have selected a specific occurrence of a person with a telephone in the defined exchange area. There are then various attributes associated with that particular occurrence – address details, telephone number. The diagram illustrates these various terms using an entity CUSTOMER as an example.

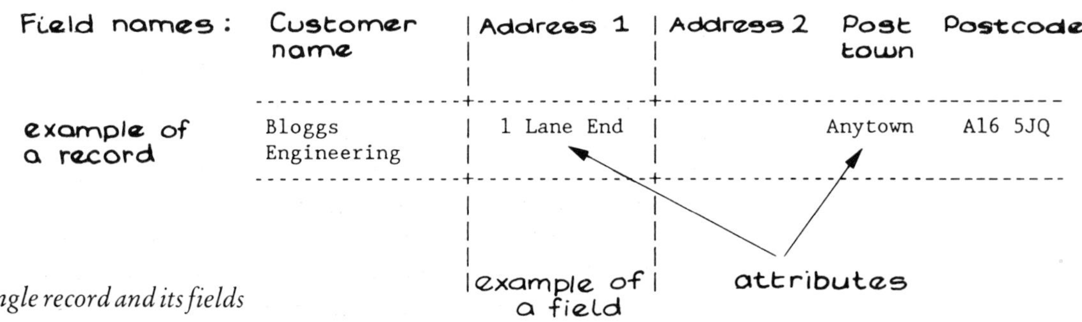

A single record and its fields

In the case of our club, the key field must be the surname of individuals or families. Key field entries should, if possible, be unique, but with most software packages, this is not an essential requirement. So there is no reason why, in such a simple application, you should not have surname as the key field, even though you may have four members by the name of Smith. There will be other features in each record, such as initials, address, subscription renewal date, etc., which will enable a particular Smith to be distinguished uniquely.

So, if SURNAME is to be the keyfield, what other fields do we need? More, perhaps, than you might think at first sight. For example, since one of our tasks is to write personalized letters to individuals regarding the renewal of their subscriptions, we must include a TITLE field, into which we would commonly enter Mr, Mrs, Miss or Ms, but which could become longer entries if we had Bishops or members of the aristocracy (e.g. a Viscount) in our club. In practice, these matters need to be thought about carefully, because the software is (usually) going to ask us to define the length of each field. In other words, we have got to say what is the largest number of characters we expect to enter for any attribute in each of the fields. We do not wish to waste space either in memory or on disk, so we are not going to specify a field to be longer than we need. However, the field must be long enough to house all *likely* entries.

If we are only likely to use Mr, Mrs, Miss or Ms, then the TITLE entry would also serve for salutation purposes, e.g. 'Dear *Mr* Smith,' (you will need this for the letter in task 4); otherwise we would probably need another field for SALUTATION. In case you have not come across the term, phrases like 'Dear Mr Smith' or 'Dear Sir' at the start of a letter are referred to as ***salutations***. We shall, of course, want a field for INITIALS; and each line of the address will need to be in a separate field so that each will take a new line when address labels are printed.

Before you go any further, try to list all the fields which you think you are going to need for this system. Against each field name, write the maximum number of characters you propose to allow for entries. When you have finished, look at page 55 and see how your data file structure compares with ours. It may be different, but that does not necessarily mean it is wrong. Remember to think about the outputs which we require, i.e. the information, address labels, letters, etc., and then decide what data must be put in to make this possible. Next think up suitable field names for the fields which will hold your data and finally decide on the maximum number of characters you are likely to want to hold in each field. Do it now.

Well, how did you get on? For our suggested list of field names we have added some explanatory notes so that if you do not have an equivalent in your own listing, you can make additions to it. The actual field names we have used may not be acceptable to some software. For example, the software you are using may not allow spaces in field names, so that rather than using 'interest group' you may have to use something like 'InterestGroup.' (If your software allows it, the use of upper case for the initial letter of each word and lower case for the rest makes it easier to read.)

The other restriction you are likely to come across concerns the length of the field name. Thus 'member classification' would be too long for many systems to handle, and we would abbreviate it to 'member class'.

Many data management systems require the fields to be of fixed length, and ask you to specify the maximum length required for each field. In the following listing we have included some suggested maximum field lengths.

Field definition

The other information which your system will ask for relates to the nature of the data to be held in each field. Basically, it will fall into one of three categories:

1 a string of alphanumeric characters
2 a number on which calculations may be performed
3 a date

and with some software, numbers are subdivided into integers (whole numbers) and real numbers (i.e. numbers which are in general not integers). Systems which do not make this distinction treat all numbers as real numbers and allow the user to specify the number of decimal places to be displayed on the screen or used in a written report.

Here are our suggested field details:

Field name	Field type	Field length	Comment
Surname	Char	25	This is the key field
Initials	Char	5	Allows for 3 initials with 2 intervening spaces
Title	Char	8	Will cover 'Mr & Mrs' but not unlikely titles such as 'the Rt Hon'. Our club is for ordinary folk!
Membership classification		1	Entries will be in the set [I,i,F,f,S,s,P,p] [1]
Interest group		1	Entries will be in the set [M,m,D,d,P,p,F,f] [2]
Address line 1	Char	30	Address lines 2 & 3 may not always be used, but we must cater for the worst case. Post towns and postcodes should always be entered in fields specifically allocated for these data in case you wish subsequently to select records on a geographical basis.
Address line 2	Char	30	
Address line 3	Char	25	
Post town	Char	20	
Postcode	Char	10	
Joining date	Date	-	Usually 10 characters, but this is often handled by the software because the length of a date field is invariable; in such cases the field length is not declared by the user.
Last sub paid	Number	-	If your system asks for a field length for a number, it is referring to the <u>display</u> of that number; the system knows how much room it needs to house a real number internally. When calculating the length required for the display of a number remember to add one space for a possible leading minus sign and one space for the decimal point if appropriate.
Sub expiry date	Date	-	Same comment as for 'joining date'.
Sub then due	Number	-	Same comment as the 'last sub paid'.
Sub received	Char	6	Why is this a character field and not a number field? See page 64 for the explanation.

1 Standing for (I)ndividual, (F)amily, (S)tudent or (P)ensioner

2 Standing for (M)usic, (D)rama, (P)ainting & drawing or (F)ilms

Some of the fields we have suggested will only be of value if your software will handle data processing as well as records processing, (i.e. will do calculations on the subscription amounts, and the date field which contains the data indicating the date through to which the subscription is paid). Most packages will do this and even if your particular software will not, it won't hurt to have one or two unused fields lying around.

So let's start this practical session by giving the computer all the information it needs about the fields. Have you switched on and loaded the operating system? Then the next step is to load your database management software. If you are unsure about how to do this, check the directory of the disk (or the first disk if the software occupies more than one) and look for a file having in its name either the name of the product or an abbreviation of it. The file extension will almost certainly be .COM or .EXE, but it is possible that the software is called through a batch file (.BAT). At the system prompt, enter the appropriate executable file name and when the software has been loaded from disk into memory, control will pass to the loaded program.

For the next few minutes you are on your own – there are so many database packages that we cannot tell you exactly how to proceed with your particular software; but the job to be done is to give the system all the information it needs about field names, characteristics and lengths. We built our system up using Compsoft's Delta software; the finished field structure was as shown here. It is important that the key field heads the list, but after that, the order in which filed names are held is not significant.

```
DELTA file name: ARTSCLUB    File Title: Arts Club membership details..
Date created: 09-05-86    Last Updated: 09-05-86    Records Used: 0
No. Fields: 15    Rec. Length: 181    Tran. Groups: 0


Tran      Field                  Fld     Fld     :   Tran      Field                  Fld     Fld
group     name                   type    Len     :   group     name                   type    len
                                                 :
 1   0    surname ........       C        25     :    2   0    initials ...           C        5
 3   0    title ..........       C         8     :    4   0    member class ....      C        1
 5   0    interest group ..      C         1     :    6   0    address line 1 ..      C       30
 7   0    address line 2 ..      C        30     :    8   0    address line 3 ..      C       25
 9   0    post town .......      C        20     :   10   0    postcode .......       C       10
11   0    joining date ....      D        10     :   12   0    last sub paid ...      2        6
13   0    sub expiry date .      D        10     :   14   0    sub then due ....      2        6
15   0    sub received ....      C         6     :
```

A file structure

Developing input screens

The next step is to provide a means of inputting data into the fields we have specified. What we need to do is to develop on the computer screen the equivalent of a blank form, which we can use later to fill in the data in much the same way as we would fill in a form. But that is later. At this stage, all we are doing is designing the form.

Notice, by the way, alternative terms which you might come across in this connection. Some people would talk about *designing an input screen*, others would refer to a *data input mask*; occasionally it is referred to as a *data input frame*. But whatever you hear it called, if you think of the process as designing a form, you won't go far wrong.

With some software, you develop your data input mask at the same time as you define the fields. Although this helps to speed up the job of developing the specific data system you want, there are disadvantages too: it may well be that you wish to deal with different data on different input screens; some fields may carry only the result of a calculation which is needed for a report, but not needed at all so far as data input is concerned.

If your software gives you the freedom to do so, lay your screen out in a way which you would find comfortable to use. Don't allow it to get too cramped, because it then becomes difficult to read. With some software, your screen prompt – that is the little message on screen which tells the user what to input at that point – need not be the same as the field name. For example, if you did use the field name TITLE, then the screen prompt might be 'Mr/Mrs/Miss/Ms etc.'. This would be more informative to a user who had not been involved in the design of the system than the term TITLE.

Here are our suggestions for three separate masks. The first of these is to input the essential data for new members; the second is to handle financial transactions; and the third is to enable periodic up-dates of annual subscriptions for the various classes of membership to be made. If your software will not handle transactions (i.e. perform arithmetic processing), then only the first screen has relevance for you.

A possible data input frame for the Club Secretary

```
                    ARTS CLUB MEMBERSHIP BASIC DETAILS

SURNAME ________________________   Mr/Mrs/Miss etc ________   INITIALS _____

MEMBERSHIP CLASSIFICATION:
         (I)ndividual, (F)amily, (S)tudent or (P)ensioner? _

INTEREST GROUP:
         (M)usic, (D)rama, (P)ainting/drawing or (F)ilms?  _

ADDRESS      ______________________________
             ______________________________
             _________________________
 (Post town) ____________________
 (Postcode)  __________

JOINING DATE __________
```

A possible input frame for the Club Treasurer

```
              ARTS CLUB SUBSCRIPTION ENTRY SCREEN

SURNAME OF MEMBER _____________________  _______  _____

SUBSCRIPTION RECEIVED: £______

++++++++++++++++++++++++++++++++++++++++++++++++++++++++++
+                  FOR INFORMATION ONLY                  +
+                                                        +
+ SUB. EXPIRY DATE: ________    PRESENT ADDRESS RECORD:  +
+                                                        +
+ ANNUAL SUB. AMOUNT: £_____    _______________________  +
+                               _______________________  +
+ MEMBERSHIP CLASSIFICATION: _  __________________       +
+                               _____________            +
+ SPECIAL INTEREST GROUP:    _  _________                +
+                                                        +
++++++++++++++++++++++++++++++++++++++++++++++++++++++++++
```

```
ARTS CLUB - SCREEN FOR ENTRY OR AMENDMENT OF SUBSCRIPTION RATES
                    ------------------------

THE CURRENT SUBSCRIPTION RATES TO BE APPLIED ARE AS FOLLOWS:


INDIVIDUAL MEMBERSHIP ... ... ...    £____________

FAMILY MEMBERSHIP ... ... ... ...    £____________

STUDENT MEMBERSHIP .. ... ... ...    £____________

PENSIONER MEMBERSHIP  ... ... ...    £____________
```

An input frame for setting and changing subscription rates

Although it's helpful to associate each of the three distinct activities with separate input frames, it's not essential to do so. So, if the software you are using doesn't allow you to do this, don't worry; the essential point is that you can communicate with your computer in a way which will allow these various inputs.

Using database software

Before we launch off into some of the more fun things you can do if your software has the capability, let us just do a couple of very simple but useful jobs which any database software should enable you to do. You should at this stage have an input screen roughly equivalent to our screen 1, and the next thing to do is to use it to input data.

Data entry

Some people regard data inputting as being boring; many people spend the whole of their working lives doing it. It is certainly not the most exciting activity in the world, but it is one in which you can take a pride in terms of speed and accuracy. Keep your fingers close to the keyboard and try to keep a steady pace even if it is not very fast to start with. You will only be able to concentrate for a limited period of time, so do say 10 records and then give yourself a couple of minutes break. Then try to input 12 records in the next batch and gradually build up like this until you can handle batches of at least 20 without losing concentration. Obviously, people with keyboard training have a tremendous advantage, but even without it you will achieve a quite useful speed.

Designing test data

But what data are you going to enter? When you are experimenting with software like this, you need to design your data so that the various facilities can be tested. For example, you want names which start with different initial letters, and you want to avoid entering them in alphabetical order. Spread the addresses over a sufficiently large region to include several different post towns, and within a major town area you need several examples where the first part of the postcode is the same. Have some addresses which use all fives lines and others using only three, e.g:

The Larches	121 High Street
57 Bridle Way	– (leave blank)
Trumpington-on-Stour	– (leave blank)
REDFORD	ANYTOWN
RD7 6JR	AN1 2PQ

You want a number of people in the same membership category – but again, you want them spread through the records, not all in a bunch. In the same way, you want people randomly spread between the four possible interest groups. What happens if two people have the same surname? (Remember, in this example we have made surname the key field.) To find out, include two identical surnames in your data. It will be sufficient to spread joining dates over the last two or three years. Right! Now you know the kind of thing you are trying to achieve, go ahead and design your data. Don't input until you have designed!

There is more to designing test data than you might have thought at first sight. And even entering data requires some thought. Are you entering it in upper or lower case? The point is that however you enter the data, that is how it will come out. For example, we are going to prepare some address labels shortly and later on we shall use the software to send personalized reminder letters to members whose subscriptions fall due in a specified band of weeks. So if we entered Joe Bloggs' name as

BLOGGS MR J

then, when we used the system to write to Joe about his subscription, the salutation would read

Dear MR BLOGGS

– not at all what we want!

To get 'Dear Mr Bloggs' we must enter our data in upper and lower case in exactly the same way as we wish to use it later:

Bloggs Mr J

Outputting information

Producing a simple report

Now that you have input your data (was your input mask as comfortable to use as you had hoped?) let's start to use it. The first task we were asked to deal with was to produce an alphabetic listing of all members, giving their names, addresses and membership categories. So we have to ***sort*** our data on the key field – field 1.

Many software packages put the two processes of specifying selection criteria and sorting together, since in general one would wish to sort selected records. But there is no need to select if we don't want to, so if your software is organized in this way, use the screen prompts to help you by-pass the selection part and get on with the sorting. Specifying the way in which you want things sorted and actually getting the system to undertake the sort in accordance with that specification are actually separate operations and some database software treats them that way. Other software merges the two processes in one continuous operation, so you must be prepared for either, depending on the software you are using.

You are on your own again. Using your software handbook, on-screen prompts, and as a last resort, by asking your tutor, get your data sorted on members' surnames ready for the next stage, which is to produce a report for the secretary. Here again, the job has two parts to it: ***specifying the layout*** you want for the report and then actually producing it using the sorted data you have just prepared.

You will need to use all the facility your software provides to get a good layout. You may not get a record all on one line unless you use a 132 column matrix printer in compressed print mode. Taking our own field listing as an example, the name and address fields use 150 characters without any spaces between fields; were we to add membership category and interest group we would have over 160 characters in which case each record may overflow on to two lines. Experiment until you get your format as you want it and then do a print run using the whole membership list as input data. Here is an example of the kind of report you might expect to produce.

09-05-86 DELTA STANDARD REPORT

Surname	Title	Initials	Membership category	Address line 1	Address line 2	Address line 3	Post town	Postcode
Jenkins	Mr	J P	I	12 Little Birch Street	Wilmsley		Blanktown	BL5 7RT
Abel	Mrs	I A M	P	Lime Tree Cottage	53 Lime Lane	Stickyford	Blanktown	BL3 8TY
Robinson	Mr & Mrs	S F	F	567 Long Road			Blanktown	BL1 1OZ
Jones	Miss	C A R	S	The Dungeon	23 Moat House Lane	Castleton	Highground	HD13 5FH
Smith	Mr & Mrs	T P	F	The New House	27 Brick Row		Blanktown	BL5 7PQ
Birtwhistle	Mr	H	S	Flat Z	123 Lower Road		Highground	HD2 4VB
Smith	Miss	A	P	101 High Street			Blanktown	BL1 2WE
Heath	Miss	M	I	Pebble Cottage	14 Short Lane	Stickyford	Blanktown	BL3 3TY
Lambert	Mr & Mrs	B	F	72 Admirals Close	Endford		Blanktown	BL4 OXR
Cooper	Mr	P	S	Coppice Hall	2-6 Main Road		Blanktown	BL2 9DR
Innes	Miss	C	P	The Pink House	29 Maple Way	Castleton	Highground	HD14 6QT
Blunt	Mrs	D	P	111 Gate Road	Wilmsley		Blanktown	BL5 2RB
Sharp	Mr & Mrs	E	F	The Nut House	Park Road	Greenton	Highground	HD6 9FW
Lee	Mr	W	P	9 Rocky Lane	Endford		Blanktown	BL4 1BT
Squirrel	Miss	L	S	Burton Hall	3-9 Long Road		Blanktown	BL1 2OR
Prince	Mrs	W	I	Flat E	45 Link Road	Greenton	Highground	HD6 8PT
Trinder	Miss	K	I	Finchley House	139 Fore Street	Stickyford	Blanktown	BL3 2BP
Lewis	Mr & Mrs	G	F	309 East Way			Blanktown	BL1 3TP
Baker	Mr	S	S	31 Elms Rise	Endford		Blanktown	BL4 7TR
Hobbs	Mr & Mrs	A	F	Manor Farm	Manor Lane	Stickyford	Blanktown	BL3 8CP

A Delta standard report

Producing address labels

Our second task was to produce address labels.

Address labels are mounted on a backing paper (sometimes called ***webbing***) either in a single column or up to 4 abreast on a wider backing paper. In all cases, the backing is driven through the printer by a tractor feed.

The software is going to want information on the field(s) to be printed on each line, the number of copies required of each label, the starting position of print for each label across the web and the number of blank lines to be advanced between each label in a column.

You will find that at some stage before the print run actually begins, you will (with most software) be prompted to say whether or not you wish blank lines to be ignored. Given this option, take it, so that if, for example, an address entry has only used address line 1, post town and postcode, you will not be left with a couple of blank lines representing the space where the data for address line 2 and address line 3 would have gone, had there been any. The diagrams on the next page show the way we set up label printing information using Delta to print two labels abreast. Your software may differ considerably in detail, but the same principles will apply. As you will see, we called for data from three fields in the first line of the address and subsequent lines called only one field each.

Delta label printing option – screen 1 (top) and screen 2 (bottom)

```
DELTA LABEL PRINTING OPTION
Line  Field name/     Additional field    Additional field
      number
  1   title .....     initials .......    surname ........
  2   Address line 1
  3   Address line 2
  4   Address line 3
  5   Post town ....
  6   Postcode .....
  7
  8
  9
 10
 11
 12
 13
 14
 15
 16
 17
 18
 19
 20
```

```
DELTA LABEL PRINTING OPTION

        How many copies of each label (1-50)      1

                 Use expanded print codes ?       N

                        Max width of label       35   (i.e. 3½" in 10-pitch)


                 Start position of label 1:       1
                 Start position of label 2:      39
                 Start position of label 3:
                 Start position of label 4:
                 Start position of label 5:

        Number of blank lines between labels      3   (the equivalent of ½ inch)

          Suppress printing of blank lines ?      Y
```

Note:
Y if blank lines within labels are to be closed up

Having set up the layout with Delta, you can run a test to see whether you have got it right. Rows of asterisks, starting at the specified position and running up to the maximum label width are printed out on the first two label rows; at this point you may edit the parameters you gave the computer or readjust the position of the labels to ensure that the address block is going to appear fair and square in the middle of your labels. When you are satisfied with it, you file this format for future use.

And that is all there is to address label printing; it really is very easy. If you don't have real labels you can use, then use the template provided on page 61 and mark out a few labels on computer print-out paper. The diagram provided is a life-size replica of one typical size of address label continuous stationery. The object of the exercise is to get at least four names and addresses nicely centred on the labels.

Label template

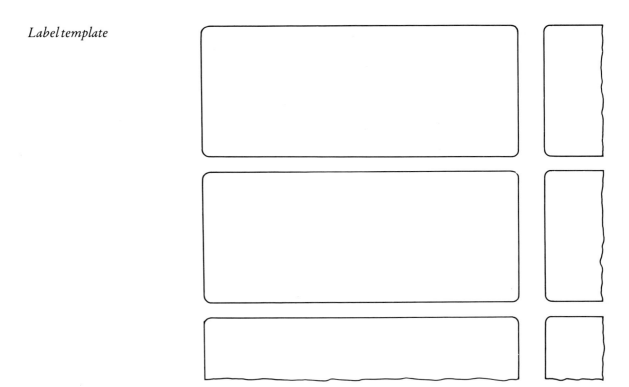

Specifying and using select/sort criteria

We could use our label format to produce address labels for every member of the club, but it is time we looked at the power of the software to select certain records according to specified ***criteria***. Let's suppose that a circular letter is to be sent to all members in the Music interest group, telling them of a forthcoming concert. Then we need to select the records only of this group and print address labels for them:

> FIELD NO. 5 = M *or* FIELD NO. 5 = m (just in case some entries were made in lower case and some in upper case)

These are not the actual words to be used with your software; they are intended to show you the nature of the criterion which you must now express in a syntax acceptable to your software.

Having specified the criterion on which selection is to be based, the next step is to run the data file against it so as to extract all those records which meet the criterion. These records are stored in a new file, usually referred to as an ***extract file***. Now all we have to do is to run this extract file against the label format which we have already designed and stored, and we end up with a perfect set of address labels for just the musicians in the club.

Review

Let's pause for a moment to look back on what we have done.

1 Having considered what the end uses of our system were to be, we set up field definitions; in doing this, we recognized that one field was to act as the key field, so that if the value of the key was known, the values of all the other attributes associated with it would also be known.

2 Next, we designed an input screen or mask so that data could be placed in the database. (We also learned a little about the design of test data in the process.)
3 Thirdly, we sorted our data into alphabetical order on the key field.
4 Then we designed a report layout and used it with the sorted data file to produce a printed report of members' names, addresses, membership category and interest group.
5 Fifthly, we designed an address label layout.
6 Finally, we specified criteria to extract certain records from the total membership file and then used the address label format to produce address labels for all the members whose records had been placed in the extract file.

This may be as far as your software will let you go; but for those of you with more sophisticated software, let's now explore some more of the typical facilities available.

Use of processing facilities

In following sections, we shall make specific reference to Delta from time to time, but the same kind of facilities are available with many other products designed for microcomputers. Software designed to run on mini- and mainframe computers is, of course, much more powerful.

The inclusion of processing facilities in database software implies a need for some work areas where intermediate answers or variable data can be held. We shall use some such areas when inputting current subscription rate data through the mask shown on page 57. This data needs to be stored indefinitely, so a characteristic of the work area used to house it must be that it is non-volatile.

If you are using very basic software with little or no processing power, then you will have to do without stored data relating to subscription levels.

We would like the computer to undertake several small processing activities, either when new records are created or when they are amended, as for example by the recording of a subscription payment. We must therefore set up ***process instructions***. Here again there are considerable disparities between the ways in which different database packages handle processing and you will need to refer either to your tutor or to the software handbook to see what is appropriate in your own case.

But to help you appreciate what kind of processing is required, consider the two process files which we developed for use with our input masks. The first process file attaches to the first of the three masks, and its contents are set out on the opposite page.

The first 15 lines cause the correct subscription rate to be entered into an individual's record in accordance with the class of membership. For example, what line 1 says in plain English is

IF member class = "I" THEN GOTO line 9

Line 2 is similar to line 1 except that it allows for the user inputting a lower case "i" in the field named "member class".

Process files for input – screen 1 (top) and screen 2 (bottom)

```
PROCESS PARAMETER FILE:- :ARTCLUB1
------------------------------------------------------

NO PROCESS GROUPS DEFINED
 1:?member class(:EQ)#'I(:9)
 2:?member class(:EQ)#'i(:9)
 3:?member class(:EQ)#'F(:11)
 4:?member class(:EQ)#'f(:11)
 5:?member class(:EQ)#'S(:13)
 6:?member class(:EQ)#'s(:13)
 7:?member class(:EQ)#'P(:15)
 8:?member class(:EQ)#'p(:15)
 9:sub then due=^27
 10:??16
 11:sub then due=^28
 12:??16
 13:sub then due=^29
 14:??16
 15:sub then due=^30
 16:?last sub paid(:EQ)#0(:18)
 17:??19
 18:sub expiry date=joining date
```

```
PROCESS PARAMETER FILE :- :ARTCLUB2
------------------------------------------------------

NO PROCESS GROUPS DEFINED
 1:last sub paid=sub received(:V)
 2:sub received=#'
 3:^1=#365*last sub paid/sub then due
 4:sub expiry date=sub expiry date+^1
```

At line 9, we have a statement which says that the value to be held in the field called 'sub then due' is to be the value held in the non-volatile ***work area*** 27.

In the same way, lines 3 and 4 deal with the situation where member class = "F" (or "f") for (F)amily, and so on. Each class of membership is referred to a different work area location, and the values in these four work areas are the current fee levels input through Mask 3.

The last three lines of that process file are used to set an initial value to the sub expiry date. But sub expiry date = joining date can only be true for a new member, whose details have to be entered before his payment of his first subscription can be recorded through the second input mask. So the ***condition*** is set down in line 16 of the process file:

IF last sub paid = 0 THEN. . sub expiry date = joining date

When we attach a process file to a mask, we have to tell the software in what circumstances the processing is to take place. The four possibilities are:

1 on operator request,
2 when a new record is created,
3 when an existing record is amended,
4 when an existing record is deleted.

In our case, we want the processing to be undertaken automatically, so we would not opt for operator request. Of the remaining three possibilites, (2) and (3) are both required; (4) would be pointless.

So much for the process file associated with the first input screen. There will also be processing associated with the input to the second screen. Let us examine this process, shown on page 63 (PROCESS PARAMETER FILE:- -:ARTCLUB2).

Remember that the purpose of the second mask on page 56 is to enable a user to input the amount of subscription received from a member. It would be very confusing if, when a particular member's record was called, there were already a value against the SUBSCRIPTION RECEIVED prompt, so the purpose of the first two lines in this second process file is to transfer the value of the 'sub received' to the field 'last sub paid' and then reset 'sub received' to an empty condition. (Note that had 'sub received' been created as a numerical field, it would display 0.00 when reset, but because it has been treated as a *character* field whose *value* is transferred to 'last sub paid', the display just shows a blank as soon as the process instructions are implemented.)

In line 3 of the associated process file, we are storing in work area 1 (which is rezeroed for each record) the number of days to be added on to the subscription expiry date as a result of the money just received. Normally, one would expect the subscription paid to be the same as the subscription due, but we have incorporated a very simple piece of processing which adjusts the renewal date in accordance with the amount of subscription paid, so that members not paying their annual subscription in one transaction can be accommodated. Line 4 of the process file simply adds the appropriate number of days to the previous expiry date to produce a new expiry date.

In attaching this process file to the second input mask, we note that processing should occur when a record is amended. The screen is not used for the input of new records nor for the deletion of dead records.

Batch processing

Right! You have just been appointed treasurer. Have you set up the current subscription rates for the several classes of membership? If not, this is your first task, using your equivalent of our input mask 3.

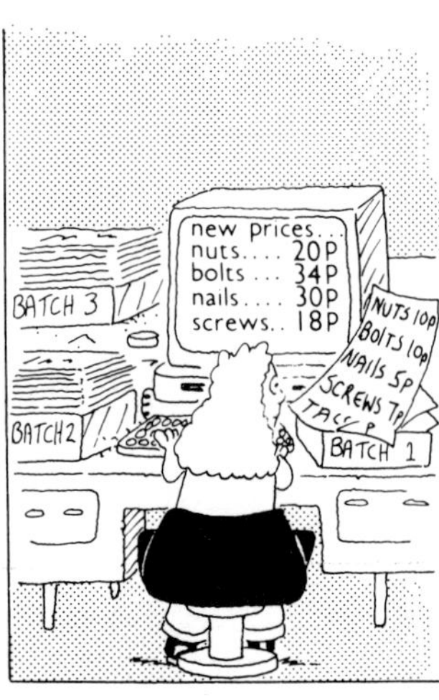

Now it is one thing to amend the data held in work areas 27, 28, 29, 30, but another thing entirely to transfer this amended data to all the records on file. What we need to do is to batch process all the records without any user intervention, and most data management software provides this facility. In Delta, for example, you would select option K from the main menu and use the first of the two process files to define the processing to be undertaken.

When you have updated all your records with the current subscription rates, the next thing is to use input mask 2 or its equivalent to enter subscriptions until everybody is up-to-date with their payments and several subscriptions are due in the coming month.

If you have used the same approach as we did in the design of the second process file, check the working of your system by inputting one or two subscriptions which are either smaller or larger than the specified sum due and check that the renewal date is adjusted accordingly.

Another pause now, just to see what we have covered since the last review. We have been concerned with aspects of *processing*. We have seen the need for temporary work areas and have made use of them; we have written process files and used them to process records immediately following creation and when amendments are input; we have used a process file in a batch processing procedure to update all records. In developing the process files we have used conditional statements and relationships involving strings, numbers and dates.

More complex selection criteria

Now let's move on to selecting the records of those members whose subscriptions fall due in the next few weels; we can then write a reminder letter to them. We have already done a very simple extraction, but we now want to do something rather more complicated and we shall consider selection criteria in more detail.

There are four distinct steps to the task we have now set ourselves, although depending on the software you are using, some of them may be combined. The steps are:

1 Establish and input the selection criteria.
2 Run the record file against these criteria and so obtain an extract file of all records which meet the criteria.
3 Design and input the letter.
4 Run the letter using data from the extract file to infill in appropriate places.

As a first step, let us look more closely at selection facilities. Usually one may select on one or more of the following bases:

1 That the content of a specified character field in the selected record is equal (or not equal) to a given character string. Usually you have the choice of observing or ignoring upper/lower case. The character string may be the content of another field or a constant.
2 That the content of a specified numerical field is less than (<), less than or equal to (<=), equal to (=), not equal to (<>), greater than or equal to (>=), or greater than (>) a given value. Again, the value may be found in another field in the same record or it may be a constant.
3 That the content of a specified numerical field lies within a given range of values. This basis of selection is not included in all software since the same effect can be obtained using criteria specified in (2) above together with the ***logical connective*** AND, e.g.

    contents of field n =>100
    AND
    contents of field n<=200

   would select all records in which the value in the nth field lay between 100 and 200.
4 as (2), but with date fields.
5 as (3), but with date fields.

With some software the user is enabled to input constant values from the keyboard at run-time, rather than embed them in the selection criteria: this is a useful facility when one wishes to change the criteria frequently. In fact, if it is available to you, this is the time to use it. On the next page is our statement of selection criteria using Delta; you should aim to achieve the same end result.

```
SELECTION PARAMETER SETUP            Current date :09-05-86
------------------------------------------------------------------------
      Fld : Op : St : Ln :Compare 1                  :Compare 2         :Case
------------------------------------------------------------------------
 1:   13    GE    1   10  #RFirst date for extract
      AND
 2:   13    LE    1   10  #RLast date for extract

 3:

 4:

 5:

 6:

 7:

 8:
------------------------------------------------------------------------
Select by key ? ...................: N (F)irst or (E)very transaction ?..: E
------------------------------------------------------------------------
Number of field to be used in comparison
Press ESC to finish
```

Screen for setting up selection criteria

Interpreting our selection instructions into plain English, we have in line 1

> Extract the record of the content of field 13 (Sub Expiry Date) is greater than or equal to a date which will be entered at run-time when the prompt 'First date for extract' appears on the screen.

But this statement doesn't stand by itself. It is linked to the statement in line 2 by the logical connective AND. So a record will be selected only if criteria specified in line 1 *and* 2 are both true for that record. The line 2 criterion is that the content of the date field (field 13) should be less than or equal to the date specified by the user when the prompt 'Last date for extract' appears on the screen.

As we indicated earlier, sort criteria are often associated with selection criteria and one may opt to specify a sorted order at this point. You know how to do this, so specify that the selected records are to be sorted alphabetically on surname.

Now that select (and sort) criteria have been set up, we can run our data file against these criteria (just as we did earlier when selecting all the musicians) to produce an extract file – that is, a file which contains only those records which meet the criteria we have specified, arranged in the order we required when specifying how we wanted them sorted. Use dates in your selection process which will allow at least four of your test records to be extracted from the main file.

Production of a standard letter

The next job is to prepare a common letter which is to be personalized for each of the club members whose records have been extracted. Many database packages will give you the facility to do this; if yours does not, you would have to prepare the letter using word processing software, 'export' the relevant data from your database file to a non-document merge file and then produce the finished letters under control of the word processing/mailmerge package.

This operation can vary quite considerably in complexity, depending on the way in which data is held by the database software and by the word processing software. At this level, you should know the general principles involved; if you have ***integrated software*** (i.e. software which is designed specifically to make it easy for users to move between database, spreadsheet and word processing functions of a total package), you will have little difficulty in actually doing the job rather than just knowing in principle what is involved.

But for the moment, we will assume that the letter can be generated within the database facility. It might look something like the one below. Save such a format so that it can be used repeatedly.

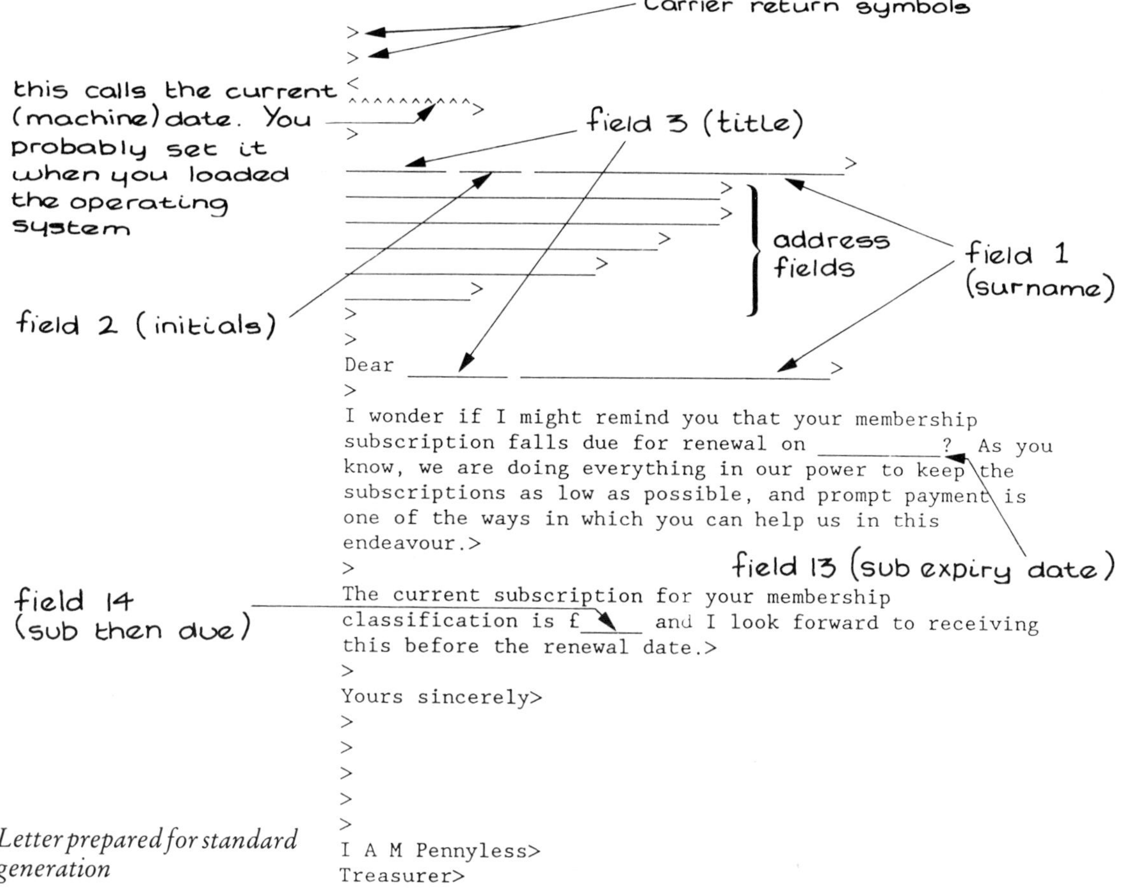

Letter prepared for standard generation

At this time, we wish to use it together with our extract file, into which we have asked the database software to place selected records – those in which the subscription expiry date falls within the dates we specified at run-time – in surname alphabetic order. The end result of this operation is a series of personalized letters of the kind illustrated overleaf. All the blank fields have been replaced by data taken from the appropriate fields of the extract file, and any fields for which there is no data (e.g. address line 3 in a short address) are omitted from the printed letter.

Having written all these letters, we need to send them out; you have already seen how to use the database software to produce address labels, so you can tackle that job without any help. It's just the same as before but with a different extract file.

To summarize: in this last part of our investigation into the use of database software, we have looked in much greater detail at

```
19-05-86

Mr J P Jenkins
12 Little Birch Street
Wilmsley
Blanktown
BL5 7RT


Dear Mr Jenkins

I wonder if I might remind you that your membership
subscription falls due for renewal on 16-05-86?  As you
know, we are doing everything in our power to keep the
subscriptions as low as possible, and prompt payment is
one of the ways in which you can help us in this
endeavour.

The current subscription for your membership
classification is £10.00 and I look forward to receiving
this before the renewal date.

Yours sincerely




I A M Pennyless
Treasurer
```

A 'personalized' standard letter

selection criteria and have used them to extract (and store in a separate file) all the records satisfying selection conditions set by the insertion of parameters at run-time. We have prepared a standard letter which is personalized when field names are replaced by data from the selected records and have produced a few personalized letters. We have reused our previously prepared address label format to produce labels for envelopes to send out our letters.

Some final points

Databases with more than one entity

We have taken you almost as far as we are going to take you on database work in this book, where the aim is to cover a range of topics at an introductory level. What we have tried to do is to help you explore some of the basic features of database software; but you should know that there are still many features which we have not touched on. Our example has been built around a single entity – Club Member – whereas many business applications involve relationships between several (sometimes many) entities. Relationships may be 'one to one', 'many to one' (or vice versa) or 'many to many'. These are illustrated in the diagram opposite. If you like, you can think of a relationship as a *verb* linking two entities – *nouns*. For example, *Customer* (entity) *places* (relationship) *Order* (entity). Customer data would be held in one file, Order data in another, and the files would have one piece of data in common (probably a customer identification number in this case). The example may readily be expanded: Orders *draw on* Stock items, and so on. Such applications exploit the full power of database software, and making an accurate data model of the physical situation can be quite complex.

RELATIONSHIPS
may be...

one to one

one to many

many to many

The bases for data relationships

Enquiry facilities

We have only hinted at the way in which single specific enquiries can be made, but the ability to obtain quickly and easily answers to enquiries such as, 'How many individual members do we have?', 'How much have we taken in subscriptions since last April?' etc. – all unplanned questions, so not built into previously prepared report formats – is an important feature of more sophisticated software. And such questions can be asked in (more or less) plain English.

We have taken you step by step through setting-up processes which, once done for a particular routine application, need never be done again; so in practice the running database software is much slicker than would appear to be the case from what you have done at this stage. With many software packages, operation can be made even faster and more convenient because the software enables you to build a menu to cover all the routine operations you require, and all the individual procedures which are involved are built into a command file (remember .COM? See page 26) which can be run direct from the operating system.

Access to large databases

Other aspects of database techniques may be running through your mind. We have seen a little of the power of relatively unsophisticated software running on relatively low-powered computers; at the other end of the scale, massive databases controlled by extremely powerful software and using large main-frame computers are in daily use. Using standard telecommunications circuits, these databases may be accessed from the other side of the world. So how can we control who has access to what data?

Essentially, control is exercised by a hierarchy of passwords, and those passwords will only allow the holders of them to access data which they are authorized to know. Techniques exist (and are used) which will exclude both specified fields and/or records from those which may be accessed by a given individual; the individual is not told (by on-screen messages or otherwise) that certain data is barred – he simply is not aware of its existence.

If you look again at the example we have developed in this chapter, you will notice that the main data input frame, intended for the Secretary's use, carries no reference whatsoever to subscriptions. Subscriptions are a matter for the Treasurer, and are dealt with on frames to which only s/he has access.

IBM internal programme for the protection of personal data

Main principles and practices

1 Purpose definition The purpose(s) of any file or application that makes use of personal data should be clearly defined and shown to be in support of valid IBM business needs.

2 Collection and use limitation Only the personal data that is needed for the defined purpose(s) of an application or file may be collected by fair and lawful means and from reliable sources. It should be correct, complete and kept up-to-date, and be used and retained on the active file only to the extent necessary for the defined purpose(s) of the application on file.

3 Access and communication limitation Within one IBM company, personal data should be made available only to data users/recipients with a well defined need-to-know. Communication of personal data outside the IBM company that holds that data should be avoided insofar as possible. Such data should be anonymised or aggregated whenever feasible in order to avoid identification of the data subject.

To data users/recipients outside IBM, personal data should be communicated only:
when required for legal reasons, or
when required for valid business reasons
when legally permitted, or
when requested by the data subject concerned.

Accountability and data security

The person responsible for an application or file that makes use of personal data must be identified. All information containing personal data must be carefully classified and protected against unauthorised or accidental disclosure, modification or destruction.

Data subject involvement

IBM honours justified requests from data subjects to have data related to them corrected, completed or updated. Insofar as compatible with its valid business interests and applicable legal requirements, IBM also honours data subjects' requests for information about data related to them that is collected, stored and used by IBM, about the sources of that data and about data users/recipients outside the company to whom such data is communicated.

The IBM data protection internal programme

Passwords, of course, can be broken, given time; so frequent changing of passwords is an essential discipline in organizations which hold sensitive data on a database. The security of data can therefore be assured, at least to a level better than the best manual systems. But then it needs to be, because manual systems do not bring such a large collection of related data together in one pool.

Data ownership and data integrity

An important concept in the use of large databases is that of data ***ownership***. A ***database management system*** must be extremely

Examples of data available through Ceefax and Oracle

well organized and one aspect of this organization is that whilst certain individuals may need access to specific attributes of a given entity, they may not be authorized to *change* data. They may read, but not write to a record. Only in this way can the integrity of the data in the database be assured.

Some simple examples of databases to which the general public in this country have read-only access include Oracle and Ceefax which are transmitted along with television signals. Prestel and a number of *bulletin boards* are available for read-only access via the public telephone network. But the read-only principle applies equally to many users of purely internal company databases.

Once a database has been established, a company or other organization can become extremely dependent on it, so the backing-up of data becomes an extremely important operational issue. We have touched on the principle of back-up in Chapter 2; the techniques are different when dealing with large computers and much more data, but the principles are the same.

A learning checklist

If you have been able to cover all the work outlined in this chapter you should now be able to:

1. Explain that a database contains data items related in terms of subject matter.
2. List the major characteristics of a database management system.
3. Explain that this system isolates the definition of data from the definition of processes to be performed on it.
4. Explain that the purpose of database software is to enable data to be retrieved easily and viewed in more than one way.
5. Define the terms *entity, attribute, field, field name, record, key field, relationship*, as applied in database work.
6. Set up field definitions for a given unrelated entity.
7. Design and use screens (or masks) through which data may be added to or deleted from the database, or updated.
8. Design and use simple processing routines to be applied to every record in the database or a specified sub-set of it.
9. Design and use simple processing routines to be applied to individual records either on creation, amendment or deletion.
10. Set up and use selection and sort criteria to extract from the database a sub-set of records having one or more common data values (or range of values).
11. Output either to screen or printer reports containing data held in specified fields of selected records.
12. Output address labels using name and address data held in a database.
13. Use specific data items held in the database to infill a standard letter or form.
14. Explain steps which can be taken to ensure data security.
15. Explain steps which can be taken to ensure data integrity.

In this chapter, we have worked through one example. It has hopefully opened up the basic concepts for you, but what you need to do now is to build up some other models for yourself. Exploit the power of your software as fully as you can. Have fun!

CHAPTER 5

First steps in word processing

Scope

Word processing can be divided into the following kinds of activity:

1 Text inputting and printing
2 Saving text to and recalling text from disk
3 Text editing
4 Page formatting (or layout)
5 Using typing production aids
6 Records processing
7 Using associated packages (e.g. dictionaries, electronic mail).

An overview of word processing activities

In this chapter we will be concerned largely with these areas:

1 *Text inputting* This refers to the process of typing text which is then held in the computer's memory until you decide whether to save or delete it. The text you type will appear on the computer screen; in computer jargon we refer to it as being ***echoed*** to screen. This screen image of what you have typed is purely for your benefit and enables you to check for accuracy and correct mistakes. Typing on a word processor is not quite like using a typewriter because the bother of having to concentrate on where to start new lines is automatically taken care of by a feature known as ***wordwrap*** (see page 81).

The appearance of certain parts of the text might be highlighted either with underlining or emboldening. Emboldening refers to darker print produced by characters being struck several times (usually three) to give a heavier image on the printed page.

Printing, either from memory (called printing in ***foreground***) or from disk (called printing in ***background***) enables you to obtain a paper record, known as ***hard copy***, of your work. If you have many pages to print, you will need to know which several types of ***paper-feed attachments*** to put on the printer, so that paper is fed through automatically and you do not have to wait by the printer to remove each printed sheet and insert another.

It will also be necessary to learn how to control the printer from the computer in order to be able to stop it and restart it in the event of a paper jam.

2 *Saving text to and recalling text from disk* This is an important feature that enables a document to be reused many times, perhaps with one or two modifications to take account of different dates or names. Alternatively, several documents may be incorporated into another one, a process known as ***boilerplating***

which enables documents to be built up very quickly from existing text without having to retype.

Although you may have heard that with the increased use of modern technology we should have no need of paper in the office, printed documents are still important to office work. But being able to recall stored text electronically and put it to repeated use eliminates a great deal of effort that was spent in retyping documents.

Reusing modified documents is particularly helpful when working with contracts or legal documents which may use the same wording, though dates or names may differ. The ability to recognize circumstances when carefully worded documents can be made to fit numerous occasions is known as ***standardizing***. You will no doubt be aware that many firms wishing to sell goods send standard letters which are identical in content but which have had individual names and addresses automatically added (***merged***). The term *mailshot* describes standard letters to be sent to several, or often hundreds, of people. Examples of these appear overleaf.

Whilst you will not be tackling the intricacies of automatic merging, you should recognize the ability to recall, modify and merge text as an important feature of word processing work. You might spare a moment or two to think about the types of documents issued by, say, a personnel department dealing with applicants for a job and consider which ones might usefully be standardized.

3 *Text editing* This refers to the facility a word processor gives you to recall documents previously typed and saved on disk and to correct typing or spelling errors. Within the scope of text editing, you can also move text from one place to another (for example, an author may decide he has written a paragraph in the wrong place and wish to see it appear elsewhere).

Print enhancements (underlining and emboldening) can be added or removed as shown below, while editing and other features, such as centred headings, can be used to improve the display of the text.

This text is emboldened; <u>This text is underlined</u>

This text is <u>**emboldened and underlined**</u>

This text is in italics

<u>*This text is in underlined italics*</u>

This is elongated

This is elongated italics

Possible print enhancements

While the text is being modified, it is held in memory only. As with inputting text, you must make a decision about saving it. You may want to replace completely the original version and would, therefore, use the same name. Alternatively, you may want to keep the original version and to create a new version and so would save the document under a different file name.

4 *Page formatting* This refers to the shape the page will take, and covers such features as the number of typed lines to a page, the

width of the typed page, the line spacing (***vertical pitch***) and the character spacing (***horizontal pitch***). Once the format is set, it too can be recalled with an existing document, the settings changed and the new version stored on disk if required.

The standardized letter without data inserts

```
01 November 1987


Dear

I am writing to thank you for your order dated
          for                  I also acknowledge
your cheque for        and enclose a receipted invoice.

Your                 will be despatched to you within a
few days.  We hope that you will be delighted with your
order, but should it fail to please, do not hesitate to
contact us.

Yours sincerely



L A Zee
Managing Director
```



```
01 November 1987

Mr I A M Weak
45 Long Lane
Shorthurst

Dear Mr Weak

I am writing to thank you for your order dated
31 October for a car door opener.  I also acknowledge
your cheque for £345.50 and enclose a receipted invoice.

Your car door opener.will be despatched to you within a
few days.  We hope that you will be delighted with your
order, but should it fail to please, do not hesitate to
contact us.

Yours sincerely


L A Zee
Managing Director
```

The standardized letter with named data inserts

Word processing features that you should be aware of but are outside the scope of this chapter are:

5 *Using typing production aids* This refers to a number of functions that not only reduce the amount of repetitive typing by enabling the operator to create boilerplated documents or merge as mentioned briefly above, but permit the substitution of phrases or words for preferred phrases or longer, and perhaps difficult (to type), phrases.

6 *Records processing* This is an additional option not always available with word processing systems. It enables the operator to control or select data almost in the way that one may use a simple database package.

7 *Using external packages* This includes for example electronic mail (transmitting text or data from one computer to another by telephone or over a special connection called a ***network***), and dictionaries (or, more accurately, spelling checkers). The spelling checker tries to match all words in the file against its

own list of words, and indicates exceptions. As well as showing wrongly spelt words, it will also throw up words which are not in the dictionary because of its limited size. It will also miss words that are spelt correctly but used wrongly, e.g. the common mistakes made with *their* and *there*). These packages and many others will become increasingly used by the word processor operator as the nature of his/her work continues to develop with the changing nature of office work.

The limitations of word processing activities

You will have gathered already that text prepared using word processors may readily be modified. But because it is so easy to make changes on a word processor, there is a temptation to become lazy and inaccurate. If you have to spend a lot of time going back and making corrections and if this involves printing many copies, then you are wasting materials and time – your time. Try to be as accurate as you can when you are typing and check your work on screen before you print. It may seem tedious, but it will save time in the long run.

Word processors are very versatile, and we shall be looking at some of the things they offer in more detail, but bear in mind they are *not* the solution to every typing problem. They are most valuable where alterations have to be made or where text already typed can be used for more than one job. They do not have any particular advantage when it comes to typing the one-off short letter, memo or envelope. If you are an accurate typist you can type and produce hard copy at the same time on a typewriter, whereas with a word processor you would have first to load the word processing software, type and *then* print, which would actually take longer to do.

The main reason for a company buying a word processor is usually to increase productivity; however the standard QWERTY keyboard, which has become an international standard, has the keys positioned in such a way that it is deliberately awkward to use. The reason for this is simply that it has been inherited from the days of manual typewriters, when it was possible to jam the typebars if one typed too quickly.

The arrangement of keys on the QWERTY keyboard

Now there is no such necessity for speed restriction, but the standard seems likely to stay.

Other styles of keyboard have been designed with keys more conveniently arranged according to frequency and ease of use. Furthermore, the shape of the keyboard – presently flat and rectangular in outline – is being experimented with and a curved shape is being advocated to reduce excessive wrist movement. These keyboard designs are the results of studies to improve the equipment operators have to use and to reduce tension and tiredness and, it is said, increase productivity. ***Ergonomics*** is the term used to describe the study of optimum equipment designs to improve the operator's comfort and working environment. However, office managers and many keyboard manufacturers are uncertain of the reaction of typists, trained on QWERTY keyboards, to different new designs. Consequently, the traditional QWERTY keyboard is still used in the manufacture of new computing equipment.

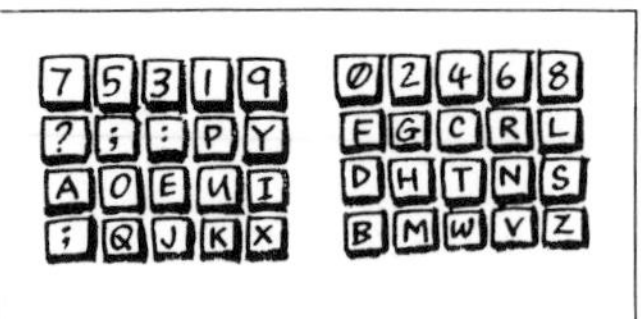

The arrangement of keys on the Maltron keyboard (left)

The arrangement of keys on the Dvŏrák keyboard (right)

What you will need before you start

You will find the work in this chapter easier if you already have some typing skills and know something about typewriter equipment and basic document layout. It is assumed that you will be familiar with margin and tab settings, and paper sizes normally used in an office. An appropriate tutor or librarian should be able to recommend a suitable text to give you this background if it is a new subject to you.

You will, of course, need a word processing package. Packages vary considerably both in the range of facilities they offer and in the way various effects are produced. It is not the purpose of this book to reproduce operational information available on-screen or in handbooks, so it is expected that, where necessary, you will consult your own reference material.

Before we begin using a word processing system, it is worthwhile just to consider how word processors compare with electronic typewriters.

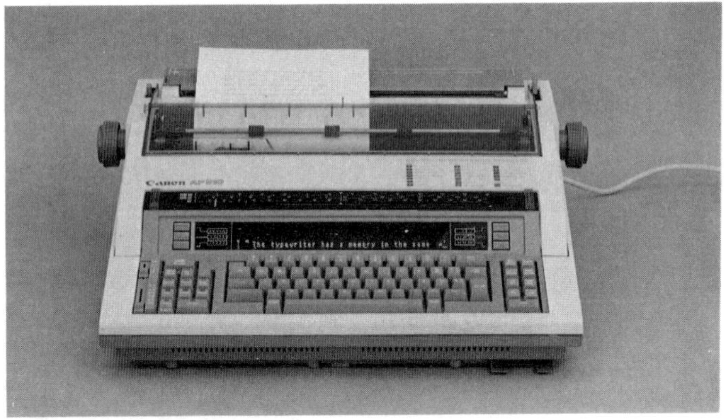

An electronic typewriter with thin window display

The path from electronic typewriters to word processors

The electronic typewriter has a memory in the same way as a computer has a memory; the typist has the opportunity to modify work whilst it is held in memory. However, the memory in an electronic typewriter is usually very small, holding only 8, 16 or 32 of the characters last typed. These are displayed in a ***thin window display*** (normally a 2-line liquid crystal display at the top of the keyboard) and only printed as the memory becomes full or upon command.

Some electronic typewriter systems can be upgraded to fully-fledged word processing systems, but this is usually not a cost-effective route to word processing.

Adding on individual items often works out more expensive than if you had bought a complete system in the first place. However, if the purchaser has a limited amount of cash at any one time, then this step-by-step approach can be useful.

The benefits of word processing on computer-based systems

Word processing on a computer-based rather than a typewriter-based system offers bigger disk storage facilities, faster processing, more sophisticated facilities (e.g. paragraph numbering, multiple columns of text to produce pages similar to newspapers, and much more) and, with the right sort of equipment, the opportunity to use other business applications software on the same machine.

Some electronic typewriters may be used to print the output from computer-based systems, but using a typewriter as an office printer is feasible only if the office does not do much printing; in other words it would be part of a lightly used system. Typewriters do not carry suitable attachments for automatically feeding paper and lack the robustness of purpose-built printers.

If it is decided that a computer-based word processing system is more suitable for a particular type of office, then the purchaser must still consider a number of factors:

1 whether to buy a *dedicated* computer or a microcomputer with a word processing *package*,
2 whether the *ergonomics* of the machine are suitable,
3 whether s/he prefers a *document-based* or a *page-based* word processing system,
4 whether s/he prefers a *menu-driven* or a *command-driven* system.

The italicized terms need detailed explanation and we will deal with them in the following paragraphs.

Dedicated word processors vs. word processing packages

A ***dedicated*** machine is one that is devoted to a single job (in this case, word processing) and nothing else. ***Package*** is a term that refers to a collection (also known as a ***suite***) of programs.

It was common in the early days of office automation for typists and secretaries to have dedicated word processors and for all other computing to be done using other equipment. The advantage was that the word processing computer stood apart from bigger systems and performed its job quickly (by the standards of those days). On a dedicated system the keyboard would incorporate non-standard keys, in addition to the QWERTY keyboard and a number pad. The non-standard keys would carry ***legends*** (i.e. prompts on the keys) such as SAVE, PRINT, SET LEFT MARGIN and so commands could be selected through the keyboard, which was operationally very convenient.

It soon became apparent that buying dedicated computers was a very expensive solution as more office procedures became automated: general purpose microcomputers were significantly cheaper, and word processing software which could be used on them was getting more and more sophisticated. Furthermore, dedicated word processors tended to have non-standard operating systems (see Chapter 2 for a discussion of operating systems) which meant they could only run the software specifically written for them. What office managers wanted was the freedom of choice to buy a suite of programs that best suited their needs from whoever offered the best value for money. Software houses found it more lucrative to write for a standard operating system that would be found on machines of different manufacturers. So microcomputers that can run database, spreadsheets, specially written programs, communications software, as well as word processing, ultimately won the day.

However, what the user won in terms of choice s/he lost to some extent in terms of convenience. Operators frequently have to use multiple-keystrokes (using more than one key at the same time) in order to perform certain functions. This calls for some skill!

What we have seen over the years then, is the decline of the dedicated computer and a massive increase in the use of the more versatile microcomputer.

The ergonomics of the equipment

We have pointed to the desirability of well-designed keyboards to assist the typist in achieving speed and accuracy and reducing the need to stretch fingers to reach often-needed keys. But ergonomics involves more than this. The resolution and stability of the screen is equally important to avoid tension of the eye muscles. It is equally important that the screen, CPU, keyboard and the disk drive (if it is a separate unit) should be placed conveniently if the operator is to work comfortably. To avoid aches and pains caused by tension, we suggest that you either use the natural breaks in your work or take regular opportunities to change your sitting position or move around occasionally to help the circulation.

To avoid eye strain through excessive concentration on a single focal point, a shift in position or a change in activity, even for only a few minutes, will help. Check to ensure that reading the screen is not made difficult by glare from surrounding light sources such as overhead lighting or direct sunlight. Well-designed VDUs tilt and swivel to enable you to make adjustment. They also have brightness controls to brighten or dull the image according to your need. If you are in a position to choose the screen's colour (if it is monochrome) amber characters on a black background is highly recommended; white on black or, worse, black on white, is tiring and difficult to read.

Ergonomic factors: ideal sitting positions for comfortable working (top); ways of rearranging computer components for working comfort (bottom left and right)

Document-based or page-based

Precisely what these terms mean will become more apparent as you type multiple-page documents but these are the main points:

1 With a page-based system there is only a limited amount of memory to deal with your typing – usually sufficient to take about 90 lines. Thereafter you must save frequently to make room in the temporary memory for subsequent pages. Typists who only deal with short documents, for example letters, do not find this a problem, but those dealing with long documents, such as long reports, find the constant interruption of saving tedious.

2 With a document-based system you can keep typing for as many pages as your computer's memory can comfortably cope with. But save fairly frequently. Remember that memory is temporary, and if there should be an interruption in the power supply, all your work since the last saving will be lost. Furthermore, if you allow files to grow too large, you will first slow the operation of the computer down to an unacceptably low level and possibly bring things to a grinding halt. In practice it is a good idea to keep files to a length of 10, 15 or 20 pages, the latter only if you have enough memory available – so when you want to set page numbers for different files containing sections of the same document it is easy to calculate.

Menu-driven or command-driven systems

These terms refer to the method of selecting the various options available under a word processing system. A menu would be a full-screen or part-screen display from which you would choose a letter or number representing a particular option. Menu-driven systems are most helpful to beginners but, unless there is a way of by-passing the menus, more advanced operators may become frustrated because of the way one may have to go through a succession of menus to get to a particular option.

Command-driven systems *appear* to offer less help (although there will be screens you can call that explain the options and how to get them) and from a learning point of view they require you to remember more from the outset. The advantage is that once you know the system, you can operate it quickly.

From the previous paragraphs, you will soon be able to identify what type of system yours is. With this background in mind, you should find the way your word processing system behaves during the following practical work more understandable.

Making a start

First, turn on your computer and load the system software. If you have not handled a computer before, then we suggest that you read Chapters 2 and 3 first. Having done this, you should be able to follow your tutor's instructions or your manual to get your computer up and running with word processing software.

Different word processing packages vary substantially in the screen layouts presented to the user. Examples of the opening screens of two widely-used packages are shown here. But although different in appearance, and in the keystrokes used to produce different effects, there is much common ground in the principles involved in using these and many other different packages.

The opening menu and directory for WordStar

```
            not editing
                  < < < O P E N I N G   M E N U > > >
  ---Preliminary Commands---      |  --File Commands--  |  -System Commands
 L  Change logged disk drive      |                     |   R  Run a program
 F  File directory     now ON     |  P  PRINT a file    |   X  EXIT to system
 H  Set help level                |                     |
  ---Commands to open a file ---  |  E  RENAME a file   |  -WordStar Options-
    D  Open a document file       |  O  COPY   a file   |  M  Run MailMerge
    N  Open a non-document file   |  Y  DELETE a file   |  S  Run SpellStar

 directory of disk A:
 AUTOEXEC.BAT  COMMAND.COM WS.COM       MAILMERGE.OVR WSMSGS.OVR  WSOVLY1.OVR
```

```
Name:                        Date: 31/07/89   File:             [DOC]    Chapter:
Col: 002/078    Line: 001/055   Page: 0001/0001    Chars free: 56425     Drive: C

*COMMAND MODE*                          Press F10 for a list of commands

_

<                                                                          >

1       2       3        4 Block  5 Block  6 Block  7 Next  8       9 Skip  10
  Menu    Help    Phrase   Copy     Remove   Insert   Line    Ruler   Units    Cont
```

The opening screen for Wordcraft

You may notice that one difference between the two opening screens illustrated is that the first system also lists the files on disk – the second does not and you would have to ask for such a list, by calling for a ***directory*** or ***index***.

It is a good idea to keep a printed (hard copy) catalogue of files on a disk for reference not only for yourself but for anyone else that needs to use your disks. A catalogue may consist of the following details:

1 its name (and extension),
2 the date it was typed,
3 the date it is to be reviewed and possibly deleted,
4 the author and typist's reference,
5 a description,
6 the reference of the disk on which it is stored,
7 the size of the file in bytes so that you have an indication of how full a disk is becoming – essential if you decide you want to copy the file to another disk and want to check that you have enough space to take it.

1, 2, and 7 can be obtained conveniently by ***quitting*** word processing software and using the operating system software to produce a directory listing which can then be printed.

You could prepare a catalogue by writing down the detail, but why bother when you have a word processor which will make it easy to maintain once it is typed?

The second screen on page 80 does not apparently offer very much! What you have here is a command-driven system with a number of reserved lines on the screen: the top two lines are ***status lines***, telling you what documents you are using, which disk drive you are logged on to, on which column/line/page the cursor is positioned (since we are not actually typing yet, this is showing the lowest values available), the amount of memory available for use, and the document type (this is a feature of Wordcraft; it is not commonly found in word processing packages). There is then a ***command line*** where you would type your instructions using ***mnemonics***, a system of letters representing the functions you wish to use. For instance, Wordcraft uses S for *save* , P for *print*, and so on. The solid bar underneath is known as a ***ruler line***, and this shows you where the left and right margins are set and will show you where tabs are set in due course.

When you have loaded the system, you will stay on the disk drive holding the system disk unless you ask to be *logged* onto a different disk drive – you can of course only do this if you have a second disk drive to change to! It is a good idea to store documents and data on a different disk to the system disk since the latter is probably very nearly full and will not offer much storage space anyway. Look for the appropriate command on the menu or on the help-screens to change from the present disk drive to the second drive. (Make sure you have a disk in the second drive!) Then use the command to make the change (for example, L to change the Logged drive in WordStar; DRive in Wordcraft: each is then followed by the appropriate drive letter). You will need to use a similar sort of routine appropriate to the software you are using.

Inputting text, printing and saving a file

Let's begin by using your system to type a short document so that you can see a fundamental feature of word processing: ***wordwrap.***

Opening a file

If you are using WordStar, you will see from the opening menu that you need to *open a document file*. Do this and give it a name of your choice, but not one that is already on the directory. (If you used the name of an existing file you would be presented with a document that had already been typed – WordStar uses the same command D to open a document file whether it is a new one or one that already exists.)

With systems like Wordcraft, you may begin typing without naming the document you are about to create. You will, however, have to move the cursor from the area known as the *command line*, a special area for instructing the word processor, located at the bottom or more usually at the top of the screen, to the larger area for typing. You would usually do this with a command or special key; for instance, with Wordcraft, as run on IBM and similar machines, you would use the ESC key.

With other systems, such as WordStar, you will not see the status line or the ruler line until you begin work on a document. With systems like this, you must select the option to create or edit a document, then name the document, before you can begin typing. WordStar uses the word *edit* even if the document does not exist. When you type in a new name which the word processing system cannot find on the directory, you will then be presented with a blank work space on the screen in which to begin your typing.

Wordwrap

We want to look at the wordwrap feature and so you will need to type in a few lines (from this book perhaps) so that you can see how word processors deal with line endings. *Do not* press the ENTER key (in the way you would in the case of ordinary typewriting) as the cursor approaches the end of the line, but continue typing and watch how the computer deals with text that it cannot fit on one line. Whilst typing, you may press ENTER if you want to finish a paragraph and then press ENTER again if you want to leave a blank line before typing more text.

Erasing an incorrect letter

If you type an incorrect letter during this exercise, then you may backspace and delete it, using either the BACKSPACE key or, if this only moves the cursor backwards, a DEL (delete) key. If you notice after you have typed a paragraph that you made a mistake further back, do not worry at this stage: you will soon learn how to go back to make corrections.

The cursor position

As you were typing, did you notice the detail on the status line changing as the cursor progressed across the screen and onto new lines? If not, then type a little more and make a point of checking the status line. It is important to take note of this information otherwise you can feel rather 'lost' if you can't remember precisely how much you have typed.

When you have typed in a few lines we shall prepare to print it, but read the following section first.

Saving your work

With some systems (WordStar is one) you must *save your work to disk* before you can print it. Systems that only 'print from disk' do not normally allow you to print the document you are working on; you should follow the saving routine for your system at this stage (with WordStar, press CTRL + K followed by D). You will then need to follow the screen prompts for selecting and using the print command.

Printing modes: background and foreground printing

The advantage of systems that can print from disk is that when you are busy at work, you can work on another file whilst the computer controls the printing in ***background***.

With other systems, you are actually allowed to print direct from screen. Indeed with one or two, Wordcraft for example, you have no choice but to print from screen, in ***foreground***.

Printing in foreground has some advantage when it comes to one-off short documents because it means you can prepare and correct the typing on screen, then print and not have to save to disk. However, try saving your file first just to experience that routine.

If you have a system that offers both *foreground* and *background* printing then you have the best of both worlds, and can choose whether you follow the guidelines for the first (save and then print in background) or second approach described above. Whichever you choose this time, make sure that you try the other approach in due course.

Preparing to print

Ensure that your printer is connected to your computer and switched on. It is best to start with the printer connected and switched through to your computer when you first load the word processing software. However, this may not be possible if you are sharing a printer. If the printer has been used recently by a different machine, it would be wise to switch the printer off, leave it for one or two seconds, and then plug it into your computer and turn it back on again. Beware: if the printer head ***resets*** itself in the process (i.e. moves back to the left-hand side of the platen) you must take care not to have your fingers – or anything else – in the way.

It is also important that your computer is set up to address the type of printer you have plugged into it. Some word processing packages will already be ***configured*** to your type of printer and you will not need to do anything. However, check to see whether or not you need to specify the type of printer before you actually use the print command. Wordcraft makes reference to some special files, called PDF files (***Printer Definition Files***) which you will probably find on your system disk if you are running this software. The popular Microsoft Word system operates on the same principle. Your tutor or manual will tell you how to call the correct printer definition file if you are using systems like these.

Once a printer has been selected, by whatever means, you will probably not need to set it again in that session, unless you change printers of course.

You may have a special paper-feed attachment on your printer – a cut-sheet feed or hopper feed for separate sheets of A4 paper, or tractor/sprocket feed for continuous stationery. With cut-sheet feeds it is normal to have to use instructions to line up the printing with the paper and, if this is the case, then we suggest that you remove the attachment at this stage and insert the paper in the printer by hand. However, most tractor feeds are relatively easy to use and so may be left on unless your tutor tells you otherwise.

When you have paper in place in the printer, then use the print command available with your machine to print the document you have just typed.

As you are using the print command, you may well come across a number of *options*: for example, to print only a section of a long document, starting at a given page and stopping at a given page; another may be to instruct the printer to pause between pages so that if you were hand-feeding paper, you could insert another piece when it came to printing further pages. Look carefully at any print options that you may come across and make sure you understand what they mean.

You have covered quite a lot so far and we suggest that you go back and practice creating, typing (using wordwrap), saving and printing again until you are satisfied that you can master this.

Text editing

When you typed your short document, you may have made some typing slips. In this section we shall concentrate on correcting text so that at the end of the section you should be able to go back and make any corrections to your own document.

If you are using the training material that accompanies this book, then you should find a file called TEXT1 on your disk; if not, your tutor will have prepared a file for you to use.

Look at the first menu, or check the help file, for the command that allows you to *edit* (i.e. work on) a file. With WordStar, the D to open a document file is also used to edit an existing file; using Wordcraft, type G for Get.

Type in the name of the file you want to work on (i.e. TEXT1) and press ENTER. TEXT1 looks like this:

```
Prof-reading is not easy.  Our eye have a way of pasing
over the line   of typescript and seeng what the mind
think is  there,  and not  what  the fingers actualy put
there.   Moreover,  the   time devoted to prf-reading is
nonproductive,  and the typist feels it necessary  to get
on with another job.     Yet proofreading is   the sol
responsibility of the typist.

When using word prcessng the opertor shoud always chek
typed work onscreen  beforeprinting.   Its a wast of time
and paper to   kep corecting   work and reprting if the
operator doesnt try to acheve a high degree of acuracy
first time.
```

When this document is presented to you on-screen, you will notice that words are misspelt; letters are missing and need to be inserted.

Moving the cursor

You can move the cursor by means of single arrowed keys (***cursor keys***) to the place where there is a mistake. You will need to place the cursor to the *right* of the last correct letter before the place you want to make an insertion. Ensure that ***insert mode*** is turned ON at this point and type the missing letter.

Think of the cursor as your 'typing point'. Wherever you place the cursor in the text, that is where your typing will appear. Remember that in word processing the SPACEBAR and ENTER keys create space so do not use them to travel about the document – as you might on a typewriter – or you will then have the added task of deleting them. Use the *cursor keys*, to travel to the point where you want to type.

Making corrections: inserting

Inserting missing text is one of two basic modes (ways) of making corrections; the other being ***overtyping***, simply typing a new character in place of an existing one.

Word processing systems are presented with either insert mode ON (and overtype mode OFF) or OFF (when overtype mode is then ON).

To find out whether the system you are using is in insert or overtype mode by ***default*** (without you having specified one or the other), type any key (other than a capital p so that it can be distinguished from the first character of TEXT1): if the character you have just typed replaces the one under the cursor, then your system is in overtype mode. If an extra character appears before the P then, obviously, your system is in insert mode. With some systems you may turn insert mode ON at any time and leave it on until you want overtype mode (as with WordStar for instance); with others you must wait until you are in the correct position to type the insertion, then turn insert ON and turn it OFF when you have finished (as with some dedicated systems, such as Philips). If you need to turn insert mode ON and can leave it on, do so now, otherwise wait until the cursor is in the position to make the correction before doing so.

Realignment

As you are making insertions, watch the end of the lines carefully. One of two things may be happening. Either words pushed beyond the end of the right-hand margin (the position of which is indicated on the ruler line) will be taken over onto new lines, i.e. automatically ***realigned***, or the line-ending will jut out beyond its original position, as is the case with WordStar, and we shall have to ask for realignment at a convenient time.

Remember when using word processing that line-endings where wordwrap took place are ***soft***, and not permanently fixed, so that when we put in extra text or take it out, the line endings may be realigned and tidied up.

Your system may not use the term realignment, so look for an alternative word, such as *reforming*. If you have to command the system to realign after corrections, it is a good idea to wait until you have finished working on one paragraph and then realign before you begin working on another. If you establish this as a routine, then you won't forget!

Hyphen-help, the hot-zone and more on wordwrap

When you are realigning, the system may stop and ask you if you would like to insert a hyphen at the point where the cursor has stopped. This happens when a word exceeds the ***hot-zone***, those last few characters (usually 5 or 6) on a line when the word processing program assesses whether the word will fit on the line or needs to be carried over to a new line (i.e. wordwrap). The line ending may not look so short if the word could be hyphenated. Some word processing systems will automatically offer hyphenation facilities, and you would need to watch the screen for prompts to use the hyphen-help correctly. It may be, however, that the author dislikes hyphens and hyphen-help could, in those circumstances, be turned off during the session.

Other systems only offer hyphen help on command, and you would need to use the appropriate command.

If you do use hyphen-help, ensure that you look carefully at positioning the hyphen and do not just accept the position the computer first offers you. Remember that with all but the most sophisticated word processing systems, the computer only counts the characters and is incapable of recognizing syllables between which hyphens should go.

Line endings

Your system may produce line endings that are automatically ***justified*** at print time or on screen as well. Justified text is where lines have been made equal in length by the insertion of more space between words. If a long word was carried over on to a new line during realignment, then the amount of space needed to pad out a line would be a great deal and would not have a very pleasing visual effect. Hyphenated words, however, can help in reducing the amount of extra space needed to justify lines.

Alternatively, your system may produce 'ragged' line endings (***unjustified***). Whatever the line endings produced at this stage, do not try to alter them yet. Remember the terms justified and unjustified and decide which your system produces by default. In a later section we will cover changing the style of line endings.

Justified and unjustified output

```
If you were asked to type

a draft document you

would choose double line

spacing to allow room for

alterations.

If the document was a
formal one, you might
choose to justify the
text. This would make
each line the same
length by inserting
soft spaces.

You might change to single
line spacing once the
final draft had been
approved. If you wanted
to highlight a quotation:

    you would alter
    the left and
    right hand
    margins like
    this to indent
    the text.
```

Saving and printing practice

When you have finished correcting TEXT1, save it to disk and then print it.

With some systems, you use the same command to save, whether the document existed before or not. With others, you use an apparently different function that updates or replaces the previous version with the new one.

Making other types of correction: overtyping

For practice, recall the file TEXT2, which contains these paragraphs:

```
If your managre asks you to tipe a draft copy of a
document, you would be well advised to ask if the
document is likley to be substansially revised or weather
the draft copy is simply to give him an idea of how it
will look when it is completed.

If the document is going to be subject to lengthy
revision, then you should type the draft in double-line
spasing (or even triple-line spacing) to give the
author sufficient room to make manuscript revisions. If
the draft is intended to show how it will look when the
job is finished, then you ahould type it in the stile
required for the finil copy.

Always mark your typing with the word draft of the
document is a draft version. Type the word draft at the
top left-hand marjin one or two clear line spaces away
from the rest of the typing.
```

Incorrect letters have been typed and need to be replaced by the correct versions. Read through the screen version you have been given and make the necessary corrections, by overtyping, before saving and printing the file.

Making other types of correction: deleting

So far we have only discussed the backspace-and-erase type of deletion during inputting. It is most useful to use this sort of deletion when your cursor is naturally positioned to the immediate right of the incorrect letter – this would be the case when you have just made the mistake!

However, on reading through a document at a later stage you may be approaching the incorrect letter from the left-hand side and so it would be useful just to be able to delete characters immediately underneath and forward from the cursor position. This you can do: your keyboard may have a DEL or DELETE key with this function; or you may need to use CTLR + key (with WordStar, CTRL + G) to delete a character underneath the cursor. Obviously, repeated delete instructions delete consecutive characters.

Where deletion would be more convenient right to left, the backspace-and-erase key or instruction would be preferable. Be warned: you may have a backspace-and-erase key or the DEL key may assume this function. Test your keyboard and see.

You may, however, cut down the number of keystrokes you have to make by using commands to delete words or bigger blocks of text. Remember that to a word processor a word is defined as a word plus space; when deleting a word, all spaces up to the next word may in fact be taken.

Defining blocks of text

To delete ***blocks*** of text, you must move your cursor to the beginning of the block and mark it in some way (with WordStar, this would be done with CTRL + K then B). Then move the cursor to the end of the block and mark it also (with WordStar, CTRL + K, then K). The blocks will normally be highlighted in some way and you would then select the command to delete it (with WordStar, CTRL + K, then Y).

When dealing with blocks of text, it is very important to remember this procedure of mark (the beginning), mark (the end) and command (in this case delete).

Now load the file TEXT3 available with this book and practice deleting words and blocks of text. TEXT3 is shown overleaf with instructions as to what you could delete.

As you are making the deletions, notice that the proof-correction marks also encompass the spaces that are to be deleted after words. Where blocks of text are to be deleted, you would obviously need to close up any gaps or remove any unnecessary blank lines that are left between paragraphs.

A year ~~year~~ ago laser printers ~~which were expensive,~~ were regarded as a somewhat futuristic and possibly expensive alternative to the more established ~~more traditional~~ types of printers, such as daisy-wheels.

But owning a laser printer no longer involves such concern as it used to. ~~But owning a laser printer no longer involves such concern as it used to.~~ Previously, owners of laser printers were concerned about the relatively short lives of the printer engines as well as incompatibility with existing ~~word processing~~ wp systems. However, it is said that following a period of use, these concerns have been overcome.

~~Laser printers are to a very large extent based on photocopier technology and the giants of the reprographic industry are active in this area.~~

Laser printers are to a very large extent based on photocopier technology and the giants of the reprographic industry are active in this area.

One of the cheapest laser printers currently available in the UK is sold at £1,367 by a firm in Essex. It is based on one of the most commonly found photocopier engines and offers eight printed pages ~~pages~~ a minute.

The major advantage of laser printers in an ~~open plan~~ open plan office environment is that they are relatively quiet compared to traditional impact printers such as daisy-wheels.

~~The problem with traditional impact printers such as daisy-wheels, is that they were very noisy.~~

You should take note of the proof-correction symbols now being shown in the text and in the left-hand margins and learn them for future use. These correction marks come from those published by the British Standards Institute and the full range can be found in the Appendix on page 173.

When you have completed the corrections, save and print this file.

Revision exercise

When you have done this, use the file TEXT4 (shown below with proof-correction symbols added) to revise and practice using correction instructions in a longer document.

Visual Diplay Units (VDU) have been in use for nearly 20 years but only relatively recently that they have become a compn feature in in offices, banks, factories and the home. Questions have arisen aobut their effects on health and there is some anxiety about the possible effects of VDUs in the long term.

Here are some guidlines that people working with vdus could follow to iprove comfort and reduce muscular tension

1. screen brightness. Do not have the screen either too bright or too faint. You will need to ajust the brightness as daylight fades or grows stronger. VDUs tend to lose their brightness with age and need replasing.

2. ambient glare. Position your VDU so that the screen does not reflect glare from over head lighting or sunshine.

3. screen height. Your screen should be at such a height that it does not cause you to strain your neck to see it because it is too high, nor to slouch because it is too slow.

4. physical tiredness. It is recommended that you take advantage of natural breaks in your work or at least every couple of hours to shift your position and thus avoid prolonged tension of the mucsles.

5. unsteady screen images. As VDUs age, they are more likly to develop faults which may cause flickering images. This is difficult to work with and it is recommended that the VDU is serviced or replaced if the fault persists.

Again, once the corrections have been made, save and print the file.

Dealing with headings

Call the file TEXT5 to screen. You will see from the print out below that it contains corrections which have been marked. Many of them you will already know, except for those affecting the first four lines.

```
[ ]      [Word Processing Practice]
[ ]      [Correcting and Printing the file TEXT 5]
[ ]      [Centring Headings]

         ---------------------------------------------------------

[ ]      [Paper Quality]
         The process for papre making results in the fibres runing
         in one direction - called the grain. The longer
         the fibres, the stronger the paper in the direction they
         run. When the grain is horizontal the paper bends more
         eazily round the type writer platten and is less likely
         to slip.

         When the grains run verticaly, is easier to make neat
         erasures. In any case, erasing strokes when using a
         typing corrector (which is pensil like in apearance)
         should always be made in the same direction as the grain.

         Some paper has a water mark, a sketch or wording which
         can be seen when the sheet is held to the light. Its
         chief value is that it identifies the right side of the
         paper. The most commonly used paper in business for
         original copies is bond. The apearance of bond paper is
         bright non-fading white, combined with an opake and
         uniform finish.

         The job you are asked to type will determine the kind of
         paper you will need to us. You must chse the quality
         and type that is most suitible. Questions that you will
         need to ask yourself might be: how much handling will the
         paper recieve? How long will it have to last? How many
         carbon coppies are wanted? (Don't forget that the
         thicker the paper before an ipact is made on the final
         carbon copy, the fainter will be the impression.) Is
         postage weight critcal? (If the typing is to be enclosed
         with other documets and then posted, then a heavier
         paper will cost more to post.)

    (A)  or if the typed document is a long one,
```

Centred headings

The square brackets indicate an instruction to centre headings. To centre an existing heading, place the cursor on the typed heading and type the centring command (with WordStar, this would be CTRL + O, then C). The heading will then automatically be centred in the middle of the line. Now do this for the remaining headings.

By using centring commands, you are beginning to work on the format, or layout, of the document rather than just the characters themselves. We shall gradually introduce more formatting commands as we progress.

Emboldening and underlining text

To give headings more impact, they can either be underlined or emboldened – features which are sometimes referred to as ***print enhancements***. The principles are the same whichever you use: the emboldening or underlining must be turned on in the right place and then turned off. Underlining and emboldening commands are usually instructions *embedded* in the text as instructions to the printer. A number of word processing systems may show you the effect of the emboldening or underlining on screen, but many will simply display control characters as ***on-screen aids***.

Place your cursor at the beginning of the first word in the first heading and insert an emboldening instruction (with WordStar, this would be CTRL + P, plus B). Then move the cursor just after the last letter of the heading and place the instruction that will indicate the end of the emboldening sequence (with WordStar and most other systems, the command to end the print enhancement is the same as the one that turned it on). When the same key sequence is used both to turn on and turn off a particular effect, it is often referred to as a ***toggle***.

Once print enhancements have been added they can always be removed – either deleted, in the way you would delete characters, or they may need special commands to delete them. Using WordStar you can remove underlining or emboldening by deleting the appropriate on-screen aids with CTRL + G or the DEL key; but with systems like Wordcraft, which will show the emboldening (by highlighting text) or underlining, you must display the on-screen aids or controls before they can be deleted.

Make use of the remaining headings in TEXT5 to practice underlining and emboldening.

Further text editing: inserting new lines and closing up space

When you have finished centring the headings, you then need to insert a new line. Ensure that you have insert mode ON before pressing the ENTER key. You will need to follow this procedure again in the third paragraph, which you will want to break into two.

When you have completed correcting the first paragraph you will see that you need to delete a line to make a paragraph run on. With systems like WordStar this is as easy as deleting characters, but with WordCraft and others you have to delete ***line controls***. This has to be done following a special procedure to display the on-screen aids.

When you have finished making the text corrections to TEXT5, then read the next section on justification before printing it.

Page formatting (layout)

In the following pages, whilst you continue to improve your text editing skills, you will begin to tackle questions concerning the format or overall appearance of your documents.

Justified right-hand margins

When you produced your own document and when you corrected and printed earlier documents, the right-hand margin would either be ragged (as it would on a normal typewritten document) or justified, depending on the default setting of your word processing system.

We have already explained that the term 'justification' means to give a 'book-like' effect to the text, that is, the lines are of equal length giving a straight appearance to the left- and right-margins. Justified text tends to be used for formal documents, such as reports, in preference to unjustified or ragged margins which look less formal and are better used in letters. You will need to be able to choose when it is appropriate to use justified text and when not.

For practice, you should try changing the default settings before printing TEXT5, i.e. turn justification OFF if it was ON before and ON if the documents were originally produced with ragged margins. With some software it may be necessary to reform the text to readjust the line endings.

With some word processing systems, what you see on the screen is exactly the way the document will appear when printed. This is not always the case, however. For instance, your screen may not be able to display in 12-pitch (12 characters to the inch) and so a document to be printed in 12-pitch will appear wider on the screen than it will be when printed. You will need to experiment with the system you are using to see if yours gives you an exact copy. If it does, it is referred to as a WYSIWYG system – standing for '*W*hat *Y*ou *S*ee *I*s *W*hat *Y*ou *G*et' and pronounced *wizi-wig*.

Not all systems will show justification on-screen and even though you have selected justified print, you may not see the effect until you produce a printed page. This is the case with Wordcraft where you do not have to select justified or unjustified text until print time.

Print TEXT5 with the altered justification settings.

By choosing between justified and unjustified text, you are making another decision about the format or the shape and appearance of the document.

You are soon going to create a file of your own but before you do, we are going to discuss how to set margins and line widths.

Calculating the margins

So far, you have been working to left- and right-margins set when the system was first installed for your computer. Let's imagine that the text you are to type is to be used as notice for display in an office and, as such, needs to be well positioned on the page. Proceed as follows:

1 The line width is to be 5 inches. If we are typing in 10-pitch (10 characters to the inch) then a 5 inch line will contain 50

characters (5 inches × 10). The typing should be centred on the page and you need to calculate where the first character position is to be. The full width of an A4 page is 210 mm – 8.25 inches, so with 10 characters to the inch there are 82 character spaces (8.25 inches × 10) across the full page.
2 Deduct the 50 character line width from 82. The remaining 32 is the amount of space that the left *and* right margins will take. If both margins are to be of equal size, then you divide 32 by 2, giving 16.
3 Conclusion? If the left margin is to be 16 characters wide, then the typing must start on the next character position, i.e. 17.

Another commonly used character pitch is 12-pitch (12 characters to the inch). Let's follow through the three steps again, but working out the settings for 12-pitch:

1 The line width is to be 5 inches, or in 12-pitch, 60 characters (5 inches × 12) but the typing should be centred on the page and you need to calculate where the first character position is to be. If we are typing in 12-pitch then we would say that in the 8.25 inches available for typing across an A4 page, there are 99 character spaces (8.25 inches × 12).
2 Deduct the 60 character line width from 99. The remaining 39 is the amount of space that the left *and* right margins will take. If both margins are to be equal size, then you divide 39 by 2, giving 19.5 (say, 19).
3 Conclusion? If the left margin is to be 19 characters wide, then the typing must start in the next character position, i.e. 20.

Another commonly used typing pitch is 15 characters to the inch. If you use a daisywheel printer, you will need to change the daisywheel you have been using for 10- and 12-pitch printing for something smaller to make it legible.

Try working through the three steps again using 15-pitch to calculate the margin settings.

Setting the margins

Having calculated the settings, you now need to use the commands appropriate to your word processing system. *Either*:

1 Set the left margin on screen at 17 and the right at 67.

or:

2 Leave the left margin at 1 and the right margin at 50 *but* use another command to shift the entire printed page 16 characters at print time. (If you choose this method, you may need to know something about ***embedded commands***, commands that change the format at print time but are visible when the document is on-screen. WordStar users will refer to embedded commands as ***dot commands*** and in this instance will use .po + value, meaning ***p**age **o**ffset* so many characters. (If you use this method with Wordcraft, the corresponding command would be width + value which would be set in the command area.)

Whichever of the two approaches described above you choose to use, the ruler line will adjust itself to the width you have specified.

A note about embedded commands

When using embedded commands, like WordStar's dot commands, you should be aware that your word processing system may be programmed to respond to a particular character from the keyboard typed in a particular column position. With WordStar, a full stop (.) typed on a blank line in column one signifies to the system that two characters will follow and, in some cases, a value to which the system must respond. Other word processing programs might use the hash (#) or a coded character in the same way.

Although embedded commands are visible on screen, they will not appear in the printed document nor will they reduce the number of typing lines on the page. If you run your cursor down the lines occupied by embedded commands, you will see that the line counter on the status line does not increase.

You will find that with many forms of embedded commands, they must also be used in special positions within the file to be properly effective. You should consult your word processing manual or tutor for guidance on this.

Which method of margin settings to use

The first method (i.e. *not* shifting the printed page) is the simplest when creating line widths and margins that together are not going to exceed the width of your VDU (normally 80 characters).

But if you are using a cut-sheet feeder, for example, and want the printing to start several inches in from the normal printing position, because the paper is guided part way along the platten, this first method may cause problems.

To leave a left margin of 3 inches using the first method, typing in 10-pitch, and allowing for a typing line of 7 inches, which is normal for 10-pitch typing on A4 paper, the right margin would need to be set at 100 and would, therefore, be off screen. You can set margins that exceed the screen width (240 characters wide is usually the maximum) but when it comes to editing, seeing only part of the document can making spotting mistakes difficult. In these circumstances it would be preferable to have either a system that adjusts the screen display to keep the typing page of no more than 80 characters wide in view, or to use an off-set command such as WordStar's .po + value. By having such a command, you keep the complete typing width for A4 paper (portrait) in view.

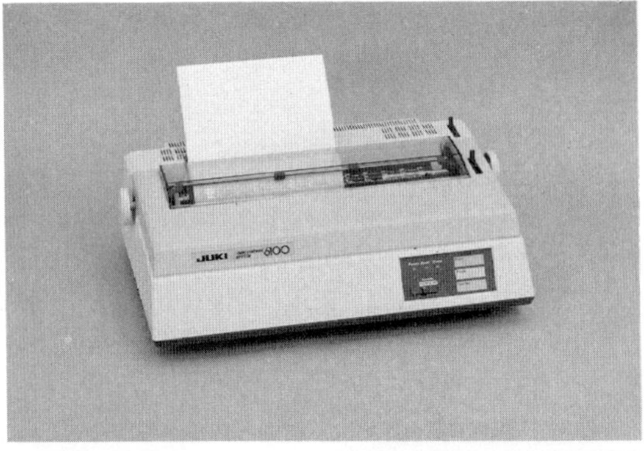

Normal paper position in the printer

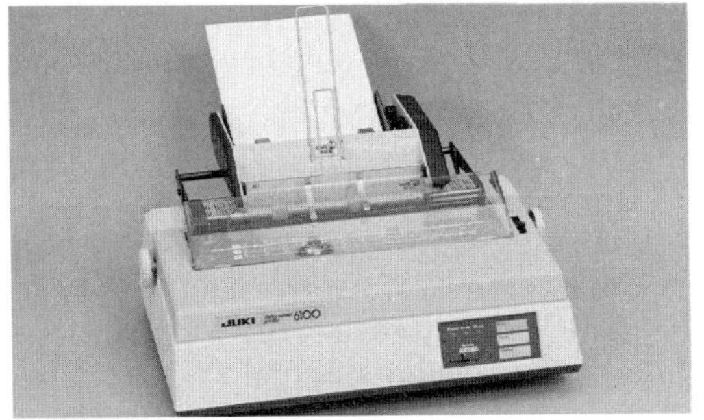

Paper position offset by cut-sheet feed

Practice in setting margins and revision of headings

Below is the text you are going to use to create the office notice that we mentioned earlier. Create your own file and follow the instructions we used to calculate margins for a centred 5-inch typing width using 12-pitch.

In this file there is also some scope for practising centred headings. You should make your margin changes before centring headings. *Centring takes place between margins.* If you centre headings and then alter margins, you may have to centre your headings again if your word processing system does not automatically recentre. You could also revise the use of emboldening and underlining but in doing so try to decide which is the most important heading of the three and therefore deserves most emphasis. Do you think emboldening or underlining makes a heading look more important? (There is no correct answer to this; it is largely a matter of taste, but once you make a decision, try and stick to it. It is very important when preparing documents to have a *hierarchy* of headings – the most important receiving the most emphasis.)

The other question you must ask yourself is whether you are going to use justified or unjustified text.

Text for typing

```
              GUIDELINES FOR VDU OPERATORS

                Positioning the equipment

If you are using computers in your work, ensure
that you adjust the screen and keyboard to
positions that are comfortable for you.  If you
are using computer equipment for long periods
then change your position from time to time to
avoid muscle tension.

                       Using VDUs

You should ensure that there is no glare on your
screen either from sunlight or overhead lighting
that makes your screen difficult to read.
Remember also that as screens get older, the image
may fade or flicker.  Adjusting the brightness or
servicing may overcome these problems for a time
but ultimately the screen will need replacing.
```

Search-and-replace

You may have noticed in the text you have just typed, that the title refers to VDUs but in the paragraphs we refer to screen. If we wanted to change *screen* to VDU to be consistent, you could spend time proof-reading the document and type in each change. However, if you use the search-and-replace function on your word processor you could take advantage of the computer's ability to look for matching occurrences of the letters *s c r e e n*, known as the ***search string***, and replace them with VDU. (In such a small document, this may appear to be a rather silly exercise, but knowing how to perform search-and-replace will become very valuable when you come to deal with long documents where depending on the human eye to spot every occurrence of a replacement string is unreliable.)

Your computer may offer you a number of options and you could spend a little time swapping VDU with *screen* and vice versa to get used to them all. In general the variations you will be looking for are:

1 A command that will search for one occurrence and one that will search throughout the whole file for all occurrences (known as a ***global search***).
2 A command that will look for *screen* as an individual word (known as an ***exact search***) and one that will pick up all occurrences of *screen* even when it starts with a capital letter or forms part of another word, for instance *screens* (known as a ***hazy search***).

Revision of margin settings and an introduction to tabulated work

You are going to create another document of your own and, using A4 portrait paper and 10-pitch, need to set left and right margins to leave a gap of one inch at both sides.

Whilst we are working on formats, the amount of space left at the top and bottom of the page is also important to us. A4 portrait paper allows 70 lines of typing, based on single line spacing at the usual pitch of 6 lines to the inch. If we decide we want a top margin of one inch and a bottom margin of 1.5 inches, we can work out on what line our typing starts and how many lines of typing that will leave on a page.

You will need to set the overall paper length in order that the computer gets the calculations correct. This value would be set at 70 and may appear embedded in the document, as with WordStar dot commands which here would be .pl 70 or may be set elsewhere, e.g. on the command line or in the PDF file for Wordcraft.

If there are 6 lines to one inch, then to leave a one-inch gap, we must start typing on the 7th line. The command used in WordStar would be a dot command, .mt 6 (mt standing for 'margin at the top'). With packages like Wordcraft, ***headers*** need to be set for the number of (blank) lines to be printed above the text. ***Headers*** – and ***footers*** – can also contain text, e.g. page numbers, to be printed on every page. Using header and footer commands ensures that text carried at the top or bottom of each page appears consistently.

To set the bottom margin to the 9 lines we need, you will either have to use a command for the bottom margin, WordStar using .mb 9, or you will have to set a page length, as with Wordcraft, and set that value to leave 9 lines.

If you are using a cut-sheet feeder, your calculations may not only need to take account of the paper length but perhaps also the small gap – called the ***phantom page*** – between the end of one sheet and the top of the next as the paper is fed through automatically. Your tutor will be able to tell you how best to set the formats for the cut-sheet feeder you might be using. With listing paper, the paper length is normally 65 lines.

Tabulated work

Having set your left and right margins, and top and bottom margins, you are going to type the document below. This document extends over two pages. But don't be daunted by its length! Notice that the programmes for each day are very similar and one of the things you are going to learn in this assignment is how to cut down repetitive typing.

Notice also that we make use of indented paragraphs and that ***tab points*** will be necessary to display the programme contents.

First, type the headings, remembering to centre and to use underlining and emboldening as shown. When you have done that, pause to read the section on setting and clearing tabs.

Display document for typing

WEEKEND CONFERENCE FOR EXECUTIVE SECRETARIES

Venue: Windrush Hall, Thudbury

Dates: Friday 3 August to Sunday 5 August inc

Delegates should arrive at Windrush Hall by 9.30 am on Friday 3 August.

Overnight accommodation for the previous evening is available on request. Evening meals will be formal occasions for which suitable dress is requested.

Windrush Hall is the beautiful setting for the 10th in this very successful development course for executive secretaries. ExecSec Limited will endeavour to make your stay both as enjoyable and as instructive as possible and would welcome any comments you may wish to make, favourable or otherwise.

Mr George Durbin will be on hand throughout each day to conduct opening and closing sessions.

PROGRAMME

Friday 3 August

9.30 am	Registration and Introductions
10.00am-11.30am	The Executive Secretary Today Speaker: Ms Lynn Thomas
11.30am-11.45am	COFFEE
11.45am- 1.00pm	Personal Skills I: Managing the Manager Speaker: Ms Deborah Ward
1.00pm- 2.00pm	LUNCH
2.00pm- 4.30pm	Information Technology I: Word Processing Demonstrator: Mrs Nicola Pierce
4.30pm- 5.00pm	AFTERNOON TEA will be served in the Lounge
5.00pm- 7.00pm	Syndicate work - case study 1
7.30pm	DINNER followed by FREE TIME

Saturday 4 August

9.30am	Syndicate reports
10.00am-11.30am	Reading the Balance Sheet Speaker: Ms Lynn Thomas
11.30am-11.45am	**COFFEE**
11.45am- 1.00pm	Personal Skills II: the Difficult Visitor Speaker: Ms Deborah Ward
1.00pm- 2.00pm	**LUNCH**
2.00pm- 4.30pm	Information Technology II: Database Demonstrator: Mrs Nicola Pierce
4.30pm- 5.00pm	**AFTERNOON TEA** will be served in the Lounge
5.00pm- 7.00pm	Syndicate work - case study 2
7.30pm	**DINNER** followed by **FREE TIME**

Sunday 5 August

9.30am	Syndicate reports
10.00am-11.30am	Report Writing Speaker: Ms Lynn Thomas
11.30am-11.45am	**COFFEE**
11.45am- 1.00pm	Personal Skills III: Dealing with Colleagues Speaker: Ms Deborah Ward
1.00pm- 2.00pm	**LUNCH**
2.00pm- 4.30pm	Information Technology III: Communications Demonstrator: Mrs Nicola Pierce
4.30pm- 4.45pm	**CLOSING SESSION** Tea will be available for those wishing to take refreshment before departure.

Setting and clearing tabs

When you have finished the headings, you will need to set a tab to ensure that the indented first line of each paragraph starts at the same point.

Your word processing system may already have tabs pre-set which you will need to clear. Look at the ruler line to see if there are any symbols representing pre-set tabs. If there are, then you will need to follow the procedure for clearing them all. (WordStar users will find this in the On-screen menu: Wordcraft users will not have pre-set tabs and so should make a point of finding out how to clear tabs using the Ruler Line option at a later stage, perhaps when we have completed this exercise.)

Then follow the procedure for setting a tab at column 5. (This is again to be found in the On-screen menu with Wordstar: Wordcraft uses the Ruler Line option.)

Ensure that your cursor is on a new line and press the TAB key on your keyboard (SHIFT + TAB for Wordcraft users) before you start typing. The cursor will jump to the tab point you have set. Follow this procedure for each paragraph and when you have finished read the next section before typing the programme itself.

Revising tab settings

Once you have finished the paragraphs, you could practise clearing a tab by removing the tab symbol but Beware! With some word processing systems whatever line you had your cursor on when you set the tab, you will find that the tab will only apply from that point down. (This is the case with Wordcraft, but not WordStar. Wordcraft users who had their cursor below the first headings when they set tab 5 should move the cursor back to line one: they will see the tab symbol disappear from the ruler line but reappear when they take the cursor back to the last typing point.)

For users of systems like Wordcraft, remove the tab with your cursor at the last typing point otherwise you are in danger of losing your indented paragraphs.

When you get to the stage of wanting to start on the programme for Friday, you will need to set two tab points: one at column 21 and one at 26.

You could then type the programme for Friday and the next heading, but then stop there. If you look closely at the programmes for Saturday and Sunday, they are very similar to Friday's and we can therefore make use of the ***copy feature*** to save a lot of work.

A word about page breaks

Before you go on with any further typing, you will have realized by now that this document is going to go on to two pages. As the document gets longer and exceeds the existing page length, there will be an indication on screen that you will be working on page 2. The page number on the status line will change from 1 to 2 of course, but another indicator will show where the ***page break*** occurs. (With WordStar, you will see a line with P on the right hand side of the screen; with Wordcraft, page 1 will be removed from view – but not from memory! – and you will be presented with a clear screen.)

The problem you may encounter is that the page break may occur in an inconvenient place, e.g. part way through the programme for one day. Instead of accepting the automatic page break, you can choose to 'force' a page break. Place your cursor in the place you think most convenient, remembering that you can't have more lines on a page than the format is set to take, and type the page break command (for example, .pa for WordStar and therefore an embedded command; CTRL + PG UP for Wordcraft).

Copying blocks of text

Do you remember deleting blocks some time ago? We remarked at the time that the principle of dealing with blocks was mark (the beginning), mark (the end) and command. The procedure remains the same for copying except that we substitute copy for delete this time.

So, mark the beginning of the block containing the activities for Friday. Move the cursor to the end of the block and mark the end. Move the cursor down a few lines and call for the copy command. If you hadn't typed Saturday's heading you could do so now, ensuring that insert is ON.

Make the necessary adjustments to tailor the programme to Saturday and then repeat the whole process for Sunday.

Moving blocks of text

Having completed the document, we are going to take the mark, mark, command procedure (see page 87) one stage further and alter the order in which the four paragraphs appear at the beginning of the document. The first paragraph should read: 'Windrush Hall . . .'

Mark the beginning of the block, move your cursor to the end of the block (the end being not the last letter, but including the space after the paragraph which is made part of the block by placing the cursor on first letter of the next paragraph), and mark it. Move your cursor to the place the paragraph is to go and use the appropriate command to make the move effective.

By extending the block to include the space after the paragraph, you have saved yourself the job of inserting blank lines to keep paragraphs separate and deleting unnessary space caused by the move.

Now decide what the best order for the remaining paragraphs would be and use the mark, mark, move procedure to make the necessary changes.

Revising search-and-replace

In order to complete this programme, you should now use search-and-replace to replace 'Speaker' with 'Lecturer' and 'Demonstrator' with 'Tutor'.

A learning checklist

By the time you have completed the work in this chapter, you should have a very sound background to enable you to undertake basic word processing tasks. There are many features still to be covered but at this stage you should be able to:

1. Describe the type of facilities word processors offer.
2. List applications for which word processors are particularly suited and applications for which they are not so well suited.
3. Compare electronic typewriters with word processing systems and explain in general terms how one differs from the other.
4. Explain how electronic typewriters can be upgraded into word processing systems and why this might or might not be an advantageous route to take.
5. Explain how the present QWERTY keyboard layout originated and became the industry standard, and what ergonomic reasons have led to the development of new keyboard arrangements.
6. Explain what is meant by the terms:
   - ☐ a dedicated word processor,
   - ☐ a word processing package,
   - ☐ document-based and page-based systems,
   - ☐ menu-driven and command-driven systems,

   and what advantages and disadvantages each might have.

7. Describe the ergonomic improvements which have been made to computing equipment to help avoid operator stress and tension.
8. Switch on a microcomputer and load word processing software.
9. Maintain a hard-copy file catalogue of a given disk.
10. Explain the function of status lines and ruler lines.
11. Input text making use of the wordwrap feature.
12. Produce printed output (in foreground or background according to the facilities available to you on your word processing system).
13. Produce printed output making use of automatic paper-feed attachments, such as tractor feeds or cut-sheet feeds.
14. Save text files using disk storage and recall them from disk.
15. Delete incorrect letters, words, line spaces and blocks of text.
16. Insert text, spaces or line spaces.
17. Overtype incorrect letters or text.
18. Centre headings.
19. Use underlining and emboldening instructions.
20. Select justified or unjustified text.
21. Set appropriate left and right margins in 10-, 12-, or 15-pitch, and use offset printing instructions where appropriate.
22. Use search and replace functions to substitute given words with preferred ones.
23. Clear tabs and set tabs for simple display work.
24. Use block copy instructions to eliminate repetitive typing.
25. Use block move instructions to achieve a desired arrangement of text.
26. Explain the term automatic page break and use the forced page-break feature.

Check this list and ask yourself if you can do these things without refering to any handbooks. If you find the answer is 'No' in some cases, then reread the relevant parts of this chapter and try the practical work, or similar practical work, again.

Check this list and ask yourself if you can do these things without refering to any handbooks. If you find the answer is 'No' in some cases, then reread the relevant parts of this chapter and try the practical work, or similar practical work, again.

CHAPTER 6 First steps in spreadsheet design and use

The spreadsheet concept

Spreadsheet techniques were in use long before computers. People who have to work with rows and columns of figures (mainly accountants) have used them for many years.

Let's look at one or two examples where spreadsheet techniques could well be used. Suppose you are a retailer. You buy goods at wholesale price and feel that to cover all your overheads, and make a reasonable profit, you must sell at 30% over the wholesale price. So when you receive an invoice from a wholesaler, you have to calculate the selling price. It is a nice job for row and column calculations. Here is a possible approach.

Col 1	Col 2	Col 3	Col 4	Col 5
Description of item	Quantity bought	Invoice total £	Wholesale cost per item (£)	Selling (i.e. retail) price per item (£)
Metal dustbins	30	360.00	12.00	15.60
Garden forks	50	900.00	18.00	23.40
Wheelbarrows	15	225.00	15.00	19.50
	data taken from invoice		Col 3 figure divided by col 2 figure	Col 4*1.3

Any figure work like this is best tackled by breaking the job down into simple steps, each step producing figures in columns as a result of calculations performed on data in previous columns. In other words, a spreadsheet technique.

Take another example: suppose that you were asked to conduct a survey of the number of people using a library in a particular month – say June. You would collect daily totals and probably present your survey data in a table like the one at the top of the next page. The kind of information you may be asked to provide from this basic data might include:

1 The total number of visitors for each week.
2 The total number of visitors for the four weeks surveyed.
3 The average number of visitors for each day of the week during the survey period.

Presenting survey data

Day of the week	Visitors in week commencing 01/06/87	Visitors in week commencing 08/06/87	Visitors in week commencing 15/06/87	Visitors in week commencing 22/06/87
Mon	250	242	230	238
Tue	202	201	198	204
Wed	208	201	203	207
Thur	310	312	305	315
Fri	203	200	202	208
Sat	315	320	317	307

How would you set about producing the required information?

Clearly, the total number of visitors each week is obtained by adding each of the columns in turn. The total number of visitors in the whole of the survey period is the total of each of the column totals. To find the average number of visitors for each day of the week during the survey period, you would need to total each row of figures and divide by the number of columns involved (in this case, four).

Quite a lot of arithmetic involved, one way or another. But in fact you would be applying the same mathematical process to each column and the same process to each row. How boring! Worst of all, when you have done it and presented the required information, people find it so interesting that they ask you to repeat the survey in July and August!

What you would like would be something to do the arithmetic for you. And preferably you would like to get away with telling it what arithmetic to do for one column and then getting it to do the same for all the other columns. The same with rows.

The electronic spreadsheet

An ***electronic spreadsheet*** provides rows and columns in which to enter data and descriptive text just like a spreadsheet drawn up on paper, but it has two very important differences: size, and the way in which calculations on the data are carried out. Even the very early electronic spreadsheets had a size of about 60 columns × 250 rows – massive in terms of the size of paper we normally use – and for the most part, large enough to contain sufficient data and calculated results to enable very large problems to be tackled successfully.

But we have come to expect more of spreadsheets. The result has been to increase the number of columns to several hundred and the number of rows to about 8500. But big is not necessarily beautiful. There is some excellent spreadsheet software around of the smaller size and you will find this more than adequate for your present purposes.

Of course, even with 60 columns and 250 rows, you would need a gigantic display to see all the cells at once. The word ***cell*** is the name we give to each junction of a row and column on the spreadsheet. And the fact of the matter is that you don't need to see them all at once. So the way the system works is that it allows you to use your computer screen to look at a small part of the total sheet – perhaps 7 columns (depending how wide you have made them) by about 20 rows. You may move your viewpoint quickly and easily to look at other parts of the spreadsheet.

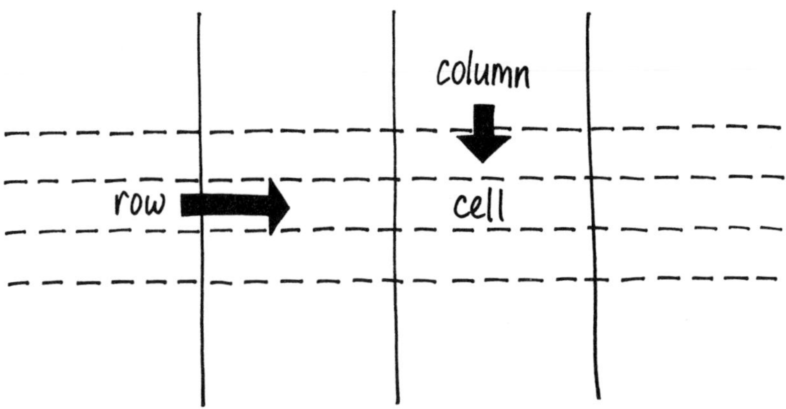

A spreadsheet row, column and cell

We said that the other important difference between manual and electronic spreadsheets related to the way in which calculations on data were carried out. With a manual system, you must of course do the calculation yourself and then enter the answer in the appropriate position on the sheet. With an electronic spreadsheet, you just specify the arithmetic process to be performed and tell the computer where you want the answer to appear; then leave it to do the arithmetic. Not only will it do simple arithmetic involving the four basic rules (plus ***exponentiation***, i.e., 'raised to the power of . . .') but, depending on the sophistication of the software, it will handle many standard mathematical, statistical and financial functions as well.

Loading spreadsheet software

Now it's time to get our hands on a computer. You know of course that you cannot load spreadsheet software (or any other software for that matter) until the operating system is in memory. Once the system prompt is displayed, you can load the spreadsheet software. If you don't know what the file is called, look at the directory to see which file names have a .COM or .BAT extension. If you are using SuperCalc, the command file is called simply SC.COM; similarly Multiplan software is normally called from MP.COM. So these are the sort of file names to be looking for.

If you cannot find anything looking the least bit likely, check the software handbook, or as a last resort, ask your tutor. We always believe that asking your tutor should be the last resort because it is so easy to rely on other people. You need to build up enough confidence to find your own answers from the software documentation or on-screen help so far as possible; if you are working to an examination syllabus, this may be expected of you by the Examining Body.

By now you have hopefully got your spreadsheet software loaded. If you have done the job successfully, you will have on screen a grid of columns and rows. Depending on what other information is displayed the grid will probably have about 20 rows and they will be numbered on the left hand side of the screen.

The columns may be identified by either letters or numbers. If letters are used, the first 26 columns are identified by the single characters A-Z and usually the next 26 by AA-AZ, then BA-BZ and so on. Some small spreadsheets with no more than 52 columns use upper case alphabetic characters to identify the first 26 columns and lower case characters to identify the next 26 columns.

Cells and their contents

The combination of a row and column reference is known as the ***address*** of the cell where the row and column meet.

The diagram below shows the top left-hand corner of a spreadsheet product which identifies columns by alphabetic characters. The address of the shaded cell is simply B5.

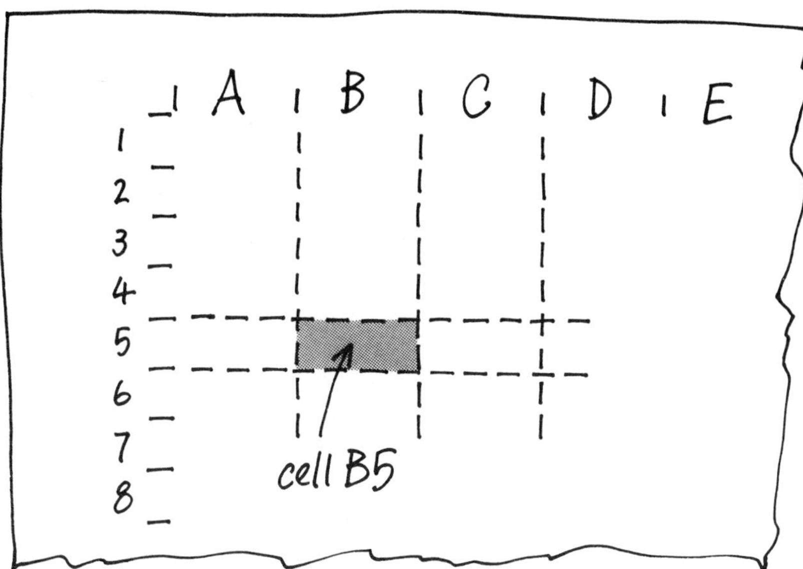

A cell address

Most spreadsheets use the column reference first, followed by the row reference as in this example. Multiplan is an exception; with this software, columns are identified by numbers rather than letters and addresses are of the form R5C2 (meaning Row 5, Column 2) which is the same thing as B5 in SuperCalc and similarly organized spreadsheets.

There are only three kinds of entries we can make into a cell: text, i.e. a string of alphanumeric characters; a number; or a formula describing an arithmetic or logical process to be performed.

Before making an entry of any kind, we have to tell the software *where* on the sheet the entry is to be made, or in the case of a formula, where we want the result of the calculation to appear. We do this by using the arrow keys to move the high-lighted cursor to the desired cell (if your computer does not have arrow keys, it will use some of the ordinary alphabetic keys in combination with the CONTROL key to produce the same effect). Whichever cell the cursor rests on, it is referred to as the ***active cell***, and you will almost certainly find the address of the active cell displayed on the screen. With both SuperCalc and Multiplan you will find it towards the bottom left-hand corner of the screen. (This is often called the ***status line***, and in addition to the active cell address it tells you about the cell contents.)

Try moving your cursor around a few cells now and see the address reference change as you do so.

Entry of strings, numbers and formulae

Now let's build a very simple spreadsheet which will involve all three entry types (a string of alphanumeric characters; a number; a formula). What we are going to do is to construct a VAT calculator.

Place the cursor on cell R3C3 (or C3) and enter the text "VALUE". Most spreadsheet software requires you either to place strings in inverted commas or at least to indicate the start of a string by using inverted commas, but this is not always the case. With Multiplan, for example, you use the Alpha command and then enter text without enclosing it in inverted commas. With highly sophisticated spreadsheet packages, the system assumes a text entry if the first character is alphabetic.

Commonly, the characters you are keying in are not transferred immediately to the active cell. They are echoed on screen in what is usually called the ***entry-line*** (often near the status line) whilst you are keying in, and are only transferred to the active cell when you press the ENTER key.

Now move the cursor one cell to the right. The active (highlighted) cell is now R3C4 (or D3). Enter more text: "V.A.T." Finally, move one more column to the right and enter the text "TOTAL".

The next step is to reposition the cursor so that R4C4 (D4) becomes the active cell. We are going to enter a formula here; what we want the software to do is to multiply whatever value is input to cell R4C3 (C4) by 0.15 and display the answer.

The technique for entering formulae varies from one manufacturer of software to another. To give just two examples: in Multiplan you would press the = (equals) key to indicate to the software that a formula is about to be input; in SuperCalc you would just enter the formula directly. In all cases the actual entry would be of the same form:

address of the variable*0.15.

For example, we may enter R4C3*0.15 or C4*0.15. As soon as we enter a formula written in a form acceptable to the spreadsheet software being used, a zero is displayed in the active cell. This is because we have not yet made an entry in R4C3 and the system interprets no entry as 0.

Let us leave data entry alone for just a moment though and get a little more practice with formulae. With R4C5 (or E4) as the active cell, enter a formula which will give the total of the two cells to the left, i.e. whatever value we enter in R4C3 and its calculated VAT in R4C4. You will probably have entered something like R4C3+R4C4 or C4+D4.

Now let's check to see if our spreadsheet is doing what we want. Enter a value in cell R4C3 (C4); we suggest something simple to start with like 100. Is there a 15 in the VAT column and 115 in the total column? If so, you have got your formulae right.

Formatting

But you may not be very pleased with the layout of your spreadsheet as it stands. There are two problems: one is that the figures are not displayed in a pounds and pence format (i.e. a format in which two decimal places are shown), and the other is that the figures are very badly out-of-line with the headings. Both problems may be dealt with through appropriate format commands. With SuperCalc, Lotus 1–2–3 and other packages, all commands are preceeded with a / (slash), so that in this case we would, with SuperCalc, use /F. Multiplan lists all its commands on screen, so we would simply select the command (F)ormat. You will find a format command of some kind whatever software you are using, and in general there are several subsidiary menus giving a wide choice of format options.

Before specifying the format you require, you must specify the cell or cells to which it is to apply – a screen prompt will tell you when to do this. In some cases you are given no option but to apply a given format to a whole column or a whole row, but the better software gives much more flexibility than this. You must follow through the prompts provided by the particular software you are using to get the numerical displays into the format *nnn.nn*, and to move the headings to the right side of their cells so that they line up nicely above the figures they refer to.

Always present your screens with the best layout possible – it doesn't take long to use the format facilities, and it makes it much more likely that your spreadsheet will be read correctly.

Now that your simple spreadsheet is operating correctly from a mathematical standpoint and is well laid out, move the cursor back on to cell R4C3 (C4); enter some other value. As you see, the new entry immediately overwrites the previous value, and the figures in the adjacent cells R4C4 and R4C5 (D4 and E4) adjust correspondingly to give the VAT of the newly input value and the new total. This shows an important feature of spreadsheets. Once you have written a spreadsheet, setting up all the headings and formulae, you may use it time and time again with different data.

Using a prewritten spreadsheet

For example, look at a spreadsheet, available with this book, which your tutor should be able to give you to copy on to your disk. It is called STOCKVAL. Before you load this spreadsheet into your computer's memory, find the command which will clear your first spreadsheet from the screen. In Multiplan you would use (T)ransfer (C)lear and then answer the verifying question with Y; in SuperCalc you would use /Z (for Zap!) and confirm your intention by entering Y. When you have found the correct command sequence for your software, use it and make a note of it. You will undoubtedly want it again!

In the same way, find out from your software handbook the command you need to load a spreadsheet and then use it to load STOCKVAL. When you have done this, note the command sequence for future use. With Multiplan the command sequence would be (T)ransfer (L)oad (path name) file name. With SuperCalc use /L as the basic load command.

Have you read the spreadsheet in successfully? If you have, you should have a screen looking something like the one on page 108. This spreadsheet has been set up for you so that it is ready to use. Its purpose is to help a small business with, say, no more than 250 items of stock to calculate the value of stock in hand. This is something a small business would do once a year as part of the preparation for drawing up annual accounts.

If you were running this business, your first use of the software must be to list all the stock items. When this is done, the sheet is worth saving, because now it is customized to suit *your* needs.

```
-1            1                  2            3            4             5
 1                  S T O C K   V A L U A T I O N
 2
 3 NB.  It is important that the unit price should refer to the same unit
 4 as it used to describe the quantity in stock.  Eg, if you have 5 cases
 5 each containing 20 bottles of a particular product, and you enter 5 as
 6 the quantity in stock, then the unit price is the price per CASE.
 7
 8      ITEM DESCRIPTION    QUANTITY   UNIT       VALUE OF    CUMULATIVE
 9                          IN STOCK   PRICE      STOCK       STOCK VALUE
10                                     (Pounds)   (Pounds)          0.00
-2
11                                                    0.00
12                                                    0.00
13                                                    0.00
14                                                    0.00
15                                                    0.00
16                                                    0.00
17                                                    0.00
18                                                    0.00
19                                                    0.00
COMMAND: Alpha Blank Copy Delete Edit Format Goto Help Insert Lock Move
         Name Options Print Quit Sort Transfer Value Window Xternal
Select option or type command letter
R11C1                                   87% Free      Multiplan: STOCKVAL.MP
```

The opening screen for spreadsheet file STOCKVAL

Saving a spreadsheet

The first thing to do is to check where the active cell is, because wherever it is when the spreadsheet is saved to disk, that is where it will be when you next load the sheet into memory. So think how you would like to see the spreadsheet positioned when you next come to use it, and place the cursor accordingly. Now you can save the spreadsheet. In Multiplan, the command would be (T)ransfer (S)ave followed by pathname and file name; in SuperCalc it would be simply /S followed by the pathname and file name.

There is no reason why you should not call your file STOCKVAL and overwrite the original file of that name, because yours, containing all the stock descriptions is more useful; it has been 'tailored' to your business.

Inputting techniques

Now you need to input data. It is always faster to keep the cursor moving in one direction, so deal with one column at a time. Work through your stocklist putting in the quantities in stock at the end of the financial year. Note that as you get to the bottom of the screen, the cursor stays still, but the spreasheet scrolls up – or to be more precise, the bottom part of it does. The top part, which carries the column headings and the cumulative total, stays put. We have arranged this by using a ***windowing*** technique when we built the spreadsheet.

What we mean by this is that we have electronically divided the screen into two independent areas. You are working on the data in the lower screen and when you attempt to input beyond the bottom of the screen, the contents of the lower part of the screen will scroll up. When this happens, the top lines in the lower area of the screen disappear – but of course you can get them back again by moving the cursor up to the top of the lower window and continuing to cursor up. But the only part of the spreadsheet which is affected is the part in the window where the cursor is – in this case it is the lower window.

You can move the cursor from one window to another (for example, with Multiplan you use the semi-colon (;) key); find out how to do it with the software you are using and make a note of it.

But now bring the cursor back into the lower window because this is where all your data entry is to take place. If you have finished entering the stock quantities, go back and enter the unit prices. As you do so, you will see that the value of each stock item is automatically calculated and that as you put in the unit prices for successive items, so the cumulative total increases.

When you have finished inputting all the values, you will want to save your spreadsheet. You know how to do that now, but just before you actually do it, let's think about the file name to be used. Why not use a name that relates to stock-taking done at a particular time? It is important that a filename should be as informative as possible, so a name such as STOCK88 might be appropriate if the stock-taking was done at the end of the financial year 1987–88. You decide what you want to call your file – but remember it should be meaningful and must not exceed 8 alphanumeric characters; when you are ready, save it to disk.

Come next stock-taking time, you would simply load your skeleton spreadsheet STOCKVAL, and there it would be, ready for you to insert current stock levels and prices. It is likely, of course, that during the year you have ceased to stock one or two items and they will need deleting from the spreadsheet. Similarly, there will probably be a few new items which have not been stocked previously and these will need to be inserted at appropriate places in the spreadsheet. But having made these small adjustments, you are all set to go and could produce a new file, STOCK89, which would contain full end-of-year stock information for 1988–89.

So you see how a spreadsheet can be used over and over again with different data. The treasurer of a small club, for example, whose annual accounts always take the same general form would simply use the same spreadsheet each year and insert current figures.

Review

What have we learnt about spreadsheets so far?

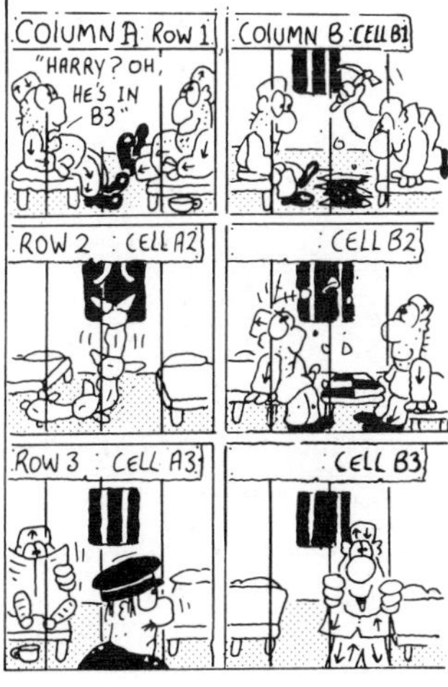

By now you should know what a spreadsheet is, and that the most important differences between a paper spreadsheet and an electronic one are:

1 that the electronic one can be very much bigger,
2 that with an electronic spreadsheet we describe by means of formulae what calculation is to be done, but the machine produces the answer, whereas with a manual spreadsheet we have to produce our own answers.

You should know what is meant by the terms ***row, column, cell, address***.

You should know how to load your spreadsheet software and use it to enter text, numbers and formulae into a spreadsheet; you should have formatted the cells containing these data to produce a well laid-out simple spreadsheet.

You have learned how to load a spreadsheet from disk into memory and how to save to disk; you have learned how to erase a spreadsheet from memory. You have had the opportunity to use a ready-made spreadsheet for a realistic small-business task, and in doing so have learned something about inputting techniques and seen a useful application of windowing techniques.

Closing the system down

Having covered all that, you may well want to take a break. If you are going to close the system down, the procedure is this:

1 Make sure you have saved any spreadsheet you have in use if it is of any value to you! (Did you remember to save it with the cursor in the position where you would like to find it when you next load the spreadsheet?)
2 Find and use the command which will transfer control from the spreadsheet software back to the operating system. Commonly, this is (Q)uit (/Q in the case of SuperCalc), and most software will require you to confirm that this is really what you want to do.
3 When you are back to the operating system prompt, remove your floppy disk(s) and switch off.

Commands used in building and changing spreadsheets

When we were outlining the use of the skeleton spreadsheet STOCKVAL as a basis for stock-taking in any year, we mentioned that there may well be a need to insert or delete lines. Your tutor will probably be able to give you a copy of a spreadsheet called GRID, which is designed to let you explore the use of these and many other commands such as COPY, MOVE, BLANK, LOCK (also called PROTECT). Those readers who do not have access to this software could construct their own quite easily. It consists essentially of rows and columns of figures as illustrated here; the figures to the left of the decimal point indicate row numbers and those to the right of the decimal point indicate column numbers.

Data from spreadsheet file GRID

```
 -1        1         2         3         4         5         6         7
  1 Program name: GRID
  2
  3 The purpose of this program is to provide a grid of figures which
  4 can be used to investigate the functioning of commands such as
  5 Blank, Delete, Insert, Lock (and Unlock), Move etc
  6
  7        7.1       7.2       7.3       7.4       7.5       7.6       7.7
  8        8.1       8.2       8.3       8.4       8.5       8.6       8.7
  9        9.1       9.2       9.3       9.4       9.5       9.6       9.7
 10       10.1      10.2      10.3      10.4      10.5      10.6      10.7
 11       11.1      11.2      11.3      11.4      11.5      11.6      11.7
 12       12.1      12.2      12.3      12.4      12.5      12.6      12.7
 13       13.1      13.2      13.3      13.4      13.5      13.6      13.7
 14       14.1      14.2      14.3      14.4      14.5      14.6      14.7
 15       15.1      15.2      15.3      15.4      15.5      15.6      15.7
 16       16.1      16.2      16.3      16.4      16.5      16.6      16.7
 17       17.1      17.2      17.3      17.4      17.5      17.6      17.7
 18
 19
 20
COMMAND: Alpha Blank Copy Delete Edit Format Goto Help Insert Lock Move
         Name Options Print Quit Sort Transfer Value Window Xternal
Select option or type command letter
R1C1     "Program name: GRID"         96% Free        Multiplan: GRID.MP
```

So if you move or copy some of the data, you will know where it came from originally. If, during your practice, the screen becomes a real mess, don't worry – simply reload the spreadsheet and start off again with a clean sheet.

Replication and similar techniques

GRID is quite useful too for learning more about ways of expressing formulae so that they may be of general application throughout a column or row, rather than tied to particular (***absolute***) addresses. Let's just consider this problem.

Formulae using absolute addresses

When you wrote your first spreadsheet, it should have looked similar to this one:

	1	2	3	4	5	6
1						
2						
3			VALUE	VAT	TOTAL	
4			100.00	15.00	115.00	
5						
6						
7						
8						

formula entered in this cell was R4C3 * 0.15

formula entered in this cell was R4C3 + R4C4

This is all right if we just want to find the VAT and total price for one item. But suppose we have a list of them, as here:

	1	2	3	4	5	6
1						
2						
3	DESCRIPTION		VALUE	VAT	TOTAL	
4	5 boxes DSSD 51/4 disks		100.00	15.00	115.00	
5	3 plastic printwheels		15.00	2.25	17.25	
6	1 metal printwheel		30.00	4.50	34.50	
7	60 printer ribbons		120.00	18.00	138.00	
8			etc	etc	etc	

The repeated use of similar formulae

If we used *absolute* addresses, we would have to write a different formula in each cell in column 4, and again in column 5. For example, in R5C4 the formula would be R5C3*0.15, in R6C4 it would be R6C3*0.15 and so on. If you had a large spreadsheet this would be a dreadful chore. Different software houses have adopted different approaches to dealing with this problem; in the following paragraphs we describe three ways which are in current use. It is likely that your software uses one of these techniques or something closely resembling it.

The first approach uses ***relative addressing*** rather than absolute addressing. Thus in R4C4, instead of the formula R4C3*0.15 we would write RC(−1)*0.15, meaning "0.15 times the contents of the cell which is in the same row, but back one column from where this formula is being entered." In this way, the formula in R4C4 is referring to the contents of cell R4C3 – but not by its *actual* address, only by its position *relative* to R4C4. If we were to copy this formula down to other cells below R4C4, it would work equally well, because the relative position of the required cell in column 3 is always the same with respect to the cell in the same row in column 4 where the formula lies. Multiplan uses this technique, and to make it even easier to use, it allows you to generate relative addresses simply by moving the cursor from the active cell to the cell which is to be addressed whilst inputting the formula.

The second approach is called ***replication***. SuperCalc, Lotus 1–2–3 and a number of other spreadsheet programs employ replication. All you do is to enter the first occurrence of the formula using absolute addresses (as for example in R4C4 in the first diagram on page 111). Then by using the replicate command (/R in Supercalc), or the straightforward copy command in Lotus (which assumes replication unless address references are made absolute by means of a $ prefix) the software will reproduce the formula in subsequent rows (or columns) using absolute addresses which have been modified automatically to refer to the appropriate cells. So in R5C4, the replicated formula would be R5C3*0.15; in R6C4 it would be R6C3*0.15 etc.

The third approach uses a command called ***name***. What this command enables you to do is to allocate a name of your choice to a cell or block of cells, which can then be referenced by name. For example, in the second diagram on page 111, we would name rows 4 to 255 in column 3 VALUE. Then with some spreadsheet software (e.g. Multiplan, but not Lotus 1–2–3) we could use an identical formula in each cell of column 4 which would simply read VALUE*0.15. In the same way, we would name rows 4 to 255 in column 4, VAT. Then the repeated formula in each cell of column 5 would be VALUE+VAT. This technique is simple to use and has the merit of helping a casual user of the spreadsheet understand more readily the process which is being modelled. Lotus in fact provides a *name* facility, but the name always applies to the whole range named and cannot be used to reference individual cells within that range.

The chances are that your spreadsheet software uses one or more of these three approaches to producing formulae which have an identical effect in each cell in a column or each cell in a row. If not, it will have its own way of providing a facility of this nature because such a facility is an essential in practical spreadsheet work.

A totalling function

Why not use GRID to practise some of these techniques? Try entering a formula in the cell which lies in the first row of the grid (that's row 7 in the diagram on page 110) and the first empty column (which would be column 8). This formula is to give the *sum* of all the entries in preceding columns in the same row. So it might be of the form SUM(R7C1:R7C7) or SUM(A7:G7) placed in column 8 (or H) at row 7.

Note that SUM( ) is a very widely used function in spreadsheet work; the convention of the colon (:) to represent the word "to" is also very widely adopted.

But whether it is wise to use *absolute* addresses depends on how your software handles the effect of replication. It is this effect we want to produce next and you must use the means most appropriate to the software available to you.

For each row of the grid, we want the final column to display the sum of the entries in all the preceding columns; and we want to achieve this without having to put in individual formulae in each row of the final column.

When you have done that, enter a formula at the foot of the first column which will automatically total the first column. Write it in such a form that its effect can be replicated for all other columns. The grid should now have a full set of column totals and a full set of row totals. Take time to experiment with GRID until you are quite familiar with entering formulae which can be replicated or are written in such a form that copying them to adjacent cells has the same effect as replication. Make sure too that you are comfortable in the use of INSERT, DELETE (or ERASE), COPY, BLANK and similar commands.

Now that you have got used to what we might call the 'mechanics' of handling a spreadsheet and have entered data into a pre-written sheet, it is time for you to try to build a simple but useful sheet of your own. Try constructing a spreadsheet to keep a record of your personal bank account transactions. If you want to model it on the layout of the spreadsheet here, we will take you through the stages of design and construction.

```
-1    1              2                 3           4           5
 1               BANK CURRENT ACCOUNT TRANSACTIONS RECORD
 2
 3               +-----------------------------------+
 4               |  The current balance is ...   120.69 |
 5               +-----------------------------------+
 6
 7  DATE     TRANSACTION DETAILS      CHEQUE No or      DEBIT       CREDIT
 8                                    PAY-IN SLIP
 9                                    REFERENCE
-2
10  01 Nov 86  Balance brought forward                              132.64
11  04 Nov 86  Dolcis Ltd (black shoes)  100102         26.95
12  12 Nov 86  cash                         124                      15.00
13
14             etc ...
15
16
17
18
19
COMMAND: Alpha Blank Copy Delete Edit Format Goto Help Insert Lock Move
         Name Options Print Quit Sort Transfer Value Window Xternal
Select option or type command letter
R14C2    "etc ..."                 99% Free            Multiplan: PERSAC.MP
```

Spreadsheet design and construction

Spreadsheet design

The first design point is to decide what outputs you require and hence what inputs you must have. In this example, it is fairly obvious – the most important output is your current balance. As a secondary matter, you may wish to view details of the transactions leading to this balance. The requisite inputs are details of expenditure and income.

Next, you must decide how you want to lay your screen out. As you will see in the last diagram, we chose to display the current balance above the column headings rather than keep a running balance in column 6. There were two reasons for this:

1 Using reasonable column widths, it would not be possible to display the running balance without moving the cursor to the right to bring column 6 into view – and when this happens, column 1 is placed off-screen.
2 The formula to produce the running balance would have to be replicated down to the bottom of the sheet, and every cell in the last used row of the spreadsheet would carry the most recent balance. This would make the sheet more difficult to read.

Both these disadvantages could be overcome by displaying the current balance at the head of the sheet.

Again in the interests of ease of use, the third design point is to recognize the need for two windows so that the title, current balance and column headings remain on the screen regardless of how many entries are made.

The fourth design point is to decide on column widths. They can always be varied later when you try out your sheet with test data, but it is helpful to get them more or less right at the outset.

Whilst you are getting used to building spreadsheets, it is a good idea to lay the design out roughly on paper first.

Spreadsheet construction

Now for the construction. First adjust the column widths to the values you worked out in the design stage.

Next enter the headings (down to row 9 in our example), but do not worry about making them beautiful at this stage. Centring and alignment come later. Make sure that the cell R4C4 is not overrun by the text "The current balance is . . ." because a formula is to be entered here in due course. Since the first entry on a new sheet will always be the balance brought forward, these words may be entered at R10C2.

The next stage is to enter any necessary formulae. There are several possibilities here; what you do will depend on the facilities available with your software. A slightly cumbersome approach, but one that should work with any software, is to place in the bottom-most cells in columns 4 and 5, formulae which will total their respective columns from row 10 (as is the case in the previous diagram) to the bottom of the sheet (typically to row 254 with the formulae themselves in row 255). The formulae will be of the kind SUM(cell ***range***). A range is, in general, a rectangular group of cells, but it may be part of a single row, column or an individual cell. Then the current balance formula to be entered in cell R4C4 (see last diagram) would be R255C5–R255C4; in other words, it is the sum of all the credits less the sum of all the debits.

The next step is to format columns 4 and 5 to display the numbers with two decimal places (in other words, a format suitable for listing financial transactions). You don't have to format each column separately; you may specify a range of cells by giving the top left and bottom right addresses. So with reference to the last diagram, we would apply a 2 decimal-place format to the range specified by R4C4:R255C5.

Testing the design

Now it is time to enter some test data to check the operation of the spreadsheet. Remember that the data must be treated as an alphanumeric string. The cheque or paying-in slip numbers should also be entered as alphanumeric strings because no arithmetic is to be performed on them, but it will not affect your spreadsheet if they are entered as numbers. Entries in the DEBIT and CREDIT columns *must* be numerical, as they are used in calculations.

Enter a credit balance brought forward in row 10 column 5 and check that the same figure appears in R4C4. Enter two or three further transactions; one should be a debit and one a credit. Check that the current balance changes correctly with each transaction.

Improving the presentation

When your formulae have been proved in this way, it remains only to improve the presentation. Use appropriate commands to move column headings so that they line up reasonably over the figures to which they refer. Line up the current balance box with the main heading and get them both as central as possible on the screen. Lastly, set the cursor to any cell in row 10 and create a second window so that the headings in window 1 always remain on screen.

Obtaining printed output

And that's it. If you have a printer available, print your spreadsheet so that you have a record of your work. Often print routines give you the choice of printing values produced by formulae or the formulae themselves. If your software does this, ask for a print of each kind so that you can see exactly what happens in the two cases. Remember that if you are printing formulae, you need also to print row and column references; otherwise no reader would understand the significance of the addresses in the formulae.

When printing a spreadsheet, you may specify the area to be printed, and the sheet you have just built gives a very good example of why this facility is necessary. Suppose you had made entries in rows up to 21. If you did not specify that you wanted to print only to row 21, the printer would churn out paper until it reached the bottom of the sheet, where we had stowed away a couple of formulae. The way to handle this situation would be to call for two separate printings, the first to cover the range R1C1:R21C5 and the second to cover R255.

Further spreadsheet applications

Now let's try another one. This time you are on your own. Try building a spreadsheet which will allow you to develop a personal budget. It might look something like this.

P E R S O N A L   B U D G E T

BUDGET HEAD	JANUARY		FEBRUARY		MARCH		APRIL		MAY	
	Budget	Actual	Budget	Actual	Budget	Actual	Budget	Actual	Budget	Actual
SURPLUS/DEFICIT b/f			25.00	0.00	22.00	0.00	22.00	0.00	22.00	0.00
Food	50.00		45.00							
Rent	100.00		100.00							
Heating & Lighting	30.00		25.00							
Laundry	6.00		5.00							
Clothing	13.00		8.00							
Travel	16.00		14.00							
Leisure activities	20.00		10.00							
Sundries	10.00		10.00							
TOTAL	245.00	0.00	242.00	0.00	22.00	0.00	22.00	0.00	22.00	
TOTAL INCOME	220.00		220.00							
SURPLUS/DEFICIT c/f	-25.00	0.00	-22.00	0.00	-22.00	0.00	-22.00	0.00		

The whole of the top part deals with your expenditure (outgoings) and all these are totalled (using a formula, of course). Then under that there must be a place to enter your total income, and the surplus or deficit is defined by a formula which subtracts expenditure from income. The only other formula is in the very first row of figures (from February onwards) where the surplus or deficit at the end of the previous month is brought forward. Notice that the formula used must *change the sign* because at the foot of the previous column, the surplus/deficit was defined in terms of positive income and negative expenditure, and when the figure is brought forward, it is treated as positive expenditure.

There is a good deal of formatting to do to make the sheet really presentable, but it is worth doing. Remember that you can format a range of cells at a time (not just single rows or columns) by specifying the addresses of the top left-hand and bottom right-hand cells in the range.

If you have the time, try developing some more spreadsheets, for there is no substitute for practice. So far you have used or developed spreadsheets for the following kinds of applications:

1 Creating a tabular record of many data items. There were calculations associated with this application, but some people use spreadsheets for tabular records even where calculation may not be involved. Often spreadsheet software includes an efficient *sort* routine which is quite useful in this kind of application.
2 Creating a transactional record – as for example a record of bank account transactions.
3 A budgetting application, like the one you have just tried.

All these types of application are common in the commercial use of spreadsheet software, and you might like to try developing different spreadsheets in each of these areas. There is another type of application for which spreadsheets are widely used; it is what is often referred to as a 'what if . . .?' type of application.

A what if? *spreadsheet format*

ANALYSIS OF PHOTOCOPYING COSTS

	NEW	END OF YEAR 1	END OF YEAR 2	END OF YEAR 3	END OF YEAR 4	END OF YEAR 5	END OF YEAR 6	END OF YEAR 7	END OF YEAR 8	END OF YEAR 9	END OF YEAR 10	END OF YEAR 11
Current value of equipment	1656.00	1159.20	811.44	568.01	397.61	278.32	194.83	136.38	95.47	66.83	46.78	32.74
Depreciation - %		30	30	30	30	30	30	30	30	30	30	30
Inflation rate - %		5.0	5.0	5.0	5.0	5.0	5.0	5.0	5.0	5.0	5.0	5.0
Likely new purchase price	1656.00	1738.80	1825.74	1917.03	2012.88	2113.52	2219.20	2330.16	2446.67	2569.00	2697.45	2832.32
Cash investment int. rate - %		10.0	10.0	10.0	10.0	10.0	10.0	10.0	10.0	10.0	10.0	10.0
Compounded cash value if inv.	1656.00	1821.60	2003.76	2204.14	2424.55	2667.00	2933.71	3227.08	3549.78	3904.76	4925.24	4724.76
Capital loss to be recovered		745.20	616.86	535.10	468.67	462.38	455.87	462.78	480.13	505.95	538.97	578.43
Maint. charge per 1000 copies		11.00	11.00	11.00	11.00	11.00	11.00	11.00	11.00	11.00	11.00	11.00
Paper price per ream		2.50	2.50	2.50	2.50	2.50	2.50	2.50	2.50	2.50	2.50	2.50
Estimated no. of copies p.a.		36000	36000	36000	36000	36000	36000	36000	36000	36000	36000	36000
PRICE PER COPY (pence)		3.67	3.31	3.09	2.95	2.88	2.87	2.89	2.93	3.01	3.10	3.21
No. of years equipment is kept			2	3	4	5	6	7	8	9	10	11
Ave. price per copy over period			3.49	3.36	3.26	3.18	3.13	3.09	3.07	3.07	3.07	3.08

Look, for example, at the spreadsheet shown above. You will find this spreadsheet on the disk which can be bought to accompany this book; it has been written to work with Multiplan software and is called COPIER. The spreadsheet has been designed to work out the real cost of producing photocopies using the same photocopier over a number of years.

It looks fairly complicated but don't worry too much about the accounting angle, unless this happens to interest you. The real purpose of including this example is to show a realistic *what if* type of application.

What if you were to buy a more expensive copier? Change the old price (it is the first entry in the first column) for a higher one and see what happens to the cost of single copies.

What if the number of copies produced each year goes up? It means that more paper and more toner is needed but is also means that the fixed costs of the copier are spread across more copies.

If you want to be adventurous you could alter the other figures as well – try increasing the inflation rate in different years, for example. (You can change anything you like that isn't a formula, but be realistic.)

You can't have helped but notice that when you have altered some figures there has been a 'knock-on' effect on the columns representing the other years. Don't worry about all the formulae tucked away behind the columns, just keep your eye on the cost of individual copies.

Using graphics

Look at the example *what if* spreadsheet again and notice that the average price per copy is relatively high in year 2, decreases thereafter, bottoming out in years 7–10 and rising again after that. You have to look quite closely at the figures to see this change in cost and this is a case where an appropriately scaled graph would show the results better than a table of figures. Many of the larger spreadsheet packages have excellent graphics facilities, usually providing a choice of at least three types of graph: line graphs, bar charts and pie charts.

You would only use a pie chart if you wanted to illustrate the relative proportions of a number of quantities which together made up a whole entity of some kind. For example, a pie chart would have been ideal to show the relative proportions of expenditure on food, rent, heating and lighting, etc., in your budgeting spreadsheet.

But a pie chart would have no meaning if we tried to use it for illustrating the year-to-year variation in photocopying costs. For this application we would almost certainly use a bar chart or a line graph. The more comprehensive packages would allow us to suppress the zero so that the year by year variation could be emphasised, and the result might be something like this:

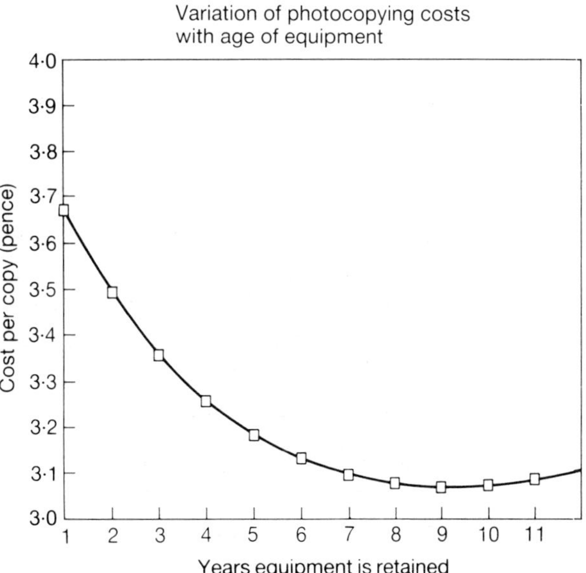

Graphic output from Lotus 1–2–3 software using the spreadsheet model COPIER

The question arises: which of the several variable factors exercises the greatest influence over the shape of this graph? In other words, to which factor or factors is the cost per copy variation most sensitive? Can we hit the minimum cost level earlier than year 8? What is it that causes the cost to rise again anyway? The way to investigate this is to vary each of the influencing factors *in turn* and observe the effect. One could try, for example, changing the depreciation rate first to 20% p.a. and then to 40% p.a., observing the effect in each case. Then, having restored it to its original value of 30%, one would make variations in the inflation rate to see what this did to the graph shape. Again, one would restore the inflation rate to its initial value before going on to vary the next factor – in this case the cash investment interest rate. And so on . . .

All we are doing is a very orderly and extended *What if* procedure, but given this orderly structured approach, you would be suprised how much useful information can be gained. There is a tendency for people to think that a *what if* application is nothing more than changing the odd figure here and there, whereas it is a powerful technique which, when properly applied, can lead to a much clearer understanding of a given problem.

There are many very useful spreadsheet techniques which have not been touched on in this introductory text, but can be explored at more advanced levels.

A learning checklist

You have covered a considerable amount and will have achieved quite a lot if you have worked through the practical exercises we have suggested. By now, you should be able to:

1 Explain what a spreadsheet is.
2 Define the terms *row, column, cell.*
3 Explain the essential differences between manual and electronic spreadsheets.
4 Load spreadsheet software.
5 Enter text, numbers and formulae into a spreadsheet.
6 Perform calculations through the use of simple formulae involving the four arithmetic rules: +, −, *, /.
7 Use the function SUM( ) or its equivalent to produce the total specified group of cells.
8 Use absolute addresses to refer to data in specified cells.
9 Use relative addressing, replication or any other appropriate technique, to enable a formula to have an identical effect when replicated and used with data one or more rows down (or columns to the right) from the positions originally addressed.
10 Perform a number of different format changes, e.g. change column widths, centre or right-justify text, control the display format of numerical data.
11 Load pre-written spreadsheets stored on floppy disk.
12 Make entries in a prewritten spreadsheet in an efficient manner.

13 Distinguish between reusable 'skeleton' spreadsheets and separately filed archive spreadsheets using the same skeleton but including data in respect of a given period.
14 File (save) spreadsheets on floppy disks.
15 Explain what is meant by a 'window' and the purpose of using window techniques.
16 Use a range of commands to BLANK cells, DELETE rows or columns, INSERT rows or columns, COPY a range of cells, MOVE a range of cells, LOCK (PROTECT) cells.
17 State at least three factors to be considered in the design of spreadsheets.
18 Design and construct a simple spreadsheet.
19 State the purpose and underlying principles of spreadsheet documentation.
20 Print out all or selected parts of a spreadsheet, with and without formulae being displayed.
21 Exit from the spreadsheet software, returning control to the operating system.
22 List a range of applications for which spreadsheet software would be appropriate.
23 Explain the place and use of graphics in modern spreadsheet software.

CHAPTER 7 Communications on computer systems

The development of access to computer systems

There was a time when computers were very large (even though their memories were small), they were very temperamental and had to be kept in a very carefully controlled environment. Temperature and humidity had to be maintained within closely defined limits, and great care was taken to keep the atmosphere dust free.

Only those people responsible for the operation of the computer would be allowed access to the computer room; programmers were not welcome and line managers whose work was being processed were not allowed anywhere near the place!

All the work was ***batch processed***, i.e. the appropriate program and data were made available to the computer, an instruction given to make the computer access the first program instruction, and after that the program would run to the end without any human intervention. At the end of the process a print-out would have been produced and this would be delivered to the appropriate department.

Then came the day when interaction with the computer during the running of a program became possible. At first, this was restricted to a single console, but as technology developed it was possible to have a number of terminals or other means of input/output all connected to the computer. No terminal had the attention of the computer all the time; the computer would look at each terminal in turn, so that each had a time slot during which it could transmit to or receive data from the computer. Such a system was called a ***time-sharing*** system.

It completely changed the nature of data processing. Certainly there were programs which could still operate effectively in batch mode – like payroll runs, for example – but the way was now open for a range of interactive computer applications.

Real time systems

One family of applications is concerned particularly with the control of dynamic processes. Such systems are usually referred to as ***real time*** systems; they are able to receive continuously varying data from sources outside the computer system, and the computer processes that data sufficiently quickly to influence the sources of data. Typical examples might be a process control system as in the production of chemicals or of paper.

Transaction processing

Another family of applications is concerned with what is commonly called ***transaction processing***. Here, terminals are connected to and controlled by the central processing unit (i.e. they are ***on-line***) and they are used to interrogate or update data files. For example, when a client calls at a Social Services office seeking help of some kind, the Social Worker needs to know before interviewing the client whether the department has had any previous dealings with the individual, and if so, what help was given. With this background information, the Social Worker can provide a much more effective service. Following the interview, the record can be updated – not with case notes, of course, but with new factual information – ready for the next time it is needed.

In the days before transaction processing was possible, such records were kept in a massive card index system which suffered from all the usual problems – missing cards, mis-filed cards, cards which hadn't been updated. And it may well be that the client had previously been in touch with an office in another location so that, even with a perfect card index system, the Social Worker would still not have the requisite background information because the card would be in another office, miles away.

A centralized system

With all the data held on a central computer and each local office having transaction processing facilities, these problems could be overcome.

At least, they could in theory. But there were two major snags. In the first place, there were both technical and financial constraints associated with connection of each office terminal over a very large area directly back to a central mainframe computer. So devices called ***concentrators*** were used. These would accept connections from up to eight terminals and then provide a single connection back to the mainframe.

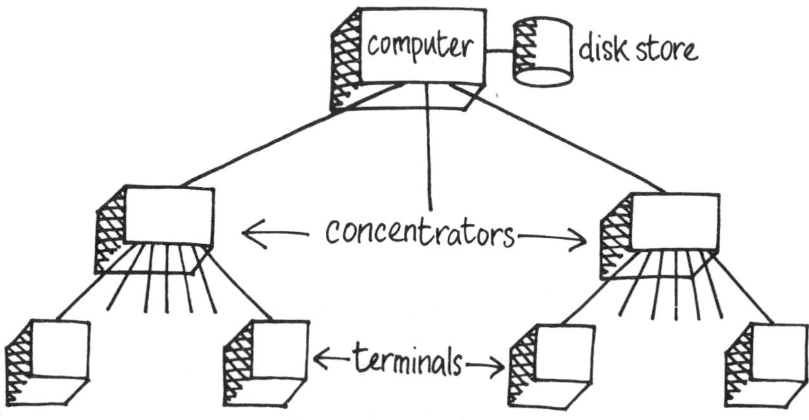

A centralized system – remote terminals connect to a mainframe computer via concentrators

The problems were:

1 As on-line enquiries and updating of data increased, so did delays arising from the use of a shared line from the concentrator back to the computer, until the system in many cases became unworkable in practical terms.

2 In the event of the mainframe computer **going down** (developing a fault which prevented its correct operation), the whole system failed. Such a system is said to have no **resilience**.

A distributed system

Technological advances helped again, for by now, powerful mini-computers had been developed with the facility to control large amounts of stored data almost as economically as could be done with mainframe computers. This enabled configurations such as that shown below to be employed. The data and the software controlling it was brought closer to the user. This is the key to modern interactive computing. You bring the data and the software as close to the user as possible.

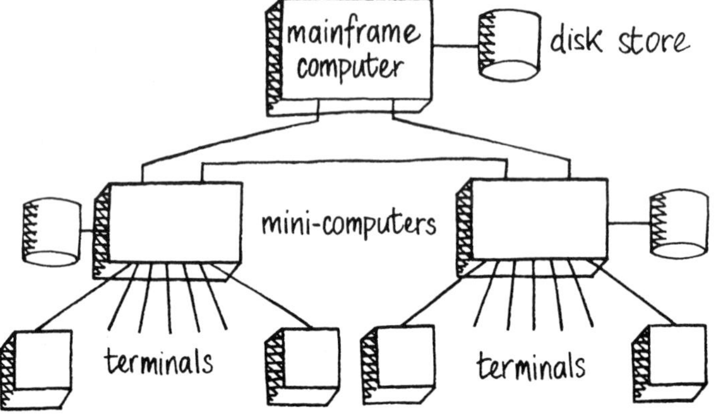

A distributed system – remote terminals from part of a Wide Area Network (WAN)

Each terminal (which may itself be a microcomputer, but needn't be) has a direct connection to a computer and the data under the control of the computer is that which is most likely to be required by the terminals connected directly to it. But data stored elsewhere can be made available, because the computers are connected to each other and can therefore access files from each other's stores.

The network gets rid of long delays for the users because of their much more direct access to the data they need, and the overall system offers a great deal more resilience. With a network system, if one computer goes down, just eight terminals out of the total system are put out of operation and only a part of the total data becomes temporarily unavailable.

Telephone circuits used for computer communication

Now if cables had to be specially laid to make connections between terminals and computer, and between computers, the system would be too expensive, and the country would soon have a jungle of wires going all over the place as more and more systems laid down their own communications cables.

There is a very good system of communications cables already existing, provided for the telephone service, and links between computers normally use telephone communications channels. The only difficulty is that the electrical signals which represent characters in computer systems are a series of electrical pulses, whereas the electrical signals which represent speech, for which the telecommunication service was originally designed, are made up of alternating current waveforms.

Modems and acoustic couplers

Therefore to transmit digital information from a terminal to a computer, or vice versa, using telephone circuits, the pulses must be coded into an alternating current waveform and then decoded at the receiving end so that they are once more in a form which a computer can handle. These two processes are called respectively *modulation* and *demodulation*. They are undertaken by a device which takes its name from these words – a ***modem*** (***mo***dulator/***dem***odulator). So every terminal connected to a telephone line is connected through a modem, and at the far end a modem stands between the telephone line and the minicomputer.

An acoustic coupler

The alternative to a modem is an ***acoustic coupler***. This achieves the same end but in a rather more round-about way. A modem simply converts one form of electrical signal to another; with an acoustic coupler, the electrical output from the computer is first converted into a coded sound signal, the sound is picked up by an ordinary telephone handset microphone and converted into an electrical signal for transmission over the telephone circuit. In the reverse direction, the received electrical signal coming in over the telephone line is converted to sound in the handset earpiece and the acoustic coupler picks up this sound signal and changes it back into a pattern of electrical pulses which can be handled by the computer.

The coupling between this device and the telephone handset needs to be quite good so that signals are transmitted and received accurately. It also needs to exclude all other noises as these may be interpreted as part of the transmitted code. Couplers work well enough with conventional handset designs, but some of the more recent designs do not fit into couplers very satisfactorily.

A dedicated telephone line is one which has been hired from British Telecom for a specific route, permanently connected all the time, between one computer and another: in such cases modems are always used. And in a typical office environment where one is not using a dedicated line, modems would always be used in preference to acoustic couplers, not just because of the inherently greater reliability, but because of ease of use.

Nearly all modems these days have ***auto dial*** and ***auto receive*** facilities, and communications software commonly used allows you to store your own file of telephone numbers, so that when you wish to transmit to or collect data from a remote computer you simply select the appropriate telephone number and let the computer and modem get on with establishing the connection.

With an acoustic coupler, you must establish the connection by dialling the number and then, when the call is established, place the handset in the acoustic coupler. This kind of device is ideal for people whose employment involves them in a lot of travelling. The coupler is often supplied to fit into the same case as a portable computer, so that it is easy for such individuals to be in touch with their company computer or their *electronic mailboxes* from anywhere they have access to a telephone. A call box is adequate.

Electronic mail

We have mentioned electronic mail. Let us just see what is involved with it. It has some of the features of an ordinary mail service but there are some important differences.

The mailbox

Like any mail system, everyone involved must have a unique address to which mail can be directed. But with ordinary mail, each letterbox is located in a different place, whereas with electronic mail, your mailbox is simply a storage space on a computer system in some remote centre, and thousands of other users have their mailboxes on the same computer system.

You don't need your mailbox situated in your own physical location, because wherever it is, it is only a 'phone call away. And having all the mailboxes on one large computer system (which may well consist of a number of large computers networked together), the distribution of messages is easy and cheap. Furthermore, every mailbox is on line to the computer system the whole time and this is an essential feature of an electronic mail (***e-mail***) system which could not possibly be achieved if the individual mailboxes were not held centrally.

Using the Packet Switch Stream service

But isn't it expensive using the telephone to connect to your mailbox if you live hundreds of miles away from it?

No, because British Telecom has developed a public data service network linking principal towns, entirely separate from the telephone service. It is called Packet Switch Stream (PSS). A local call to the nearest town with a PSS exchange is virtually all it costs you. The electronic mail service you are using will pass back to you an appropriate portion of the total charges they pay for using PSS facilities, but this is small and much more economical than dialling the computer direct from a long distance. The reason packet switching is so cheap is that is uses the transmission line very intensively. Your signals will be interspersed with those from other users in a system which is known technically as ***time division multiplexing***. Packet switching is available internationally as well, but, so far as e-mail is concerned, your only need is to connect to your own mailbox.

Multiplexing on a PSS service

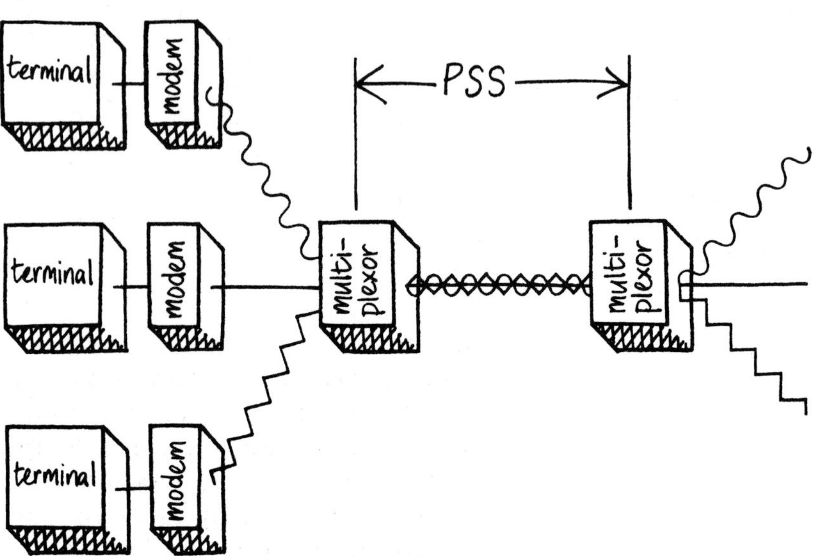

An incomplete communication medium

Of course, you can only use e-mail as a communication medium if the people with whom you wish to communicate also have mailboxes. But even that is not enough. They must have mailboxes provided by the same mail service that you are using yourself. There are several e-mail services in the UK: Telecom Gold, One-to-one and Easylink are probably the most widely known. Subscribers to one service can only send mail to or receive mail from other subscribers on the same service. These companies operate in other European countries and in the USA and Canada, so overseas communications is as simple as communication with a subscriber ten miles down the road. But . . . you can only communicate with subscribers to the same service.

Because of this problem, and the fact that everyone wants to have access to as many people and organizations as possible, the tendency is for new subscribers to join the service which already has the largest number of subscribers, so that the strong become stronger. Hopefully this will in the end lead to a single service, or at very least, cross-linking between services, for at the moment the commercial battle is doing nothing to help the subscribers.

Let's see the procedures we must follow to get into our mailbox.

How the system operates

The first stage is to dial up the nearest PSS exchange. The number we dial will not only set up the connection; it will also tell the exchange at what rate we are going to send our data. We shall see in the next few paragraphs why it needs to know this. In Chapter 3 (page 39) we talked about *serial* and *parallel* transmission of data. When it comes to transmission over a telephone line, which is only a 2-wire circuit, we must use serial transmission.

This diagram shows the electrical voltage levels making up a typical byte (what character does it represent?) and sums up the distinction between serial and parallel transmission.

Data transmission

Digital information (1 or 0) is represented by two electrical voltage levels.
With ***parallel*** *transmission there is a separate circuit for each bit of the byte and all bits are transmitted simultaneously*
With ***serial*** *transmission the electrical signals representing the binary digits are sent sequentially over the same cable circuit*

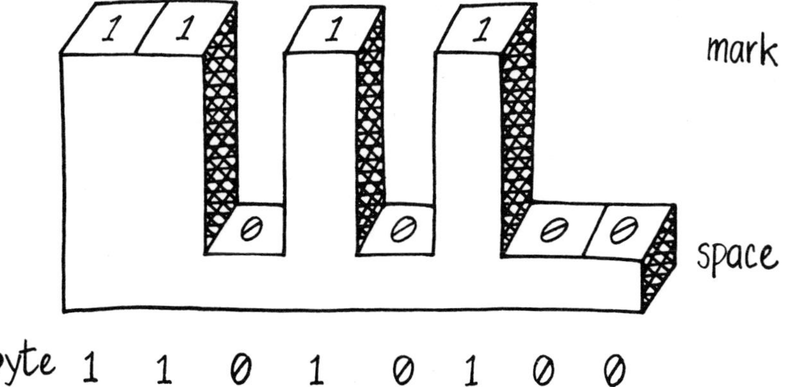

Unless the sending and receiving ends are in step (***synchronized***), there are two main problems which arise for the receiving end of the system (at this stage, the PSS exchange to which we are about to send digitally coded information). Firstly, out of a whole stream of electrical pulses, it must be able to detect where each byte begins and ends; and secondly it must be sure that it has sampled the voltage level of each pulse (bit) in each byte.

With non-synchronized (***asynchronous***) systems the first problem is dealt with by the sending end preceding each byte with a ***start bit*** and ending it with a ***stop bit***. (Some systems operating at low speeds use a longer end-of-byte marker, and 1.5 stop bits or 2 bits are standards which you might come across.) How a byte is embedded between start and stop bits is shown below.

Bits required to transmit a single character

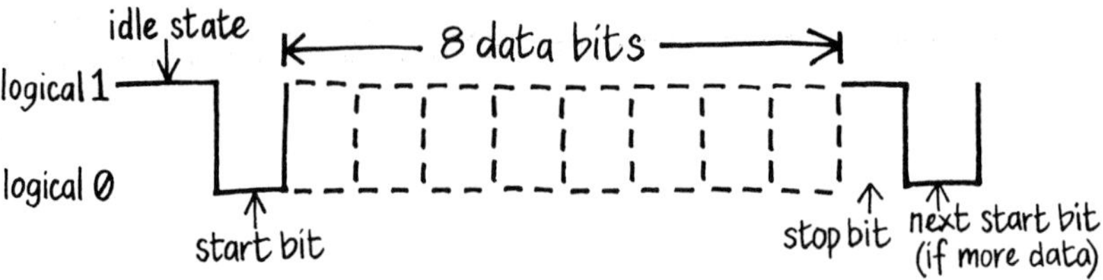

The purpose of the start bit is to start a clock at the receiving end which will enable the line to be sampled eight times (to receive an 8-bit character). The stop bit(s) are there simply to allow the receiving terminal to return to a condition where it can recognize the start bit preceding the next character.

The second problem for the receiving terminal which we mentioned above was that of ensuring that every bit in the byte had been sampled. We now know that following the start bit, eight samples will be taken; but what we need to ensure is that they are taken at the same *rate* as the pulses are arriving. If, for example, the byte in the diagram on page 125, were sampled at twice the rate at which the pulses were being sent down the line, the receiving computer would think the transmitted character was 11110011 (letter *s* transmitted with an even parity bit). What we actually sent was 11010100, the letter *T* with an even parity bit.

So the sampling rate must be the same as the rate at which pulses are being sent down the line, and it is for this reason that, when dialling our PSS exchange, we have to use the number which is appropriate to the speed at which we wish to send data.

Data transmission speeds are measured in ***Bauds*** – a Baud is a bit per second, so a transmission rate of 300 Baud (which is typical) means that we are transmitting up to 30 characters per second. (Remember that each character is *ten* bits long when transmitted because of the additional start and stop bits.)

Practical aspects of electronic mail

Logging on to the system

So we have dialled our local PSS exchange and our computer is now connected to it, either through an acoustic coupler or directly through a modem. The exchange sends back a message which appears on your computer screen. It simply reads:

NUI?

What it is asking for is a Network User Identity code.

Most people will not be registered PSS Network Users – you need to be using packet switching a great deal to make it financially worthwhile – but for the purposes of electronic mail, the companies providing the mail service allow subscribers to use their NUIs, recharging the PSS cost to the subscribers concerned in their monthly billing.

So if, for example, we were using Telecom Gold, we would enter in response to the prompt NUI? a string of characters starting NTLGOLD and continuing for a further six characters which are not echoed to our screen.

Immediately this is accepted, the prompt ADD? appears on our screen, and we respond by entering the Network Users Address (NUA) of Telecom Gold immediately followed by the number of the computer system in which our mailbox sits.

There is a response from Telecom Gold indicating that you are now connected to your computer, and the next prompt invites you to sign on. There are two stages to this. First, we must enter our own Identity Number in the form ID ABC1234 (in practice, the number of figures involved may be 3, 4 or 5). Then comes the prompt:

PASSWORD?

and we enter our private password (of at least 6 characters) which we can (and should) change frequently.

At last we are in! You may be relieved to know that all the steps we have described can be fully automated if you use a good communications software package and are prepared to write an appropriate command file. It is worth the effort to do so.

Sending mail

Faced now with the prompt >
there are a number of services we can request. But let's stick to mail for a moment. So, again the prompt, we enter:

MAIL

Back comes the host computer:

Send, Read or Scan?

Let's suppose we want to send a message, so we enter

SEND

(actually SE is sufficient for the computer to understand our intention). Immediately the prompt

To:

appears on the screen and we enter the address (i.e. the ID number) of the subscriber to whom we wish the message to be delivered. As soon as the ENTER key is struck, the next prompt appears.

Subject:

Here one needs to enter a few well-chosen words so that if the recipient of our message chooses only to scan his/her mail, s/he can have a fair idea of what the full text of the message is about. All that appears on screen if you scan your mail is the name and mailbox address of the sender, when (date and time) the message was 'posted', and the subject of the message. So it is important that the subject is brief and meaningful. Next, the prompt

Text:

appears and it is at this point you type in the message you wish to send. At the end of the message on a new line we enter

.SE

which is a command to the computer system indicating that we have finished entering the message and wish it to be sent. The concept of distinguishing commands by entering them on a new line and starting with a dot (full stop) is similar to the way commands are embedded in word processing text using WordStar, although of course the commands themselves are different.

There are a whole range of commands available within electronic mail, but it would be beyond the scope of this introductory text to go into further detail. It is enough to say that you can, for example, send copies of your message to other addresses for no extra charge; you can ask for an automatic acknowledgement to be returned to you indicating that the recipient has received your message (including the date and time it was read!). And more . . .

Signing off

When you have sent your message, the computer at the far end confirms that it has been sent and gives the appropriate screen prompt to enable you to send another. We do not wish to do so on this occasion, so we use the ENTER key until we are returned to the > prompt. If we wish to sign off at this stage we simply type

OFF

(the system also recognizes BYE). The mainframe computer responds with a message telling you how long you have been on the system and the time of disconnection. It stores this information, and when you next sign on, will tell you when you were last on.

In this 'blow by blow' account of an encounter with an electronic mail service, we have used Telecom Gold as our example. Had we chosen one of the other services, the prompts would have been rather different, but the principles involved are the same.

Preparing text off line

A final word about e-mail before we move on to other aspects of communication between computers. In the basic description we have given in the last few paragraphs, we described the kind of interaction which takes place between the user and the big computer network operated by the e-mail service when a message is being sent.

But if the message were of any appreciable length, it would be foolish to type it at the keyboard whilst on line, because the telephone and computer time charges would be mounting. You could not, even if you were a brilliant typist, type as fast as the computer can send text down the line. So you prepare the text beforehand, using either a simple text editor which is almost always included in a communications software package, or a word processing package which produces simple ASCII code files.

Then, when it comes to sending your text down the line, you simply instruct your computer to open and send the contents of your text file (either by use of an appropriate function key, or by means of instructions stored in a command file – it depends on the communications software you are using).

In commercial practice, where one might be sending out a number of messages to different addresses in one session with the computer, the various text files would also include the recipients' addresses and would be batched so that they were sent one after the other in quick succession.

Efficient collection of mail

In much the same way, you can save on-line time when you are collecting mail from your mailbox by reading all mail straight into a disk file (which you could call MAIL) and then deleting the contents of your mailbox. You can then look at the contents of the file MAIL off-line, edit them to remove material of which you do not want a hard copy record, and print the edited file.

Do you remember all the COPY commands you practised when working through Chapter 2? Well, here is another application of the same command, because the computer operating system MSDOS/PCDOS treats the printer in the same way as a file. So, with the system prompt A> on the screen, we may enter at the keyboard

```
COPY MAIL PRN
```

and the contents of the file MAIL will be output to the printer which will immediately produce the required hard copy.

Services other than e-mail

Your access to the computer on which your mailbox exists gives many more facilities than just electronic mail. For example, it is linked in with the telex service and you may use the system both to send and to receive telex messages. It also gives you access to various Bulletin Board services. For example, the Telecom Gold bulletin board, accessed at the > prompt by entering NOTICEBD, includes a range of categories even including one for LONELY-HEARTS!

Gateways to databases

Electronic mail systems also offer ***gateways*** to public access databases providing specialized information services. (A gateway is an interface, perhaps between networks, perhaps between a network and a major computer system, and it usually involves both hardware and software.) The information services available through e-mail system gateways are aimed mainly at the businesses; some, for example, give financial information on companies registered in the UK, others deal with marketing information, give up-to-date information on available Government and EEC financial assistance for companies, and so on.

Obtaining information from these databases is not free. Obviously the initial setting-up and the continual day-to-day updating of information involves heavy costs, and the providers also expect to (and do) make a profit. That is what they are in business for. Prices vary quite widely, but will probably be in the range £1 to £3 per minute of access.

A very useful (and relatively cheap) database of value to the travelling public is OAG – the Official Airline Guides. Not only does the database give a great deal of information on available flights and fares, but it has been extended to include extensive hotel information as well. It may be accessed, for example, from your Telecom Gold computer, simply by entering OAG at the > prompt.

Direct access to major computer systems

In addition to being able to access these data sources through gateways from the electronic mail system to which you are connected, there are numerous *dial-up* facilities totally independent of any e-mail system. Of these, the obvious one to mention is the Prestel service which has around 250,000 pages of information, most of which is free (apart from the standing quarterly charge for using the national Prestel network computers).

There have been attempts to use the Prestel network as the basis for armchair shopping. One or two banks and building societies have tried this. The necessary hardware is provided on either a rental or outright purchase basis (free if you invest lots of money with the bank or building society).

Facilities include being able to review your building society account, pay bills from it or transfer funds between it and a current bank account, purchase goods from the limited number of stores taking part in the scheme and, of course, have all the Prestel information available to you.

Local area networks

Up to this point, we have been talking about communicating over considerable distances, but short-distance communciation between components of a computer system is also very important. For example, within a building (or even a large room) or, with a larger organisation, spread across several buildings on one site, computers can communicate with each other, share common peripherals, e.g. printers and substantial hard disk data storage.

In such cases, equipment may be linked for communication purposes by a ***local area network (LAN)***. This is specifically a digital communication network, so no modems are needed. Because of the relatively short distances involved and the communication systems used, very high speeds of data transmission can be used (up to 100 million Baud) – much faster than we could use on the Public Switched Telephone Network (PSTN) which we talked about in the first part of this chapter.

Network topologies

There are three basic shapes (***topologies***) for local area networks.

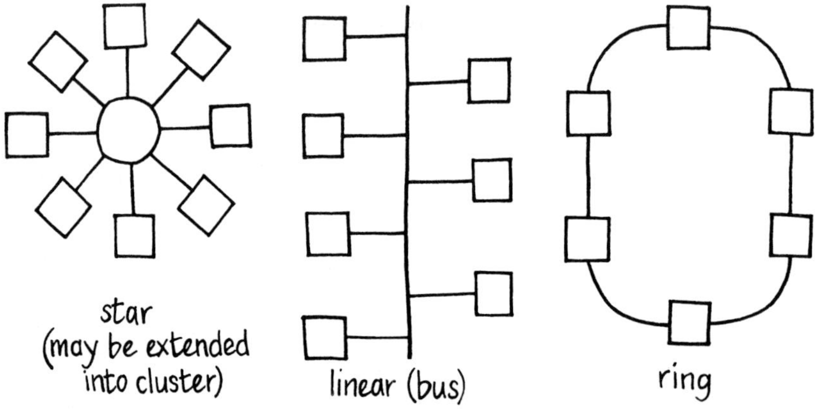

Examples of network topologies

The square boxes represent any hardware which is linked into the system. One might be a hard disk drive with its controlling microcomputer (called a ***file-server*** in this application), another a laser printer, others may be microcomputers of varying size and power.

Datagrams

Any LAN can be seen as a mechanism for transporting ***datagrams***. The important features of a datagram are:

1 It involves one-way communication only.
2 It carries both destination and source addresses.
3 The data contained in it may be of variable length.
4 It involves direct transmission – there is no call set-up or closedown, nor is there any way in which the data can be stored and forwarded later (both features of e-mail which we discussed earlier).

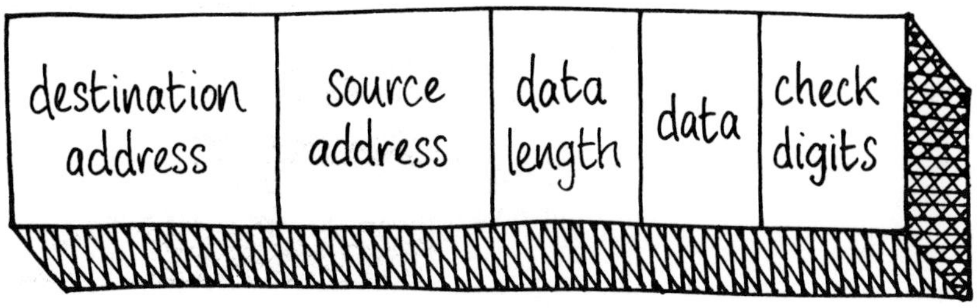

destination address	source address	data length	data	check digits

A datagram

The structure of the datagram is more or less self-explanatory, but we need to say something more about the ***check digits***, because we have not mentioned this term previously.

Check digits help eliminate errors

Check digits are used widely, not just in data transmission, but in many other cases where sequences of numbers are being transferred from one part of a system to another. They are computed by a fixed arithmetic sequence performed on the numbers in question. Then to check that the data has been transferred accurately, the same calculation is carried out again after the transfer and the new computer check digit(s) is compared with the originals.

A common example of the use of a single check digit is in the design of mail order catalogue reference numbers. Suppose you were ordering something, but in writing down the catalogue reference you accidentally transposed two figures (for example wrote 2776453 instead of 2776435). The description of the item which you also write on the order form might well be sufficiently general to apply to a whole range of products, and if a check digit was not incorporated in the catalogue reference, you could end up with the wrong goods.

But with a check digit system, as soon as the order clerk enters into the computer system the reference number you have given, the check digit is computed and it is found not to agree with the check digit incorporated in the number you have quoted. The error has been detected.

Using exactly the same principles, but with more complex calculations procedures and up to 16 check digits, the validity of the address information and the data itself in a datagram can be checked and errors detected. When a system detects an error, it automatically requests a repeat transmission of the datagram.

Illustration of check digit computation.
Consider a 6-figure stock item code which does not include a check digit e.g. 458612
Stage 1: multiply successive digits by 1, 2, 3, etc.
Stage 2: add the products and divide the result by 11, so as to produce an integral quotient & remainder

4 * 1 = 4
5 * 2 = 10
8 * 3 = 24
6 * 4 = 24
1 * 5 = 5
458612 → 2 * 6 = 12
79 ÷ 11 = 7 rem. 2
check digit ↑

The new stock item code becomes 4586122

An example of how a check digit is used

But a check digit system will not trap *all* errors. The only 100 % check is for the receiving terminal to send back its version of the received datagram to the originating station where a bit by bit comparison of the entire data field (and the address of the terminal to which the datagram was originally sent) may be carried out. But with clever *algorithms* (see page 156) and a reasonable number of check digit bits, a very high level of protection against errors occuring during transmission can be achieved. There is always a trade-off between the amount of additional (or ***redundant***) information in the form of check digits, and the probability that an error will be detected.

Practical local area networks

Now we know something about datagrams, let us look at the more important LAN systems which will transport them and see how they work.

The contention problem

The big problem that any network has to deal with is that of ***contention***. This may take two forms:

1 The same station being addressed by more than one station at the same time (e.g. two microcomputers fighting over the same printer).
2 More than one station trying to transmit over the same piece of cable at the same time.

There are several quite different approaches to this problem; we shall examine the principles of three of them.

Ethernet principles

The first we shall consider is the CSMA/CD access method, generally referred to as ***Ethernet*** because it originated in a proprietory system of that name. The string of initials refers to Carrier Sense Multiple Access with Collision Detection – and once we can unravel what the words mean, we shall see that this is a very concise description of the way the system works.

Ethernet is always used with a *linear* or *bus* type of network (see page 130 again). A terminal which wishes to transmit a datagram 'listens' to find out if the line is already in use, and if it detects no signal it assumes the line to be free and starts transmission. If the line is not free, it waits for a random period and then tries again, in much the same way that if you were telephoning a friend and got the engaged tone, you would try again a little while later. But of course, the LAN works on a much shorter time scale.

So that's carrier sense multiple access: many terminals have access to the line (multiple access) and before they transmit they sense that the line is clear (carrier sense). It sounds like a foolproof system. So why is collision detection necessary? The simple fact is that although electrical signals travel extremely quickly down a cable, they do take a finite time – the transmission speed is about 20 cm/ns. (A nanosecond (ns) is a thousand millionth (10^{-9}) of a second.) So, it is possible for two terminals at different points on the line both to seize the line, believing it to be free because the signal from the other station has not yet arrived. A moment later the two signals collide.

The system is designed so that the collision is detected by every transceiver (the hardware which stands between each terminal and the cable highway) and as a result of this, all terminals trying to access the highway withdraw in an orderly fashion so that the line is clear again. Then, after a random delay period, each station wishing to send a datagram tries again. Should the same problem arise on restart, the delay periods are increased until successful entry to the highway is achieved. Statistically, the number of collisions occurring is quite small; nevertheless, the system must be able to cope with them when they do occur – hence collision detection.

Token-passing principles

Other approaches to LAN design avoid the possibility of collision altogether. Of these approaches, ***token-passing*** is the most important technique of which you should be aware. It takes its name from the token-passing technique which used to be employed on stretches of single track railway line to ensure that collisions could not occur. There was only one token and a driver could not enter the single track section without it. If it was not available, he knew that the track was in use and would have to wait for the token to become free.

The LAN token-passing principle is identical, although in this case, the token takes the form of a coded signal block to which a terminal wishing to transmit may attach its datagram. There is only one token, and if it is in use, no other station can transmit.

Token-passing principles may be used with either ring or bus configurations. Token ring systems are more common.

Polling principle

The third technique which we will mention briefly is that known as ***polling***. Here, a master station addresses each station connected to the line in turn, to see whether it has any data to send. It is a relatively slow technique, because every station is given the opportunity to transmit even if it doesn't want to. Thus it tends to be used mainly in industrial process control applications where data transfer rates need not be particularly high, but where data integrity (i.e. errors are not introduced) is of greatest importance.

Summary of facilities provided by LANs

So, in broad terms, you now have an idea of how the major LAN products work, and the lengths the system designers go to in order to ensure that the data you are sending down the line to a printer, or receiving from the central database, arrive at their destinations as accurate copies of the originals. We note the advantages of being able to access shared data easily and being able to utilize under-used peripherals more intensively (one printer can easily serve several users without causing a bottle-neck – but watch out for practical difficulties with remote printing if there are several standards of paper size or different pre-printed stationery items involved).

In addition, of course, you may have your own internal electronic mail system since any terminal can address a datagram to any other. In many ways the priniciples involved are the same as those described earlier in this chapter in regard to national and international electronic mail. Perhaps the most obvious difference is that with a local system, you will get an on-screen message either at the top or bottom of your screen, whilst you are working, to tell you that a message has arrived in your mailbox, whereas with a public service you have to dial up the mail service computer and look in your mailbox to see if there is any mail waiting for your attention.

Linking LANs

There are in theory limits to LAN sizes, both in terms of the physical distance and the number of terminals involved. Practical products currently available have limits much smaller than the theoretical figures, but this does not present difficulties that cannot be overcome. You simply have several individual LANs with gateways allowing transfer of data from one to another, in just the same way as you would expect a LAN to have a gateway to the outside world.

A learning checklist

The time has come to summarize what we have covered in this chapter. It is the only one, apart from the introductory chapter, where we have not offered some specific practical work. A good many readers may not at present have access to the hardware and software necessary to enable communication with other computers; but the situation is likely to change quite rapidly, for it is in the field of computer communications that we have seen the most rapid growth in recent years.

So we hope that even without specific practical work, this chapter will have given you some feel for what is going on in this area and some understanding of the principles involved.

At this point you should be able to:

1 Explain what is meant by and distinguish between:
   - ☐ batch processing,
   - ☐ real-time processing,
   - ☐ transaction processing.

2 Explain the advantages of distributed systems over centralized systems.

3 Describe the principles of international electronic mail systems.

4 Explain the economic advantages of using PSS for sending data over long distances.

5 Explain the significance of start and stop bits in asynchronous data transmission.

6 Explain why it is important that the receiving terminal knows the rate at which data is being transmitted.

7 Describe the typical steps in the dialogue involved in establishing contact with a public electronic mail service.

8 Appreciate the extent to which contact with an electronic mail service can be automated.

9 Define the term *gateway*.

10 List some kinds of service available through gateways from public electronic mail systems.

11 Describe some other computer services available to the general public over the public telephone network.

12 Define the term *local area network*.

13 Explain the uses of a LAN in terms of the efficient use of shared resources (physical and data) and the provision of an internal e-mail system.

14 Sketch and name some network topologies.

15 Define the term *datagram* and name its constituent parts.

16 Explain the problem of contention on a LAN.

17 Describe the principle of operation of an Ethernet system.

18 Describe the principle of operation of a token-passing system.

19 Describe the principle of operation of a polling system.

CHAPTER 8 Applications software

Applications software defined

In previous chapters we have dealt with some aspects of general-purpose software: database, word processing, spreadsheet and communications. Each of these could be used for many different applications. For example, the database software might be applied to stock control, or the same software could be used differently and with different data to create and maintain an address/telephone directory of personnel in a company.

Applications software is not like this. It is written to do a specific job – things like seat-reservation systems, payroll, keeping the company accounts, etc. What we want to do now is deal with features which are often found in such software. We will illustrate the points made by looking at some simple accounts software (available on the diskette associated with this book).

Economic considerations

Software houses (i.e. companies whose business is writing and marketing software) do not make their money out of doing one-off jobs. They are quite prepared to write software from scratch for one client provided there is the potential to sell it (in modified form) to a wider group of purchasers. The reason for this is simple: there are very few clients who would be prepared to pay the true development cost of the package, so the marketing policy is to regard the original client's job as a 'loss leader' and get back the full cost by selling to a wider market.

Vertical markets

This policy often leads to what are called ***vertical markets***. A vertical market is the description given to the concentration of marketing activity on one particular specialist area, rather than marketing on a broad front. For example, a particular software house may specialize in software for hotels, another might specialize in farming applications, another in hairdressing and so on. Each of these areas would be called a vertical market, and the reason they tend to develop is that before any applications program can be written, the job that it has to do must be thoroughly understood by the system designer. Once someone in the software house has become really familiar with the business side of hotel work, farming, or whatever, then that knowledge can be used to base a range of useful software products in the particular specialist field. The products might range through all the different levels of a business activity, in hotels for example from planning prices and bookings throughout the year, down to seating plans for restaurants.

PARADOX - *extra*ordinary
solution to a *classic* problem

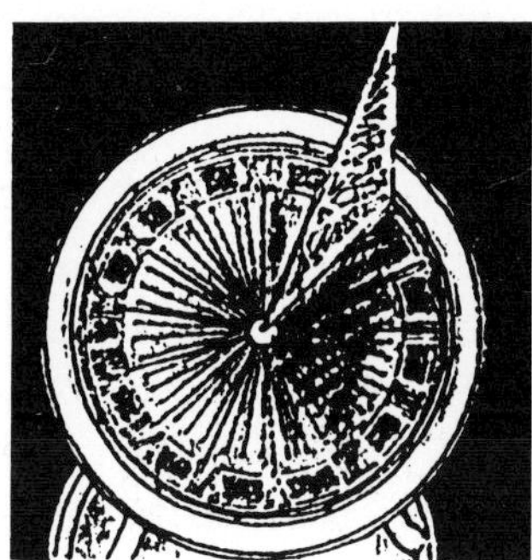

Paradox Version 2.0 is the first true multi user relational database and is now available in the UK.

So Why Paradox 2.0?

- Easy to use.
- Full training and support from Ansa.
- Customised applications.
- True Multiuser for all IBM and 100% compatible networks.
- PC to Mainframe communication via Paradox SQL link.

Stand alone Paradox retails at £595.00
Paradox network pack retails at £795.00
NB: To run the Network pack you do not require Paradox single user.

Paradox is the Answer.

For further information, please complete the coupon.
Return to: Ansa Software (UK) Ltd, 2 Bedford Square, London, WC1B 3RA.
Tel: 01-580 4766 01-631 4798

Name ____________

Company ____________

Address ____________

____

Telephone ____________

ANSA

Circle No 108
Fast Facts ☎ 01-200 0200

An advertisement for a software package from the top of the range

Software for a wider market

A product or range of products for a vertical market is, from the vendor's point of view, a great deal better than producing a package for one specific client, but the market is still somewhat limited and this tends to be reflected in the software price. The wider the market (a ***horizontal market***), the greater the sales *potential*, and because that potential is there, the individual selling price can be reduced.

The actual cost of the diskettes on which the programs are sold, the transferring of programs from master disks on to these diskettes, and the supporting documentation (e.g. operator manuals), is no more than a few pounds. Yet one commonly pays several hundred pounds for applications software for use on microcomputers and often thousands of pounds for larger scale applications on minis or mainframes. The tremendous price difference between the small direct costs and the selling price is in part due to the need to recover development costs (marketing costs and profit margins account for most of the balance).

One type of software which has found a very wide market is accounting softeware. Every business needs to keep accounts, and because this is such a large market there are many competing products. But the accounting needs of a very small one-man business are quite different from the accounting needs of, say, a business employing 50–100 people; the accounting needs of a firm which provides professional services for clients (such as solicitors, for example) are quite different from those of a firm which carries considerable stock for reselling. The firm that has employed particular practices for many years (both in terms of bookkeeping techniques and the layout of various forms used) wants the least possible change and disruption when it moves across to a computer system.

The need for flexibility

It is very difficult for one piece of software to be 'all things to all men', but within broad limits, this is what the software houses attempt to produce. Flexibility is of great importance to a successful product and it implies:

1 modular construction,
2 a facility for allowing the product to be customized,
3 a facility for changing parameters.

The other key factors are that the software must be 'comfortable' to use, and seen as being fast in operation.

Firstly, what do we mean by ***modular construction***? It simply means that instead of selling a comprehensive piece of software in one very large program, it is broken down into self-contained units, each of which can be bought separately. But each piece is designed to work with every other piece, so that it seems as if it all works together as a unit. In fact, the ***source code*** (that's the code written in a programming language, like COBOL) of any program of large size is written in quite small modules anyway; this enables the programming effort to be managed on a team basis, with each member of the team working on a different module. It also makes testing and debugging much easier, and it also makes easier the reading of the program during development. There is a later spin-off too. Perhaps in response to user comments, perhaps because of a change in government legislation (e.g. in regard to taxation law), the software house may wish to update some aspect of its program and issue a new version. With modular construction, it is easy to get at just those parts of the total program which require modification.

But modular construction of source code does not in itself mean modularity of ***object code*** – the .COM program file (see Chapter 2) – which is provided for the user. This object code is a translation of source code into a binary form which controls the computer operation. It may bring together a number of separate source code modules into one command file. So if there is to be modularity at the command file level, the writers must make a conscious decision to produce a series of .COM files, each of which deals with a separate area of the total product. For example, one accounts product may have separate command files containing object code for individual modules to deal with the following:

sales ledger
purchaser ledger
nominal ledger
invoicing & sales order processing
stock control
job costing
payroll
bill of materials preparation

A small business might well want only the first three modules, at least to start with. Together they would be described as a ***suite*** of programs.

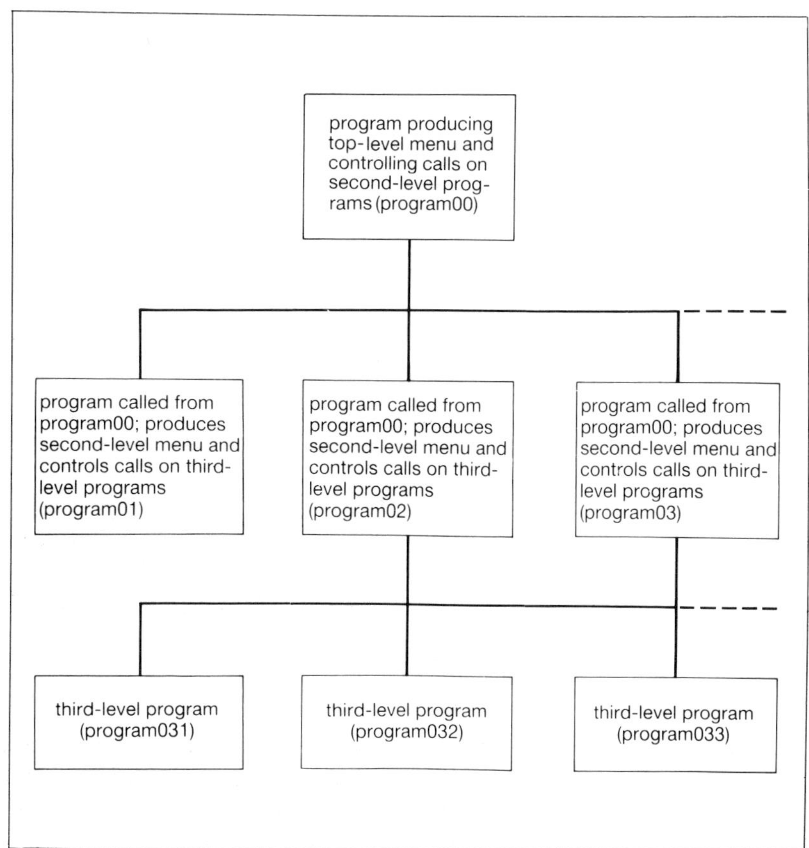

Modular construction

Another product may present a range of ***groupings*** of modules and the group of modules selected by a particular end user will be combined in a single .COM file. If the user subsequently wishes to extend his system, the supplier replaces the previous disk with one which includes in the command file additional code to provide the new facility. In either of the two approaches described, the idea of a modular approach is maintained, although it is more obvious in one case than in the other.

Customized software

The second point we listed as an important aspect of flexibility was that the product should have a facility for allowing the user to ***customize*** it. For example, a farmer using a computer system to record and cost out all the chemicals and fertilizers which he applies to each of his fields, does not want to refer to his fields as 001, 002, 003, etc. He knows them as 'Lower Meadow', 'Spinney Piece', 'Ford Meadow' and other such names. And he wants to be able to use these names, or perhaps just their initial letters.

Too often the authors of computer programs have not considered enough the way in which the user wants to work, and have tried to impose on the user a rigid system which is quite unlike the manual system previously employed. The new system may be very good in terms of what it does and it may be very efficient; but if it upsets the user because it requires him to change his established ways of working to bend himself round the system, the end result may be very unsatisfactory.

So, if the software product is marketed as a package of broad application suitable for a wide range of businesses, it must allow a degree of customization. If you have access to the supporting diskette associated with this book, you will have the opportunity to customize the simplified accounts software included on the disc. We will tell you how to do this a little later in the chapter.

User-controlled parameters

The third point we made about this kind of software was that it should include a facility for changing ***parameters***. What is a parameter? It is simply a name or a value made available by one program module to another (or others).

For example if a module, such as an invoicing module, were to include the calculation of VAT, it would not be a good idea to build into the program statements involving the factor 0.15 simply because the VAT rate is currently 15%. Actually there are two VAT rates at present, but the second one happens to be zero. And who is to say the Chancellor of the Exchequer may not change either or both of these rates next budget day?

Were this to happen, then a great deal of time and effort would be needed to modify programs which had the VAT rates built as constants into various statements. A far better approach is to make them variables whose values are contained in a ***parameter file***. The contents of this file can be reset from a separate module designed to allow the inputting of current values of all parameters.

Menu-driven software

So much for flexibility. Our next criterion was that the software should be ***comfortable*** to use – the common jargon for this is ***user friendly***. In terms of applications software this is usually taken to mean that the program shall be ***menu-driven*** – a term we have touched on in (Chapter 3, page 35).

But just to refresh your memory, by menu-driven we mean that when the software is loaded and run, the first screen (after any 'commercials' and warnings about copyright) contains a list of options from which the user chooses whichever one s/he wants. The top diagram shows a typical opening menu. This may be described as a ***top-level*** or ***first-level*** menu. Depending on the option chosen, the user may be presented with another (***second-level***) menu. For example, if in response to the input request on the first screen, we had chosen 6, then a second-level menu (see bottom diagram) would have been displayed.

```
COMPANY ACCOUNTS SYSTEM
INFORMATION PROCESSING SERVICES LTD
30 Westgate, Oxford, OX1 1NZ

AVAILABLE OPTIONS
1 PREPARE INVOICES
2 ENTER INCOME
3 ENTER EXPENDITURE
4 A/C BALANCES and TRANSFERS
5 VAT PAYMENTS/REPAYMENTS
6 REPORTING FACILITIES
7 UTILITIES

Please enter the required option number...
If no option is required, you may remove
your diskettes now.
```

An opening menu

```
REPORTING OPTIONS

1  Current debtor details
2  List income for specified months
3  List expenditure for specified months
4  List income and/or expenditure by account head
5  List transfers between accounts
6  Return to top level menu

Please enter option choice (1 - 6)...
```

A second-level menu

Often systems have three or more levels of menu; if you are working at, say, the third level, you climb back out by going back to the second-level menu and then to the first, retracing the route you took when starting out, as shown here.

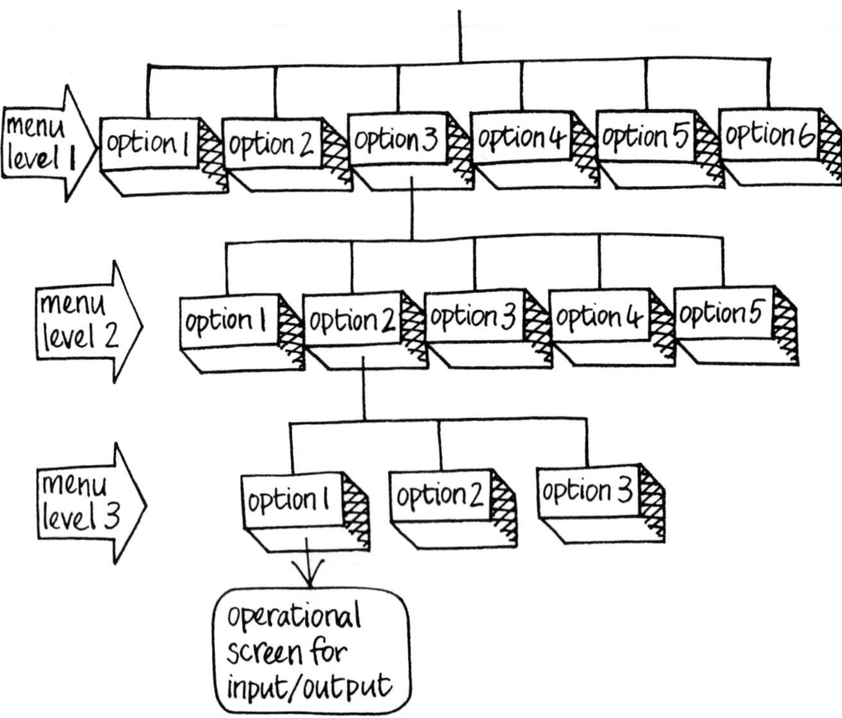

The structure of menu-driven software

Sometimes the return from the lowest level to the next higher level is automatic on completing the selected task. The return to a higher level may also be carried out by a menu option reserved for that purpose (see, for example, option 6 in the lower diagram on page 141). Another method employed by some software writers is to use the ESCAPE key for return to the next higher menu level.

Command-driven software

People find menu-driven software easy to use because if the option titles are as meaningful as they should be, the user is guided progressively through to the part of the program s/he needs. However, once a user has become thoroughly familiar with the software, s/he may feel quite frustrated with having to go through successive menus to get to the required screen and might much prefer to get there by striking just one or two keys.

Software which is written in a style known as ***command-driven*** may be preferred in such circumstances. There are no menus, and very often no on-screen list of commands available to the user, although they would all be well documented in the handbook supplied with the software. To use such a system efficiently, the user has to know it very well. When this is the case, it can be much faster to use than a more *friendly* system. But for the most part – because of staff turnover or stand-in staff having to take over in the absence of regular users – menu-driven software seems to be preferred.

Validation checks on inputs

Another very important aspect of user-friendly software is that the user must be protected so far as possible from making input errors.

There are several techniques which can be used to reduce input errors. So far as data input is concerned, the golden rule is that it should pass through as few stages as possible before reaching the computer. You will be aware of some input techniques, such as the reading of bar codes, which cut out human intervention altogether, and by building in special checking systems into the bar code construction, the chance of an input reading error is very small. There are a number of different direct input techniques like this – the automatic reading of the magnetic ink character at the foot of a cheque is another example – but in many cases there is no alternative to manual input.

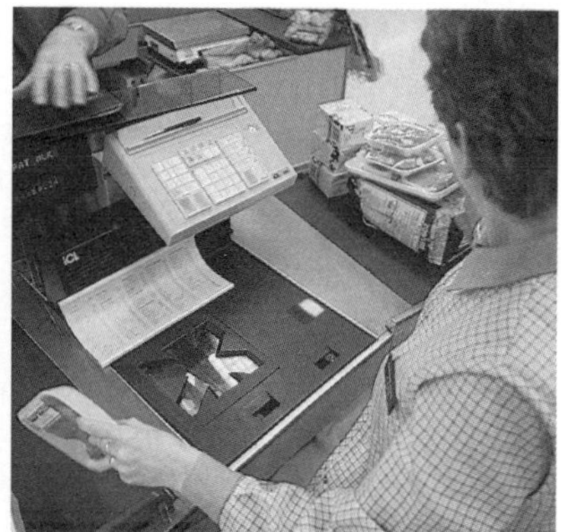

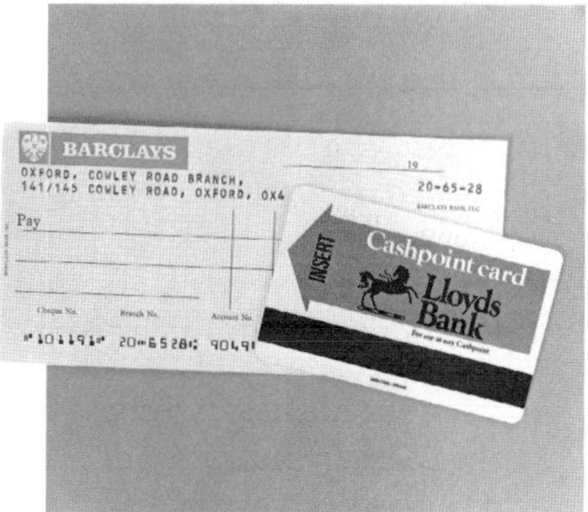

Types of non-manual input systems: a graphics tablet (top left); a bar code reader (top right); a cheque with magnetic ink characters and cheque card with magnetic strip (bottom left); a document scanner (bottom right)

Manual inputs at the keyboard fall into one of four groups:

1 A valid input is one of a small known set of characters, as for example, when responding to a Y/N type of question presented on the screen. Only the character Y, y, N or n would be acceptable, and the software would be so written that any other input would be rejected.

2 The input is a number of known and constant value, such as a part number for a stock item, or an account number for a customer. In these circumstances, the numbers used would not be sequential, but would incorporate a *check digit*. The check digit is the last figure of the number and it is calculated by applying a particular arithmetic procedure which involves all the other figures in the number. When such a number is entered at the keyboard, the computer program undertakes the same arithmetic procedure and compares its calculated check digit

with the last figure of the input number. If they are the same, there is a presumption that the whole number has been correctly input, and there is an extremely high probability that this is the case. (Other applications of check digits are discussed in Chapter 7, pages 131–132.)

3 The input is a number which could have any of a wide range of values. Here there is less validation possible, but we can usually apply what is called a ***gross error check***. By this we mean that although we have no means of checking that the input was necessarily correct, we do know the expected total range of numbers within which the input should fall. For example, we might arrange for a program which controls the printing of gas bills to refer back for checking any domestic bills exceeding, say £800 per quarter, because it would be expected that domestic bills should normally be for less than this amount.
4 The input is a string which could have any value. Very often there is a limit to the acceptable length of such a string, and the only validation possible is that the length of the string can be measured. If it exceeds the pre-determined maximum number of characters, it is then disallowed and the program is so written that the input is cleared from the screen and the user advised to re-input.

As we have indicated, checks by the computer program help, but there is no substitute for accuracy of input. Always take the initial opportunity to check your input, because what you key in is echoed on the screen, but is not actually input to the computer as a variable value until you press the ENTER key. Always use this opportunity – it is much quicker to correct faulty keying at this point than later.

Opportunity to edit or re-input

But usually, when you have completed data input using a particular screen, a message will be displayed under your input asking you to confirm that the entries are correct. If you say *No* at this stage, none of the entered values are filed, and you are either given the opportunity to re-input the whole screen or put into an edit situation where you can change specific entries. Once you confirm that all entries are correct, processing continues and files are updated with the new data.

Processing and I/O speeds

Finally, we suggested that for applications software to be acceptable, it must be fast in operation. How fast is fast? At the end of the day, this comes down to a user's judgement. For example, if it takes the computer, say, four seconds to file the last input and offer a fresh screen for the next input, this will seem like an eternity if the operator has nothing to do during this time. But if one has to place a document in an 'entered' heap and look at the next piece of paper for some specific data like, say, an invoice number, the four seconds has passed and one is not held up by the system at all.

So really, what we are suggesting is that a system may be considered to be satisfactorily fast provided it does not introduce delays into the user's work flow.

Applications built on database software

Some systems which are marketed as having been designed for a specific application, have not in fact been written using one of the many available programming languages, but have been developed usng standard database software. Programs can be developed much more quickly in this way, but they are usually quite a lot slower in execution than programs compiled from source code written in such languages as, say, Pascal or COBOL.

A practical example

Let us now turn to an example which is supported by software associated with this book. This is accounts software and it is ***modular*** in construction. After initial installation it contains seven *command* files, each called by a corresponding *batch* file. Two of these command files are built up of several modules of source code, which are combined at the time of compilation.

Generally, we would arrange a system so that data files were kept either in a separate sub-directory (in the case of a hard disk), or on a disk other than the program disk. However, so that the software may be accessible to users with only single disk drives, we have organized it so that it creates all data files on the program disk. There should be sufficient room on the disk for all the data you are likely to create, as you are unlikely to want to run to your accounts over more than one financial year. Should you wish to do so, this can be done, but it is handled more easily when data files are kept separate from program files.

Just a word of caution before you rush to experiment with the software. Do not use the original disk. Copy it first, and if you are using a 'stand-alone' single-disk system, copy it to a disk to which you have already copied the operating system at the time of formatting. You could follow the same procedure for a twin floppy system, but to leave rather more space on the Accounts disk, you may prefer to keep a 'booting' (i.e. operating system disk) in drive A and run the accounts from a non-system disk in drive B.

With a hard-disk 'stand-alone' system, a simple floppy-to-floppy copy is all that is required; run the accounts from floppy drive A. If you are using a networked system, each user should have his own copy of the accounts software in his own sub-directory. This is because each user will set up a data file containing details of his company's name and address, in the course of initial installation. This file is called FIRMDATA.DTA and so that there should not be multiple attempts to write conflicting data to this file, each user should have his own area of the hard disk.

Installation: setting up the files

One way or another, you should now have a copy of the original software on disk, and in order to run the software you must log on to the disk or sub-directory, where the copy software is being held. At the system prompt enter ACCOUNTS. By doing this, you are telling the computer to execute the batch file ACCOUNTS.BAT. Since this is the first time you have used the software, the batch file will run a program, which asks you to enter your company name and address. We suggest you use upper case for the company name and ordinary upper and lower case for the address.

Next, you will be asked if your company is a registered company in the UK. You must respond with Y or N, and if you enter Y for 'yes', you will immediately be prompted to supply the registered number. Typically, this comprises seven figures, so for present purposes you could make one up if you wished to.

Finally, you will be asked if you are registered for VAT. In real business situations, the government sets turnover limits, above which one must register. These limits are not very high, so it is likely that your enterprise will need to be registered. If you respond Y, the next prompt asks for your VAT number. Again, you can be inventive, but note that to be realistic, it should be of the form *nnn nnnn nn*.

There is a last chance to change your mind about entries, but once you enter Y in response to the question 'Are these entries correct?' there is no further opportunity for change. Your company details are filed, the program that created the file is destroyed and the main menu appears on the screen.

The details you have just entered should appear on any invoice you raise; by inputting them at this stage, they will be automatically printed on every invoice. You will also notice that the company name and address appears at the head of the main menu of the accounts program. The data for this is also taken from the file FIRMDATA.DTA which you have just set up. This is an example of *customizing*, which we mentioned earlier in this chapter.

From the main menu, choose option 7, utilities, and when the utilities menu appears, choose option 1, which allows you to access the installation utilities. You are now presented with a third-level menu; from this, start with option 1, which allows you to enter the current VAT rates. The system asks you to enter the current primary VAT rate (rate 1) and then the secondary rate (rate 2). Your entries are stored in a parameter file, which is referred to by the software whenever VAT values are required. If VAT rates change, you simply use menu option 7.1.1 (i.e. option 6 from the top level menu, option 1 from the second-level and option 1 from the third-level) to input the revised values. They are then used throughout the whole accounts system.

Next select option 2 from the third-level menu. This allows you to set up values for:

1 All serial numbers used in the system (e.g. invoice numbers, transaction numbers).
2 The balances in the bank (we have made provision for three bank accounts: current, deposit and investment; but in many cases, firms will have only one account).
3 VAT input and output totals, together with the total values of inputs and outputs in the current VAT period.

We would suggest starting invoice numbers at 1000, income

transaction numbers at 2000 and expenditure transaction numbers at 3000. There is nothing special about these numbers, but you may find it helpful to have clear separation between sets of numbers used for different purposes. The system adds the prefix IN to all income transaction numbers and E to all expenditure transaction numbers.

If you are starting the accounts system from scratch you will want to set all bank account balances to zero since at this stage you have not received or paid any money. The VAT balances should also be set to zero.

Now select option 3 from the third-level menu. This enables you to set up a group of data files associated with the cash transfer operations and loans.

The first of these is a small file called CASHTO.DTA which will contain a list of any sub-accounts which will receive cash from or pay cash to the company bank accounts. For example, a Director may have made a long-term loan to the business for start-up or capital expenses. This would show as a negative sum in the Director's loan account, with a corresponding positive amount in one of the company's bank accounts.

Similarly, directors or others may run a short-term loan account to cover personal expenditure on behalf of the company. Such loans would probably be cleared by monthly transfers from the company bank current account. Not only does this part of the program set up CASHTO.DTA; it also sets up a series of files ACNAME01.DTA, ACNAME02.DTA, etc, one file for each of the sub-accounts in the file CASHTO.DTA.

In addition to the files which you have knowingly set up during this procedure, other files have also been created to receive data, which you will generate in due course as you use the system. These files are DEBTS.DTA, in which records of all outstanding debts will be held, and TRANSFER.DTA, in which records of all cash transfers between accounts are held.

Setting up accounts headcodes

You have now created nearly all the files you need to run the accounts program, but you are not yet ready to go, because there is one important piece of preparation yet to be undertaken.

At the end of the year (and maybe sooner) you will want to be able to analyse what kind of things you have spent your money on, and how much each of your several business activities has contributed to the total income of the company. To enable you to do this – or rather, to enable the computer system to produce the information for you – you must allocate account headcodes to the various kinds of transactions. For example, you would want a code for expenditure on Rent and Rates, another code for Heat, Light and Power, others for Printing and Stationery, Telephone and Postage, and so on.

You can make your system as complicated or as simple as you please, but we suggest that if you have ten or a dozen expenditure heads, this should be adequate for the present purpose.

Now you want to do the same sort of thing for income. It is more difficult to make helpful suggestions here, because your account heads will depend on the kind of business you have chosen to run.

The point is that from the account heads you can find out which areas of the business are bringing in most income and which the least. This could give a pointer as to how you should be developing the business.

A VAT return form

If you select option 4 from the installation utilities menu, you will be able to tell the system what codes you want to use for which purposes. There are one or two restrictions to watch, the most important of which is concerned with the correct recording of VAT information. Most of the bills you pay will include Value Added Tax. When you enter such expenditure in the accounts system you will be asked by screen prompts to enter the amount before VAT is added and the amount of the VAT. These two figures are added to the total value of 'inputs' and the total 'input VAT' respectively, and these figures are used on the VAT return to Customs and Excise.

H M Customs and Excise

Return of Value Added Tax

For the period

01 04 86 to 30 06 86

To be returned not later than 31 07 86

These dates must not be altered without the agreement of Customs and Excise.

For Official Use

Registration No | Period 06 86

075 348 6382 24 100 06 86

015268

Please complete the whole of this form. The notes on the back and *Filling in your VAT return* will help you to do this. Return it, with any VAT due, in the enclosed envelope to the Controller, VAT Central Unit, H M Customs and Excise, 21 Victoria Avenue, SOUTHEND-ON-SEA X

SS99 1AF

Complete all boxes (writing "none" where necessary). If an exact amount of pounds is to be entered write "00" in the pence column. **Do not** put a dash or leave the column blank.

REMINDER

As from 1 October 1986 the receipt of returns and tax payments after due date may lead to surcharges.

W11858 100 RT06 *

SPECIMEN

FOR OFFICIAL USE

		£	p
VAT DUE in this period on OUTPUTS (sales, etc), certain postal imports and services received from abroad	1		
Underdeclarations of VAT made on previous returns (but not those notified in writing by Customs and Excise)	2		
TOTAL VAT DUE (box 1 + box 2)	3		
VAT DEDUCTIBLE in this period on INPUTS (purchases, etc)	4		
Overdeclarations of VAT made on previous returns (but not those notified in writing by Customs and Excise)	5		
TOTAL VAT DEDUCTIBLE (box 4 + box 5)	6		
NET VAT PAYABLE OR REPAYABLE (Difference between boxes 3 and 6)	7		
Value of Outputs (excluding any VAT)	8		00
Value of Inputs (excluding any VAT)	9		00

Please tick only ONE of these boxes:

box 3 greater than box 6 — payment by credit transfer ☐ — payment enclosed ☐

box 6 greater than box 3 — repayment due ☐

How to pay the VAT due

Cross all cheques and postal orders "A/C Payee only" and make them payable to "H M Customs and Excise". Make credit transfers through account 3078027 at National Girobank or 10-70-50 52055000 for Bank Giros. You can get pre-printed booklets of credit transfer slips from your local VAT office. In your own interest do not send notes, coins, or uncrossed postal orders through the post.

Please write your VAT registration number on the back of all cheques and credit transfer slips.

Please tick box(es) if the statement(s) apply:

box 5 includes bad debt relief ☐ box 8 includes exempt outputs ☐ box 8 includes exports ☐

Retail schemes If you have used any of the schemes in the period covered by this return please tick the box(es) to show all the schemes used.

A B C D E F G H J

Failure to make a complete return or to pay the full amount of VAT payable by the due date is an offence.

DECLARATION by the signatory to be completed by or on behalf of the person named above.

I, ... declare that the
(full name of signatory in BLOCK LETTERS)

information given in this return is true and complete.

Signed .... Date .... 19 ......
*(Proprietor, partner, director, secretary, responsible officer, member of club or association, duly authorised person) *Delete as necessary

FOR OFFICIAL USE

VAT 100 F 3790 (April 1985)

Code for VAT exempt items

But some items of expenditure are VAT exempt, such as rent, rates, salary payments. Not only do you not pay VAT on these items, but they should not be included in the total value of 'inputs'. So the program is organized for specified groups of expenditure codes to be treated differently from others and items using codes in these groups do not affect the VAT input totals. These codes should be used for VAT exempt items and for VAT payments to Customs and Excise.

In the same way, it is possible that some of your activities from which income is derived may be exempt from VAT, so there are also groups of codes for exempt 'outputs'. Note, by the way, that VAT exemption is not the same thing as a service being zero rated. Anything which is zero rated attracts zero VAT, but it is not exempt from the VAT regulations, whereas items which are VAT exempt are totally excluded from the VAT system.

In general, you are liable to account to Customs and Excise for VAT you are collecting on their behalf from the date of the invoice (known as the 'tax point') even though you have not received the money from your client or customer. So the system adds to the running total of outputs and output VAT when the invoice is raised, not when the account is settled.

On the matter of invoices, you will find that we have provided a choice of two layouts: one is designed for firms offering a range of professional services; the other is appropriate to the sale of goods. The two layouts are illustrated here and overleaf.

Invoice layout – option 1 – for professional services

```
                INFORMATION PROCESSING SERVICES LTD
                  30 Westgate, Oxford, OX1 1NZ

                                      Registered in UK No 1633731
                                               VAT No 348 6382 24

                              INVOICE

          Please pay this Invoice: Statements are not issued



I M A Student                                 Invoice No. 1000
204 High Street
Lowfield                                      Tax Point: 16/09/86
Middle Wallop
Glos
GL15 7TY


To professional services as detailed below:   £127.00

Value Added Tax ...........................   £ 18.00
                                              -------
                                      TOTAL   £145.00
                                              =======

Training services:

Course leading to a City and Guilds of London Institute skills
competence certificate in Word Processing at Introductory level.
(This is a module within the Information Technology series).
Course fee: 120.00 plus VAT: certification fee: 7.00 (no VAT).
```

```
                INFORMATION PROCESSING SERVICES LTD
                   30 Westgate, Oxford, OX1 1NZ

                                           Registered in UK No 1633731
                                                  VAT No 348 6382 24

                             INVOICE

           Please pay this Invoice: Statements are not issued



I M Cashman                                Invoice No. 1001
Cashman Merchant Bank
Cheapside                                  Tax Point: 16/09/86
London
EC1A 2QQ


Stock No.      Description               Unit cost  Qty   Total cost   VAT

12345     IBM XT 512K +20 M1 hard disk     2300.00    3      6900.00     1
12350     Hercules Colour Card              150.00    3       450.00     1
12360     High resolution colour monitor    310.00    3       930.00     1

                                           TOTAL         8280.00
                                             VAT         1242.00

                                   INVOICE TOTAL         9522.00
```

Invoice layout – option 2 – for the sale of goods

When you have thought about your income and expenditure codes and have used option 4 of the installation utilities menu to create a file containing them (this file is HEADCODE.DTA), print a listing of them (there is a menu option for this purpose), for you will find it useful to refer to when you input income and expenditure later on.

Using the system

The setting up is now all but complete. Return to the second-level menu headed Utilities and select option 2 (preparation of new annual data files). Then select option 1 at the third-level. The warning message need not worry you, since you are setting up the system for the first time; enter Y in response to the question 'Do you wish to proceed?', press any key when prompted to do so and the files BANKIN.DTA, BANKOUT.DTA, VAT.DTA will be created. Finally take option 3 followed by option 4 in order to climb back to the main menu. You are now ready to start business. No business can run without capital, so probably your first move will be to transfer funds from a long-term loan account to one of the company accounts.

So, start by selecting option 4, which includes transfers. Using the on-screen prompts as your guide, transfer say £15,000 from a long-term loan account to one of the company accounts – perhaps the deposit account. You can then transfer some of this money into the current account for immediate use. If you check back on your balances now using menu option 4 again, you will see an entry of

–£15,000 in the long-term loan account, and corresponding positive entries totalling £15,000 in the company bank accounts. From now on, you can run your simulated business as realistically as you like. If you are working within an organized class group, it is possible that your tutor may form you into several inter-trading companies. But to understand fully how the system is working, you need to have a banker as well. For the bank to be able to carry out its part, you must have cheques to issue (with sequential serial numbers), paying-in slips for your bank accounts (also numbered sequentially, with different number series for current and deposit accounts), and transfer slips to ask the bank to transfer money from deposit to current account or vice versa. Your tutor should be able to provide you with these; alternatively you could generate your own cheques and paying-in slips using programs CHEQUEBK.COM, PAYINCUR.COM and PAYINDEP.COM which are provided on the disk assocated with this book.

Spreadsheet generated bank statements

The chief function of the bank is going to be the clearing of cheques and linked with this, the debiting and crediting of accounts. To keep track of these transactions and to provide bank statements from time to time, the bankers could design a simple spreadsheet for themselves – see Chapter 5 if you don't yet know how to do this. The kind of finished result the bankers are aiming for should be something like this:

```
                    BANK CURRENT ACCOUNT TRANSACTIONS RECORD

                    +-------------------------------------+
                    |  The current balance is ...  220.69  |
                    +-------------------------------------+


DATE        TRANSACTION DETAILS       CHEQUE NO. of   DEBIT     CREDIT    BALANCE
                                      PAY-IN SLIP
                                      REFERENCE

01 Nov 86   Balance brought forward                             132.64    132.64
04 Nov 86                             100102          26.95               105.69
12 Nov 86   Cash/cheques              552124                    115.00    220.69

            etc ...
```

Bank statement simulation

Account reconciliation

When you, the company accountant, receive a bank statement, you will need to *reconcile* your accounts. The balances shown by your accounts system may not be the same as the balances shown by the bank, because some of the cheques you have issued may not have been presented for payment yet. You will find menu options 6.2 and 6.3 of the accounts system helpful in accounting for any difference between the balance as shown by the bank and the balance as shown by the system. If you use the hard copy option, you can tick off each transaction against the bank statement.

Links between computer system and vouchers

Remember that both for audit purposes and to satisfy the requirements of Customs and Excise when you offset against Output VAT, the VAT you have paid for goods and services, you must pay against invoices which are subsequently archived. The system asks you to mark up these with the machine-generated transaction number (these numbers are prefixed with the letter E (expenditure) in our system).

In the same way, you can keep a copy of all invoices you issue, and mark them up with the IN (income) transaction numbers when you receive payment against them. In this way you have full documentary evidence for your auditor and for inspection by Customs and Excise should they wish to look at your activities.

Data for the VAT return

You have to account to Customs and Excise for VAT at the end of every VAT period. A period might be quarterly, or in some cases monthly; if you refer again to the diagram on page 148, you will see it shown as 06 86 near the top right corner of the form. This return was for the period ending on the last day of June 1986.

In your use of the accounts software, when you come to the end of the VAT period, use option 5 from the main menu and then option 1 from the VAT sub-menu to reset the VAT balances to zero ready for the next period. You should make appropriate entries on the VAT100 form at this time.

When you have done this, you can go back into the VAT sub-menu if you like and select option 4. The record displayed will not yet be complete, because you have not yet paid the Customs and Excise the net VAT which you have accrued over the last period. It is always possible that your VAT deductable on Inputs was greater than the VAT you collected on outputs, in which case Customs and Excise will pay you the difference for the quarter. But you can't have many quarters like that if you are going to stay in business for long. Whichever way it is, use option 2 or 3 of the VAT sub-menu to enter the financial transaction when it takes place. The income or expenditure record file (whichever is appropriate) will automatically be updated when you do this.

Other trading activities

You may carry on trading for as long as you like. The opportunity exists not only to use applications software but, as we have indicated above, there is scope for simple spreadsheet design and use and you could easily find reasons for using word processing software for a range of purposes within your business operation. Similarly, database software could be used to keep records of all your customers or clients.

Analysis by account head

But in due course (usually at the end of your financial year), you are going to want an analysis of what you have spent your money on and how much income has been derived from each of your activities. This is the time for you to run the program called by menu option 6.4. Following through the screen prompts, you will produce a listing of all income and expenditure by accounting head. In the event of a headcode having been used which is not in your file of headcodes which you created at the outset, the transaction(s) which cannot be allocated will be listed by the computer. It is then open to you either to reallocate the transaction to an existing headcode (using option 7.3 of the main menu) or to generate a new headcode in your file using option 7.1.4.2.

Review

Let us pause for a minute and see where we have been.

1 We started off looking at commercially produced applications software and we saw how economic pressures led to the design of software which would appeal to the widest market possible.

2 We saw how this could lead to uncomfortable compromises between user expectations and software performance, and how the situation could be improved by some built-in facilities for tailoring or customising the software.

3 We looked at the advantages of modularity, both in terms of program maintenance and in terms of a user being able to restrict his software purchases to meet just his current needs, whilst maintaining his options open for the purchase of other integrating modules at a later stage.

4 We considered various aspects of 'user friendliness' including consideration of menu-driven versus command-driven software, screen layout, input validation facilities, error correction facilities, program robustness so that nothing disastrous can occur even when the user does something wrong, etc.

5 Finally, in this section of the chapter, we illustrated many of the points by reference to some simple commercial accounts software.

Some aspects of programming

For readers whose main interest is in getting to grips with the use of general purpose and specific applications software produced commercially, this book has taken you as far along the road as is appropriate for an introductory text. But there will be some who, as well as using other people's programs, would like to know just a little of how they are constructed. Some might like to write simple programs for themselves. The rest of this chapter is for them.

Programming language levels

When, shortly, we start to look at a programming language, it will be a high-level language.

It would take forever to write even a simple program in machine code. In the early days of computing there was no alternative, but as technology advanced it was found possible to use simple codes which were a little more easily recognizable and shorter to write. The reason this was possible was because programmers working for the computer manufacturers were able to write programs in machine code which would translate the more recognizable code back into binary code which the machine could handle.

The code the programmers wrote in is what is known as an ***assembly language***, and the software which converted it to a binary version is called an ***assembler***. Programmers will still write short sequences in assembly language where very fast operation is required, but for the most part they now use languages which are very much nearer to ***natural language*** (English in our case). As an illustration of language levels, consider the case of adding two numbers together to produce a third. It might, for example, be a case of

Total = Price + VAT

This would be an acceptable statement in many implemenations of BASIC, but some interpreters will not handle such long variable names, so it would be safer to write

```
T = P + V
```

Although we have said what we want the computer to do in one statement, this has to be interpreted to the computer as three distinct steps. These are seen if we look at the same task written in a typical assembly language. The statements might be:

```
LDA P
ADD V
STA T
```

If a process is to be carried out on a variable, it must first be loaded into a ***register*** called the **accumulator** because the Arithmetic and Logic Unit operates on data which is held in this register. So what we are saying in the first of the above statements (LDA P) is 'Load the accumulator with the value represented by the variable P'.

The second statement (ADD V) adds the value represented by the variable V to the contents of the accumulator (P) and the result of this addition replaces P in the accumulator.

Finally, the present contents of the accumulator need to be stored in memory under the variable name T, and the third statement (STA T) does this.

We could go back a stage further and see what this same group of statements might look like if translated right back to machine code. (Remember – translation from an assembly language to machine code is done by a program called an *assembler*). The machine code might be:

```
10100101 00001111
01100101 00010010
10000101 00010011
```

In each case, the first group of figures would describe an operation, i.e. the function to be performed and the address of the register (in this case the accumulator) associated with the function. The second group of figures represents the address where the data associated with the operation is to be found (or in the case of the third instruction, where it is to be sent to).

Notice that now we are at machine code level: we are dealing in actual addresses, not variable names.

Interpreters and compilers

As in the case of programs written in assembly language, programs written in the nearer-English (high-level) languages such as FORTRAN, COBOL, BASIC, Pascal, have to be converted back to machine code by programs written specially for that purpose. These programs are either ***interpreters*** or ***compilers***. We told you a little about interpreters in Chapter 3 (see page 33). At that time we were asking you to run the program BIRTHDAY.BAS, written in the high-level language BASIC. To do this, you had first to load the BASIC interpreter (held in a command file) and then, with control transferred to this interpreter program, call and run the program BIRTHDAY.BAS. The program was interpreted line by line into binary as it was run.

Such a procedure has several disadvantages. For example, you cannot run the program without also having the interpreter present; operation of the program is relatively slow because of the time taken to translate instructions into machine code; the program has to be reinterpreted every time it is run.

Source and object code

The alternative is compilation – a process done by a piece of software called a ***compiler***. In this case, the compiler reads the high-level language program, converts it into binary and then saves the binary coded version in a command file. The program as written by the programmer is called the ***source code***; the machine code translation of it is called the ***object code***. Usually the compiler includes extra code to cover standard routines on which the program might call – these are called ***library routines***.

Once the command file has been created by the compiler, the source code is not used again unless the program needs to be amended at some later stage. Every time the program is run, it is the object code file which is used, and because this is in machine code, it is run simply by typing in the file name against the operating system prompt. It is fast in execution because no time is taken in interpretation.

When software is sold, it is normally in binary code, carried in command files on diskettes. This is convenient for the user, and it means too that the programmers' detailed construction of the program is not readily accessible to the purchaser. In this way the programmers' ideas cannot easily be stolen and used by others; also, it is difficult to change the program, and then blame the original programmers for any problems.

The accounts software referred to earlier in this chapter was written in Pascal, but supplied on disk in compiled form. The chances are that you do not have a compiler available to you; we shall work in the assumption that you have a BASIC interpreter, and this will do fine for our present purposes.

Basic skills

Before we go any further, let's just list the things we need to be able to do in order to produce some simple software.

1 First and foremost, we must decide how we are going to tackle the particular problem which we wish to handle using the computer. Having analysed the problem, we must reduce it to a set of simple steps or instructions (this is called an ***algorithm***). Never try to code before you have done this.

2 We must know enough about the use of programming languages to be able to:

   2.1 Produce text on the screen and lay it out as we want it (as, for example, in a menu).

   2.2 Instruct the computer to accept data input from the keyboard.

   2.3 Instruct the computer to perform arithmetic operations on numerical data.

   2.4 Use conditional statements: IF this is true THEN do that ELSE do some other thing. Statements of this kind are fundamental to most computing work. You will find equivalents in spreadsheet software and database processing software. The actual words IF . . . THEN . . . ELSE are common to many programming languages.

   2.5 Output either to screen or to printer.

3 We must be able to structure the program so that it is easily readable and can be easily modified. (This is easy if you have worked out a good algorithm in the first place.)

There are several other *desirable* things, and some of these will be picked up on the way; those listed above are just the bare essentials.

A case study

We are going to design a program which will enable a user to enter at the computer keyboard any income s/he receives and any payments s/he makes, and which will maintain a running total of the amount of money the individual has.

Sounds simple? Well, it can be, but simple approaches tend to be very crude. We shall try to do something rather better. First, let's develop the algorithm and then see if we can break the program down into small self-contained blocks. Our concern in this book is much more the program design than the actual coding. We shall make some reference to code, but we are assuming that you will have separate practice in producing correct code.

An algorithm

A possible algorithm for our problem might be:

1 Set initial values, especially user's name and starting balance.

2 Produce menu on screen.

3 Validate, and if OK accept, the option choice.

4 If option = 1, clear screen and display current balance; return to step 2 under user control.

5 If option = 2, clear screen, accept validated input of expenditure, compute new balance and display it; return to step 2 under user control.

6 If option = 3, clear screen, accept validated input of expenditure, compute new balance and display it; return to step 2 under user control.

7 If option = 4, confirm that user wishes to end the session; if not, return to step 2 above.

Program design

We now need to outline a program structure which will handle this algorithm efficiently. There are a number of ways such an outline might be presented; it could look like the one below.

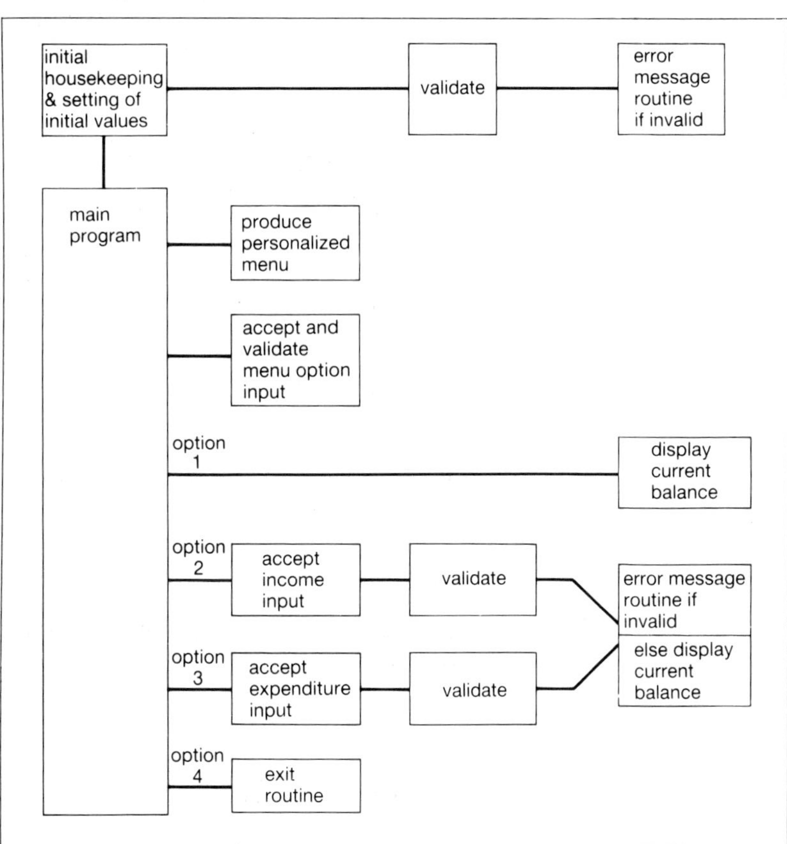

Model outline of a program structure

Notice that every time a user input is accepted, we make sure validation checks on it are possible.

A corresponding realization of the program structure

Let us now look at the program, listed at the end of this chapter (pages 170–172), and see where the various steps in this algorithm are undertaken.

1 Initial values are set in lines 100–210.

2 Menu is produced by subroutine 1000.

3 Option choice is validated, and if valid, is accepted, in subroutine 2000.

4 Current balance display is handled in subroutine 3000; this is used not only in step 4 of the algorithm, but in steps 5 and 6 as well.

5 The input of income is accepted in subroutine 4000; the validation of the input string takes place in subroutine 6000 and, once validated, the value of the input updates the current balance back in subroutine 4000.

6 The input of expenditure is accepted in subroutine 5000; again, validation of data is undertaken in subroutine 6000 and, as in 5 above, the current balance is updated – this time, in subroutine 5000.
7 The end-of-session routine is undertaken in subroutine 8000, which controls the termination of or return to an indefinite loop round the main program.
8 Subroutine 7000 is brought into play if unacceptable inputs are detected in subroutine 6000 and does not relate to a specific step in the algorithm we have developed.

Notice that when dividing a program up into useful blocks, the first one is concerned with what is often called the *initial housekeeping*, e.g. the setting of initial values of certain variables.

The main program

Next comes the main program. This should be short, calling on subroutines or procedures for each self-contained block of the total program. In our solution to the problem, the main program contains only 12 lines of active statements. Each of the subroutines relates to the whole or part of a step in the algorithm. The main program (lines 300–450) is designed to keep going round in an indefinite loop until the user chooses to leave the program. This is a basic technique for menu-driven software which is worth remembering. In our listing, it takes the form:

```
320         WHILE G=0
                WHILE 0$<>"4"
                    CLS
                    GOSUB 1000
                    GOSUB 2000
                    IF 0$="1" THEN CLS: GOSUB 3000
                    IF 0$="2" THEN GOSUB 4000
                    IF 0$="3" THEN GOSUB 5000
                WEND
                GOSUB 7000
            WEND
450         END
```

Indefinite loops

Notice the pairing of WHILE (condition) and WEND – a short form of 'WHILE END'. These, with the statements within them, form a ***pre-condition*** indefinite loop. Not all implementations of BASIC include support for WHILE . . . WEND. A good many of those which don't do so, provide REPEAT . . . UNTIL (condition) instead. Statements of the REPEAT . . . UNTIL kind could be applied to our main program like this:

```
REPEAT
    REPEAT
        CLS
        GOSUB 1000
        GOSUB 2000
        IF 0$="1" THEN CLS: GOSUB 3000
        IF 0$="2" THEN GOSUB 4000
        IF 0$="3" THEN GOSUB 5000
    UNTIL 0$="4"
UNTIL G<>0
```

The essential difference between WHILE . . . WEND and REPEAT . . . UNTIL is that the first produces a ***pre***-condition loop whereas the latter produces a ***post***-condition loop, in which all the program steps within the loop must be executed at least once because the condition isn't known until after this. With a pre-condition loop, if the condition specified is not met, the statements in the loop will not be executed at all.

Notice from our example, by the way, that you can have ***nested*** loops, i.e. loops within loops.

There is an interesting illustration of the technique for re-entry to a pre-condition loop in the program we are studying. When subroutine 8000 is entered, O$="4". If the user then opts *not* to leave the program after all, the program follows the route 8050, 8070, 8100, 440.

If at this point, O$ still had the value "4", control could not pass back to line 330. So, to cope with the pre-condition loop round the main program, O$ is set to some value other than "4"; this is done in line 8070.

If you have a limited subset of BASIC in which neither WHILE . . . WEND nor REPEAT . . . UNTIL are implemented, all is not lost! You can get the same effect using IF . . . THEN . . . with GOTO. But do keep the GOTOs to an absolute minimum throughout any program you write. One of the major factors in bad program construction is the unthinking sprinkling of unconditional jumps (GOTOs) throughout the program. They make it very difficult to trace the logic of the program, and so many logical errors creep in.

To show how to manage without either WHILE . . . WEND or REPEAT . . . UNTIL, look at lines 160–200 in the housekeeping section of our program.

```
160 LOCATE 12,10
170 INPUT "Please enter the starting balance in your
    account: £",B$
180 X$=B$
190 GOSUB 6000: 'Input validation routine.
200 IF F=1 THEN CLS: GOTO 160
```

This is a post-condition loop with the condition being set in line 200. F is normally 0, but is set to 1 in the subroutine starting at line 7000 if the input at line 170 is invalid.

Coding – some dialect variations

Since you may be worrying about some of the code we have been using in these examples, we will set the all-important logical design of the program aside for a few moments to discuss some of the coding used.

One of the things we have to arrange is for messages to appear on-screen for the user. And we want to be able to say exactly where on the screen we want the text to appear. The means of controlling the cursor position varies in different dialects of BASIC. Some use PRINT @ x,y; others use PRINT TAB (x,y); GWBASIC and BASICA use LOCATE row, column, and this is the syntax used in the example.

Every implementation of BASIC uses INPUT statements to make the execution of the program wait for an input from the keyboard. Some, however, do not allow the inclusion of a prompt within the statement. In such cases, the syntax used in, for example, line 170, would have to be modified by using a PRINT statement to display the prompt and then a separate INPUT statement (with no prompt string) to take in the data represented by the variable B$ in this program.

On the subject of separate statements, do you know about the use of the colon (:) to separate two statements written against the same line number? There is an example in line 190 where the statement GOSUB 6000 is separated from the following REMarks statement by a colon. Notice, by the way, the substitution of a single quote mark (apostrophe) for the keyword REM. It is an acceptable shorthand in many implementations of BASIC.

Subroutines (or procedures in some BASIC dialects)

We need to say something about ***subroutines***. They are used to contain blocks of statements, and there are several reasons why we might want to handle statements in blocks like this. For example, a particular routine performed by a block of statements might be called several times from different parts of the program, and we don't want to have to write identical program lines over and over again. If we can direct the control of the program to the same block each time, we save ourselves quite a lot of work.

In the program whose design we are studying, the subroutine starting at line 6000 is called three times: once from line 190, once from line 4070, and again from 5070. Similarly, the subroutine starting at line 3000 is also called from three places in the program.

Another reason for using subroutines: suppose that following a conditional statement (IF (condition) THEN (statement) ELSE (statement)) you wanted a block of statements to be executed. You could just keep repeating the condition:

```
IF (condition) THEN (statement1)
IF (condition) THEN (statement2)
IF (condition) THEN (statement3)
& so on.
```

But how cumbersome! How much better to say:

```
IF (condition) THEN GOSUB (line number)
```

Then, starting at the specified line number, you have your block of statements, and to tell the computer when the end of that block has been reached, you terminate it with the statement RETURN.

When the program is being run and the BASIC interpreter encounters the word RETURN it immediately executes the next statement following the one containing the GOSUB statement which sent it to the subroutine. Think of it, if you like, as carrying on from where if left off when it diverted to work through the subroutine.

We have already touched on another reason for using subroutines. It is to keep the program in tidy blocks which relate to the original algorithm. This helps to get the logic right and it aids the process of testing and ***debugging*** (finding the logical errors in your program).

One more word about subroutines. BASIC allows disorderly programming, and it is possible to jump out of subroutines, using, for example, conditional GOTO statements: IF (condition) THEN GOTO (line number outside the current subroutine). Don't do it!!

An example of acceptable practice can be seen in the program we are considering. The subroutine starting at line 6000 is designed to trap inputs which contain non-numerical characters (other than the decimal point) and inputs which exceed £99999.99. When it detects an unacceptable input, control is returned to the main program which immediately calls the menu again, since O$<>"4". But this return is not effected by a direct jump. Control passes via line 6120 to the next statement following the one which called the subroutine. This might, for example, have been 4080, if line 6000 had been called from 4070.

Because the 'flag' F has been set to 1, 4080 immediately passes control to 4120, the RETURN statement which takes control back to 390 and hence back into the indefinite loop of the main program.

If your dialect of BASIC uses procedures instead of subroutines, all the principles which we have discussed above still stand; but instead of using GOSUB (line number) you will call the procedure by name, and instead of terminating the procedure with the word RETURN, you would use ENDPROC.

Input validation

Let's look at another principle of programming. We want our program to be *robust* – i.e. it should not misbehave in any way if the user fails to use it correctly. For example, if the program is expecting the input of a number, but an alpha character is input, BASIC comes up with a rather unhelpful error message: ?REDO FROM START. How much better to take your variable data in as a character string, check it to see that it is indeed a number, and only then assign its value to the appropriate variable.

One way of checking each character is shown in lines 6030–6110 of our program. The input data has been assigned to the variable X$. The essential lines of the program read:

```
6030 FOR N=1 TO LEN(X$)
|
|
|
|
6040   W$=MID$(X$,N,1)

6100 IF ((ASC(W$)=<48 AND ASC(W$)<>46) OR ASC(W$)>57 THEN . .
     GOSUB 7000
6110 NEXT N
```

(The subroutine starting at line 7000 produces error messages and sets the 'flag' F to 1.)

So there is a loop set up by lines 6030 and 6110, and the number of times the loop is cycled depends on the length of X$. At line 6040, W$ represents a single character extracted from the string X$. MID$ is another BASIC keyword – a word which has a special meaning within the programming language. In this case it is a keyword which is the name of a function. In the brackets which follow it, there are three entries separated by commas. The first entry is simply the name of the variable to which the function is being applied – in our case, X$. The purpose of MID$ is to extract from the string X$ a substring starting at the character defined by the second entry in the brackets and having a length defined by the third entry.

It sounds very complicated, but it isn't, really. Let's take an example. Suppose we assign the value "WEATHER" to a variable A$. Then

MID$(A$,2,3)="EAT". We started at the second character and took a total substring length of three characters.

Try again.

MID$(A$,3,5)="ATHER". You could try this out on your computer. Do something like this:

```
LET A$="YOURNAME": PRINT MID$(A$,N,M)
```

where N and M are integers you choose for yourself – but note that they should be realistic and not ask the computer to try to go beyond the end of your name. See that the computer does what you expect it to do.

Now, going back to our little program extract, we had the assignment statement W$=MID$(X$,N,1) embedded in the loop

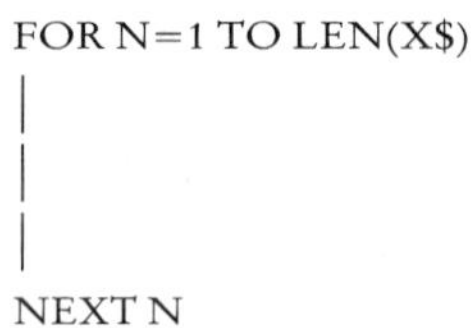

So the first time the FOR statement is reached, N=1 and W$= MID$(X$,1,1) i.e. W$ represents the first character of the string X$. When the execution of the program gets as far as the NEXT N statement, it immediately goes back to the FOR statement, increased N by 1, provided that by so doing the new value of N does not exceed the length of the string X$. So, the second time round, N=2 and W$ has assigned to it the second character in the string X$.

The use of ASCII codes in validation

So the program continues, with W$ representing each character in the string X$ in turn. Each time, we apply a test to the character to see whether it is a number or a decimal point. We do this in line 6100 using the values of these particular characters in the ASCII code. (See Chapter 2 pages 16–17 for an introduction to ASCII codes.) Now the ASCII code (expressed as a decimal number) for a decimal point is 46 – the corresponding binary code is 0101110. The codes for the figures 0–9 are 48–57 inclusive.

Most implementations of BASIC have a very useful function called ASC. ASC(Z$) would return the ASCII code (expressed as a decimal number) of the first character of the string assigned to the variable Z$. Now W$ is only one character long, so ASC(W$) will give us a complete check on each character as we come to it, because if ASC(W$) is neither a decimal point (code 46) nor a number (codes in the range 48–57), then we know that Z$ is unacceptable. This is the test which is taking place in line 6100. If the character fails the test, subroutine 7000 is invoked. This produces an appropriate error message and sets the flag F to 1. We have already seen the effect of this.

Building a library of useful routines

Ideas like the one we have just described for validating numerical input are worth keeping in your own software library. There is no point in reinventing the wheel! You could have simple sort routines and many other useful programming ideas stored away on your disk ready to use when the occasion demands.

Further validation checks

Our subroutine 6000 does more than just check that the input characters are either figures or a decimal point. We decided that even entries which satisfied these criteria should be regarded as invalid if the entry were for an amount of £1 000 000 or more. Line 6060 traps such entries because E becomes 1 as soon as the variable W$ represents a decimal point (see line 6050). So if N is greater than 5 and a decimal point still hasn't turned up, we know that the input figure will be at least £1 000 000 and could be a lot more. In this event, line 6060 routes the program to the error message subroutine.

The only other kind of incorrect entry we guarded against was the possibility of a user entering more than two characters after a decimal point. Such errors are trapped in line 6080.

You will perhaps be able to think of other kinds of unacceptable input which we haven't trapped, but hopefully we have got all the likely ones. It is usually a matter of judgement as to how far you go in this direction: each extra step you put in the program makes it a little slower in operation because you have given the computer more jobs to do. But you do need to protect the user so far as is reasonable from running into trouble because of inputting mistakes.

Some good habits

We have been holding out on you. Quite deliberately, perhaps unkindly – but we want to make a point and make it strongly.

As you have been looking at our program listing at the end of this chapter, you have almost certainly been saying, 'What is F?' 'What is X$' 'What is G?' 'What is O$?'. Why aren't the variables defined? Why indeed? Simply to bring home as forceably as possible the need to do so!

In many programming languages (and some implementations of BASIC) you can use long variable names which indicate – if carefully chosen – what it is that the variable is representing. In such cases there is less need for a definition than in cases where a variable is identified by a single character; but even so, it is a good practice to maintain a list of all variables used and what they have been used for.

It can be acceptable to use the same variable for different purposes at different times. We have one example of that in the program we are looking at: Y$ is used in line 3060 to represent any value input from the keyboard, but once past line 3070, Y$ has served its purpose and can be used again in a similar context but for a completely different end result in line 8050 and thereafter.

But take care about the reuse of a variable; make sure that you really have finished with it before using it again, and if you do decide to reuse, make sure that it does not carry forward into the subsequent use a value assigned to it previously.

It is good practice to list your variables as you go along with the coding of your program. You would be suprised how easy it is unintentionally to use the same variable more than once even in a program with only two or three hundred statements.

Where will you list them? It could be in the documentation associated with your program, but our own preference is to place them in a series of REM statements immediately following the details of the programme name, date, author and updating details. Then they are always available to anyone reading the program, whereas separate documentation may not be (although it should). So far as our program is concerned, you are going to have to flip between this page and the end of the chapter to relate definitions to the program. Here are our definitions with some added comment:

B$ a string variable representing the starting balance input at the keyboard.

B a variable representing initially the value of B$ after it has been validated, but more generally, B represents the current balance.

E$ a string variable representing any of several error messages to be displayed on screen in appropriate circumstances.

E a variable which is used as a 'flag' and acts like a Boolean variable. It has only two possible values, 0 and 1; it is preset to 0 and is set to 1 when a decimal point is detected in an input string representing a numerical input.

F a variable which is used as a 'flag' like E; it is normally 0 but set in 1 in subroutine 7000 which is only called if an input amount is unacceptable.

G another variable which is used like a Boolean variable which may have only two values – true and false. G is normally 0 and is only set to 1 when the user confirms that s/he wishes to leave the program.

I$ a string variable representing income as input at the keyboard.

I a variable representing the value of I$ (when validated).

M$ a variable assigned to the personalized heading string at the top of the menu screen.

M an interger variable determined from a calculation involving the length of M$ and used to set the starting column position for the screen presentation of the personalized heading M$.

N$ a string variable representing the user's name as input at the keyboard.

N,P integer variables used to count the number of passes round pre-determined loops within FOR . . . NEXT statements.

O$	a variable assigned to user input at the foot of the menu screen. BASIC does not distinguish between string and character variables; if it did, O$ would be a character variable since its only permitted values are one character long.
S$	a string variable representing expenditure as input at the keyboard.
S	a variable representing the value of S$ (when validated).
W$	a variable representing in turn each character contained in the string represented by X$.
X$	a string variable to which any input string must be assigned if it is to be validated in subroutine 6000.
Y$	a variable assigned to any single-character input from the keyboard (mostly, but not always, captured by INKEY$).

What else could help someone reading our program to understand how it functions? Probably the most useful tool we could offer would be a suitably annotated flow diagram of some kind.

Flowcharts

Never think you are going to get your flowchart in a good orderly shape at the first attempt. It takes a genius to do that! But do attempt to produce one. Some people draw up a flowchart at the outset and develop their coded program from it. Our own preference is to state the algorithm carefully, then produce a design outline from it and use this as the basis for coding. Then a flowchart can be developed as coding proceeds. In this way, you can always see at a glance where you have got to and you can check your logic as you go along.

Once you have drawn a flowchart in this way, you can move your boxes around to make a more understandable diagram for anyone else who needs to read your program. There is no single 'correct' flowchart for a given program; the extent of detail will vary from one author to another, but of course the logic must be the same.

The diagrams overleaf show a possible flowchart corresponding to the program listed at the end of this chapter. To simplify the reading of this flowchart we have used the connectors A, B, C to link the two sections together. To make the flowchart more useful, line numbers or references to subroutines should be shown against each step on the flowchart. We have not done this on our diagrams. Your tutor (if you are working in a tutored group) may be able to give you a photocopy of the two diagrams so that you can, from your own reading of the program, put line numbers on it in appropriate places.

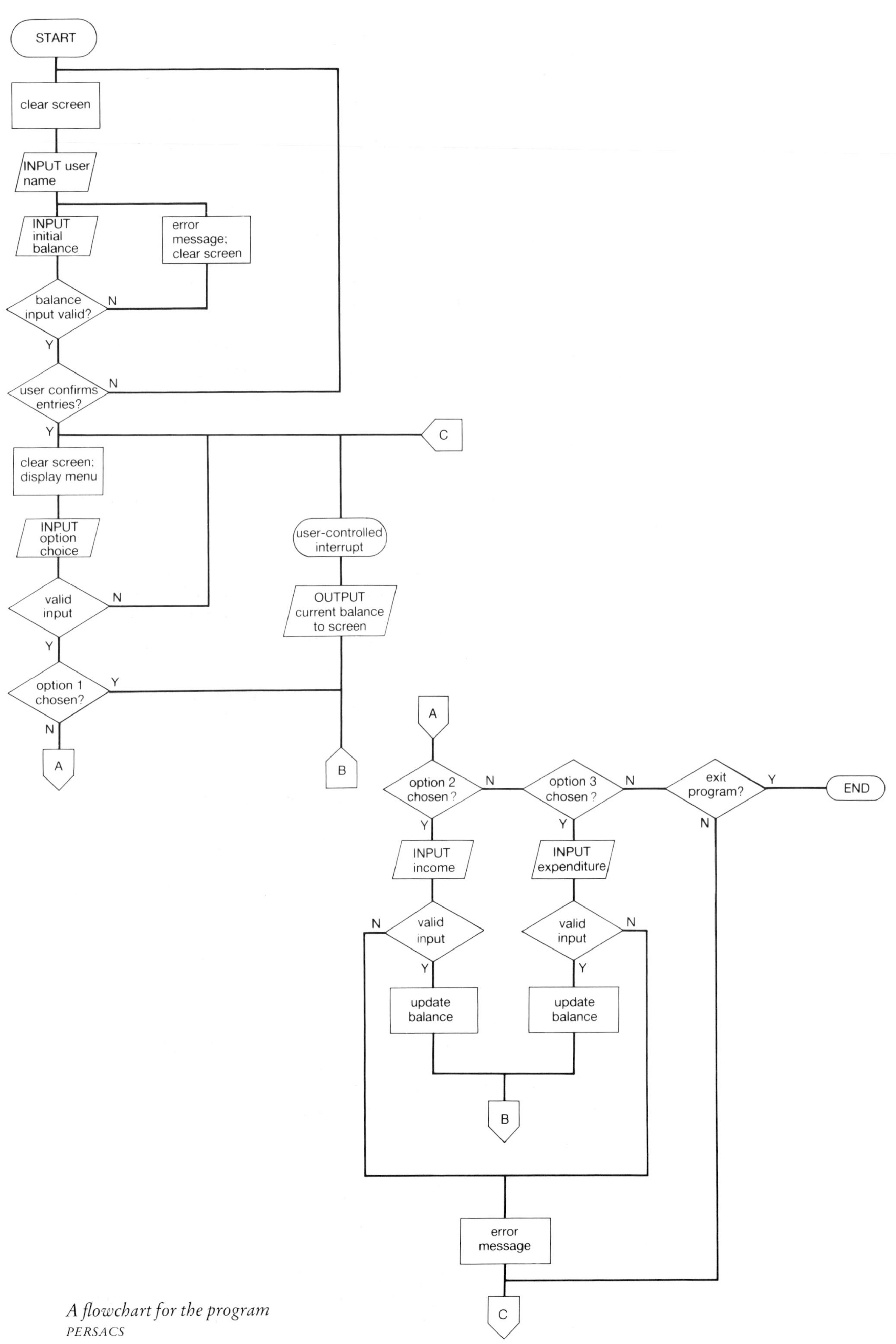

A flowchart for the program
PERSACS

A learning checklist

What we have aimed to do in this part of the chapter is to illustrate with reference to a simple example some of the principles and procedures involved in producing software for end-users. Our simple illustration shows an example of customization and the principle of menu-driven software. It stops short of being of real practical value, since to make it so we would need to file at least the user name and current balance, so that they can be recalled when the program is next used, rather than re-input. But file-handling is rather beyond the level of an introductory text.

Nevertheless, we have covered quite a lot of ground. If you have stayed with us, you should know how to:

1 Analyse a simple problem and produce an algorithm for it.

2 Design a program structure which will give effect to the algorithm.

There is a considerable difference between knowing how to do something and actually being able to do it. Practical proficiency can only come from repeated practice. Many readers will settle for an appreciation: for those wishing to take programming more seriously, we have at least provided a starting point. In addition to an appreciation of analysis and design, you should be able to:

3 Know when and how to use indefinite loops.

4 Understand the effect of, and distinguish between pre- and post-condition loops.

5 Understand the concept of subroutines or procedures and why they are used.

6 Understand why numerical input is best handled as a string until validated.

7 Understand and use a number of validation techniques.

8 Understand the purpose of developing a library of useful routines.

9 Produce documentation for a program including a list of variables and their significance, and a flowchart.

We have made no attempt to teach you coding in BASIC, although there have been some references to code where we felt it might be helpful. What we have tried to do is to point to good practice, so that if you do learn to code, you will be able to write well-structured and documented programs.

Two assignments

If programming is part of your course, or you think it would be fun to do some, here are a few ideas for you to try. We have not provided you with solutions to the problems (although your tutor may well have some), and they are not difficult to program. But just because they are relatively simple, don't jump in with both feet and try to code before you have developed the algorithm and designed your program.

Health warning . . . Programming is usually addictive!

1 Write a program which will convert input temperature values in the range −273 °C to 10 000 °C from degrees Celsius to degrees Fahrenheit and vice versa.

The opening screen should look like this:

```
TEMPERATURE UNITS CONVERSION

You may...

1. Convert from degrees Celsius to
degrees Farenheit

2. Convert from degrees Farenheit
to degrees Celsius

3. Exit from program

Choose 1, 2 or 3...
```

As soon as a valid option is chosen, the screen should be cleared. If option 1 had been selected, the next message to appear on screen would be:

Please enter temperature in degrees Celsius:

As soon as a valid input is entered, the computer should respond (3 lines lower) with:

The corresponding temperature in degrees Fahrenheit is *nnn.n* (where *nnn.n* is a number displayed rounded to one decimal place.)

So for example, a completed screen could look like this:

```
Please enter temperature in degrees
Celsius: 14.2

The corresponding temperature in degrees
Fahrenheit is 57.6


Press SPACEBAR to continue . . .
```

Operationally, choosing option 2 is similar to choosing option 1. In both cases, pressing the spacebar (but *only* the spacebar) should return the user to the opening menu, from which s/he may exit from the program if no further conversions are to be computed.

Use a standard exit routine which allows the user to change his/her mind and come back into the main program should this be desired.

In case you have difficulty with the mathematics involved, you may find the following helpful.

Look at the thermometer at the top of the next page. There are two fixed points on it which we know about: the temperature of melting ice is 0 °C or 32 °F and the temperature of boiling water at atmospheric pressure is 100 °C or 212 °F.

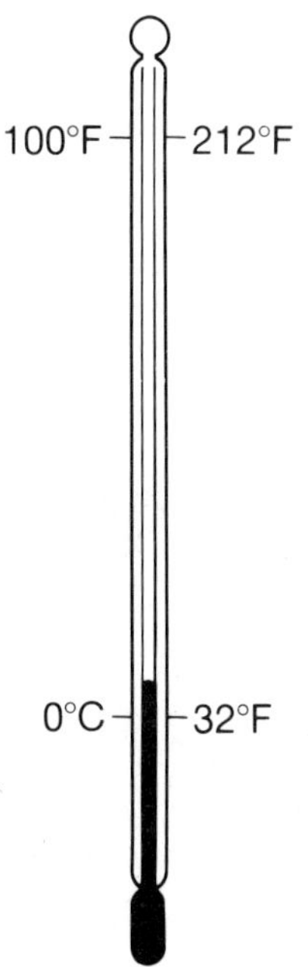

Comparative Celsius and Fahrenheit temperature scales

So a temperature rise of 100 °C is the same as a rise of 180 °F, or a rise of 1 °C is equivalent to a rise of 1.8 °F.

But if we speak of a temperature of 15 °C we mean 15 °C higher than 0; to relate temperature in °F to the same base (melting ice), we must take off 32.

So Temperature (°C) = (Temperature(°F)−32)/1.8
Temperature (°F) = Temperature(°C)*1.8+32

2 Write a program which will accept flight bookings and issue tickets specifying the seat allocated to the named individual whose ticket it is.

Your company, SAFEWAY AIR SERVICES, operates aircraft with three different seat layouts, which you can refer to as types 1, 2 and 3.

Your system should perform according to the following outline:

The first screen should allow the input of initial data which should include the Flight No., Destination, Leaving time and date, and the Seating type.

The next screen is the working screen which will be used for making the bookings. In the top half of the screen, there should be an appropriately numbered seat diagram. It might look like this:

1A	2A	3A	4A	5A	6A	7A	. . .etc
1B	2B	3B	4B	5B	6B	7B	. . .etc
1C	2C	3C	4C	5C	6C	7C	. . .etc
1D	2D	3D	4D	5D	6D	7D	. . .etc
1E	2E	3E	4E	5E	6E	7E	. . .etc

There should be up to say 15 rows of seats (this would take up about 60 columns of an 80 column screen).

Below this, the user should be prompted to enter the passenger's name and the desired seat number.

If the desired seat number is valid (i.e. it exists within the seating pattern and has not already been booked) it is removed from the display of bookable seats and a ticket is printed.

Details of the passenger are then deleted from the screen and preparations made for the next input. The program continues to run until an asterisk (*) is input instead of a passenger's name.

We suggest that the ticket print-out should look something like this:

SAFEWAY AIR SERVICES

TO: ....

Flight No. ____________________

Destination ____________________

Leaving LONDON (HEATHROW) __________ on __________

Passenger name ____________________ Seat No. ______

It would, of course, be more realistic if you could save current data to disk and call it back to continue bookings on a later occasion, but we have assumed that at this stage you will not have dealt with data files.

What you will need in order to tackle this project successfully is reasonable skill in screen layout and printer control, and a good facility in string handling. Like the previous example, we have designed it to give you practice in producing simple algorithms and well-structured programs. The basic idea which we have given here can be enlarged on in many different ways if you wish to develop it into a more demanding project.

Case study program

```
10 REM In this and the following lines you would record details of the program
11 REM name, the date it was written and the author's name.
12 REM
13 REM If there were a subsequent updating or revision, then the version number
14 REM and date of the revision would be added and there must be room for this
15 REM to be done.
16 REM
17 REM There also needs to be a very brief description of the purpose of the
18 REM program - no substitute for adequate documentation, but enough for a
19 REM user who is reading a program to know that he has correctly identified it
20 REM
21 REM
100 REM *** HOUSE-KEEPING; SETTING OF INITIAL VALUES ***
110 REM
120 G=0
130 CLS
140 LOCATE 10,10
150 INPUT "Please type in your name in UPPER CASE:",N$
160 LOCATE 12,10
170 INPUT "Please enter the starting balance in your account: ",B$
180 X$=B$
190 GOSUB 6000: 'Checks validity of input.
200 IF F=1 THEN CLS:GOTO 160
210 B=VAL(B$)
220 CLS
230 LOCATE 10,10:PRINT "Your name is ";N$
240 LOCATE 13,10:PRINT "Your starting balance is ";USING "#####.##";B
250 LOCATE 18,10:INPUT "PLEASE CONFIRM THAT THIS IS CORRECT (Y/N) ",Y$
260 IF ASC(Y$)-89 OR ASC(Y$)=121 THEN 320
270 IF ASC(Y$)=78 OR ASC(Y$)=110 THEN 130
280 PRINT CHR$(7):LOCATE 18,52:PRINT "        ":GOTO 250
290 REM
300 REM *** MAIN PROGRAM ***
310 REM
320 WHILE G=0
330 WHILE O$<>"4"
340 CLS
350 GOSUB 1000: 'Produces menu on screen.
360 GOSUB 2000: 'Accepts input of menu option and checks for valid entry.
370 IF O$="1" THEN CLS:GOSUB 3000: 'Prints current balance on screen.
380 IF O$="2" THEN GOSUB 4000: 'Produces income input screen.
390 IF O$="3" THEN GOSUB 5000: 'Produces expenditure input screen.
400 REM The last three statements could have been replaced by a CASE statement
410 REM but the keyword CASE is not to be found in many dialects of BASIC yet.
420 WEND
430 GOSUB 8000: 'Ending routine.
440 WEND
450 END
990 REM
1000 REM *** PRODUCES PERSONALISED MENU HEADING AND MENU ON SCREEN ***
1010 REM
```

```
1020 M=INT(80-(LEN(N$)+19))/2
1030 IF RIGHT$(N$,1)="S" THEN M$=N$+"' PERSONAL ACCOUNTS" ELSE M$=N$+"'S PERSONAL
ACCOUNTS"
1040 LOCATE 2,M
1050 PRINT M$
1060 LOCATE 5,15
1070 PRINT "AVAILABLE OPTIONS:"
1080 LOCATE 9,20
1090 PRINT "1.  Display current balance"
1100 LOCATE 11,20
1110 PRINT "2.  Enter income"
1120 LOCATE 13,20
1130 PRINT "3.  Enter expenditure"
1140 LOCATE 15,20
1150 PRINT "4.  Exit from the program"
1160 LOCATE 19,15
1170 PRINT "ENTER OPTION CHOICE and press RETURN... ";
1180 RETURN
1990 REM
2000 REM *** INPUT OF MENU OPTION AND VALIDITY CHECK ***
2010 REM
2020 INPUT O$
2030 IF LEN(O$)<>1 THEN 2050
2040 IF ASC(O$)>48 AND ASC(O$)<53 THEN 2060
2050 PRINT CHR$(7):LOCATE 19,55:PRINT "          ":LOCATE 19,55:GOTO 2020
2060 RETURN
2990 REM
3000 REM *** PRINTS CURRENT BALANCE ON SCREEN ***
3010 REM
3020 LOCATE 14,10
3030 PRINT "YOUR CURRENT BALANCE IS ":USING "#####.##";B
3040 LOCATE 22,10
3050 PRINT "Press SPACEBAR to continue ..."
3060 Y$=INKEY$:IF Y$="" THEN 3060
3070 IF ASC(Y$)<>32 THEN 3060
3080 RETURN
3990 REM
4000 REM *** ACCEPTS INPUT OF INCOME AND UPDATES BALANCE ***
4010 REM
4020 CLS
4030 LOCATE 10,10
4040 PRINT "Please enter the income amount: ";
4050 INPUT "",I$
4060 X$=I$
4070 GOSUB 6000: 'Input validation routine.
4080 IF F=1 THEN 4120
4090 I=VAL(I$)
4100 B=B+I
4110 GOSUB 3000
4120 RETURN
4990 REM
5000 REM *** ACCEPTS INPUT OF EXPENDITURE AND UPDATES BALANCE ***
5010 REM
5020 CLS
5030 LOCATE 10,10
5040 PRINT "Please enter the amount spent: ";
5050 INPUT "",S$
5060 X$=S$
5070 GOSUB 6000: 'Input validation routine.
5080 If F=1 THEN 5120
5090 S=VAL(S$)
5100 B=B-S
5110 GOSUB 3000
5120 RETURN
5990 REM
6000 REM *** VALIDATES INCOME AND EXPENDITURE INPUTS ***
6010 REM
6020 E=0:F=0: 'Resets flags if previously set.
6030 FOR N=1 TO LEN(X$)
6040 W$=MID$(X$,N,1)
```

```
6050 IF ASC(W$)=46 THEN E=1: 'Sets flag to show that decimal point has been used
6060 IF E=0 AND N>5 THEN E$="INPUT TOO LARGE A NUMBER":GOSUB 7000
6070 REM Detects cases where there are too many intergers in the input.
6080 IF ASC (W$) =46 AND LEN(X$)>(2+N) THEN E$="INPUT A NUMBER CONTAINING FRACTION
OF A PENNY":GOSUB 7000
6090 REM Detects cases with more than 2 figures after the decimal point
6100 IF ((ASC<W$)<48 AND ASC(W$)<>46) OR ASC(W$)>57 THEN E$="INPUT A CHARACTER
OTHER THAN A FIGURE OR A DECIMAL POINT":GOSUB 7000
6110 NEXT N
6120 RETURN
6990 REM
7000 REM *** SETS ERROR FLAG F AND PRINTS ERROR MESSAGE ON SCREEN ***
7010 REM
7020 PRINT CHR$(7)
7030 F=1
7040 CLS
7050 LOCATE 10,10
7060 PRINT "UNACCEPTABLE INPUT.  All characters must be numbers, with the "
7070 PRINT TAB(10);"exception of the decimal point separating pounds and pence."
7080 PRINT :PRINT TAB(10);"Maximum value allowable is 99999.99"
7090 PRINT :PRINT :PRINT TAB(10);"YOU HAVE ";E$
7100 FOR P=1 TO 4500:NEXT P
7110 N=LEN(X$)
7120 RETURN
7990 REM
8000 REM *** ENDING ROUTINE ***
8010 REM
8020 CLS
8030 LOCATE 10,10
8040 PRINT "YOU HAVE OPTED TO LEAVE THE PROGRAM.  ARE YOU SURE? (Y/N) ";
8050 Y$=INKEY$:IF Y$="" THEN 8050
8060 IF ASC(Y$)=89 OR ASC(Y$)=121 THEN G=1:GOTO 8100
8070 IF ASC(Y$)=78 OR ASC(Y$)=110 THEN O$="":GOTO 8100
8080 GOTO 8050: 'If Y$ is neither Y nor N (upper or lower case) the input is
8090 'unacceptable.
8100 RETURN
```

Appendix: BSI proof correction marks

Notes on the use of the marks
(clauses **4.5, 4.6, 4.7** and **4.8** of BS 5261:Part 2: 1976)
"Marks extracted from BS 5261: Part 2: 1976 by permission of British Standards Institution, 2 Park St., London W1A 2BS. Complete copies of this or a special reduced version BS 5261C can be obtained from BSI."

Proof corrections should be made in coloured ink thus:
(a) printer's literal errors marked by the printer for correction: green;
(b) printer's literal errors marked by the customer and his agents for correction: red;
(c) alterations and instructions made by the customer and his agents: black or dark blue.

Group A General

Instruction	Textual Mark	Marginal Mark
Correction is concluded	None	/
Leave unchanged	.... under characters to remain	✓ (encircled)
Remove extraneous marks	Encircle marks to be removed	X
Push down risen spacing material	Encircle blemish	⊥
Refer to appropriate authority anything of doubtful accuracy	Encircle word(s) affected or in doubt	? (encircled)
Set in or change to bold type	~~~~ under character(s) to be set or changed	~
Set in or change to bold italic type	~~~~ under character(s) to be set or changed	
Change capital letters to lower case letters	Encircle character(s) to be changed	≢
Change small capital letters to lower case letters	Encircle character(s) to be changed	≠
Change italic to upright type	Encircle character(s) to be changed	
Invert type	Encircle character(s) to be inverted	
Substitute or insert character in 'superior' position	/ through character or ⋏ where required	under character e.g.
Substiture or insert character in 'inferior' position	/ through character or ⋏ where required	over character e.g.
Substitute ligature e.g. ffi for separate letters	through characters affected	e.g. ffi
Substitute separate letters for ligature		Write out separate letters
Substitute or insert full point or decimal point	/ through character or ⋏ where required	⊙
Substitute or insert colon	/ through character or ⋏ where required	: (encircled)
Substitute or insert semi colon	/ through character or ⋏ where required	;
Substitute or insert comma	/ through character or ⋏ where required	,
Substitute or insert apostrophe	/ through character or ⋏ where required	'

Group B Deletion, insertion and substitution.

Instruction	Textual Mark	Marginal Mark
Insert in text the matter indicated in the margin	⋏	New matter followed by ⋏
Insert additional matter identified by a letter in a diamond	⋏	⋏ Followed by for example (A)
Delete	/ through characters or through words to be deleted	
Delete and close up	through character or through character e.g. charaácter charaéctor	
Substitute character or substitute part of one or more word(s)	/ through character or through word(s)	New character or new word(s)
Wrong fount. Replace by character(s) of correct fount	Encircle character(s) to be changed	⊗
Change damaged character(s)	Encircle character(s) to be changed	X
Set in, or change to italic	under character(s) to be set or changed	
Set in, or change to capital letters	under character(s) to be set or changed	≡
Set in, or change to small capital letters	under character(s) to be set or changed	=
Set in or change to capital letters for initial letters and small capital letters for the rest of the words	≡ under initial letters and = under the rest of the words	
Transpose a number of characters or words	3 2 1	123
Transpose lines		
Transpose a number of lines		4 3 2 1
Centre	enclose matter to be centred	[ ]
Indent		
Cancel indent		
Set line justified to specified measure	and/or	
Set column justified to specified measure	e.g. 26p/e	
Move matter specified distance to the right	enclosing matter to be moved right	
Move matter specified distance to the left	enclosing matter to be moved left	
Take over character(s) word(s) or line to next line, column or page		
Take back character(s) word(s) or line to previous line column or page		
Raise matter	over matter to be raised and under matter to be raised	

Substitute or insert single quotation marks	/ through character or ⅄ where required	‘ and/or ’
Substitute or insert double quotation mark	/ through character or ⅄ where required	“ and/or ”
Substitute or insert ellipsis –	/ through character or ⅄ where required	...
Substitute or insert leader dots	/ through character or ⅄ where required	(...)
Substitute or insert hyphen	/ through character or ⅄ where required	|-|
Substitute or insert rule	/ through character or ⅄ where required	|—|
Substitute or insert oblique	/ through character or ⅄ where required	(/)

Group C Positioning and spacing

Instruction	Textual Mark	Marginal Mark
Start new paragraph	_⌐	_⌐
Run on (no new paragraph)	⊂⊃	⊂⊃
Transpose characters or words	⊔⊓ between characters or words, numbered when necessary	⊔⊓
Lower matter	over matter to be lowered and under matter to be lowered	
Move matter to position indicated	Enclose matter to be moved and indicate new position	
Correct vertical alignment	||	||
Correct horizontal alignment	Single line above and below misaligned matter e.g. misaligned	=
Close up. Delete space between characters or words	linking ⁀ characters	⁀
Insert space between characters	| between characters	Y
Insert space between words	Y between words	Y
Reduce space between characters	| between characters	↑
Reduce space between words	↑ between words	↑
Make space appear equal between characters or words	| between characters or words	X
Close up to normal interline spacing	(each side of column linking lines)	
Insert space between lines or paragraphs	—(or)—	
Reduce space between lines or paragraphs	← or →	

Index